EXPLORING
PERSPECTIVES

EXPLORING PERSPECTIVES

NEIL GRAHAM
Co-ordinator of English
Scarborough Board of Education

McGRAW-HILL RYERSON LIMITED
Toronto Montreal New York Auckland Bogotá Caracas
Hamburg Lisbon London Madrid Mexico Milan New Delhi
Paris San Juan São Paulo Singapore Sydney Tokyo

Exploring Perspectives

ISBN: 0-07-549876-6

       7 8 9 0 TRI 0

Printed and bound in Canada

Canadian Cataloguing in Publication Data

Graham, Neil
  Exploring perspectives

ISBN 0-07-549876-6

1. English language - Rhetoric. 2. Exposition (Rhetoric). I. Title.

PE1408.G73 1991   808'.0427   C90-095029-3

Cover and interior design: *Michelle Losier*

Sponsoring Editor: *Janice Matthews*

Senior Supervising Editor: *Lenore Gray*

Illustrations: *Stuart Knox*

Cover and Topic pages image © 1990 M. C. Escher Heirs/Cordon Art,
Baarn, Holland.

The cover image by Dutch graphic artist M. C. Escher (1898-1971) *Other
World* is a wood engraving and woodcut dated January 1947. *Other World*
places the viewer in a room where front, back, left, right, up, and down can
be interchanged depending on which window one looks out of. Escher's
experiments with perspective and optical illusion made him world famous.

Our life is what our thoughts make it.

Marcus Aurelius Antoninus

ABOUT THE AUTHOR

Neil Graham is Co-ordinator of English with the Scarborough Board of Education. He is co-author of *Thinking Through the Essay*, and author of the Ontario Ministry of Education Teacher Resource Document, *Student Evaluation in English*.

ACKNOWLEDGEMENTS

The author would like to thank the following people for their encouragement, suggestions, and contributions:

Patricia Graham, teacher-librarian, Dr. Norman Bethune Collegiate Institute, Scarborough Board of Education

Sheryl Freeman, Head of English, Bendale Business & Technical Institute, Scarborough Board of Education

Frank McTeague, English Co-ordinator, Board of Education for the City of York

Trevor Owen, Teacher of English, Riverdale Collegiate, Board of Education for the City of Toronto

Peter G. Smith, Head of Languages, Sir John A MacDonald High School, Halifax County-Bedford District School Board

Janice Matthews, Sponsoring Editor, McGraw-Hill Ryerson Limited

Denise Shortt, Associate Editor, McGraw-Hill Ryerson Limited

List of Topics

Using Exploring Perspectives

If a copy of this text were set on a desk in the middle of the classroom, everyone would see it from a different point of view, a different perspective. Some would see the title right side up, some at an angle, and others upside down. Those close to it would be able to read the title; those farther away would see only size, colour, and shape. In addition to these differing visual perspectives, observers would also respond from different emotional perspectives. For example, those who don't like the colour blue might react differently from those who do, and those who don't enjoy reading might react differently from those who do. Obviously, a variety of perspectives produces a variety of responses.

It is much the same with our thinking about ideas and issues. If we see them only from our own perspective, then our response to them can often be very narrow and one-sided. However, if we develop the habit of thinking things through by exploring them from various perspectives, we expand and deepen our ability to respond.

Exploring Perspectives is designed to help you expand and deepen this ability.

Exploring Perspectives focuses on nine selected topics from a variety of perspectives. You are invited to broaden the perspective on each topic even further and update the information presented by locating other related and relevant material. Once you have explored the topics in the text and developed the perspectives habit, you may wish to select other topics of interest and expand and deepen your ability to respond to them by collecting material that explores each one from a variety of perspectives.

The ability "to think things through" also depends on being able to select and apply a range of thinking patterns and processes when considering ideas or issues. To help develop these thinking skills, *Exploring Perspectives* sets up a three-stage approach for exploring the ideas and issues contained in each topic.

FOCUSING IN: In this first phase, you identify your initial reactions to the topic by exploring your own perspective, your own thoughts and feelings.

FINDING OUT: In this phase of the unit, you read, view, and *explore* the topic from various perspectives, noting similarities and differences, and analyzing relationships and patterns. It is important to note that you are not expected to agree with all perspectives represented in the text. Rather, your goal is to objectively evaluate these viewpoints by examining evidence and support, and weighing information and bias. Through these activities you will ultimately broaden your own perspective on a given topic.

FOLLOWING THROUGH: In this final phase, you apply your wider perspective to a situation that has personal meaning for you, either as a group or individually, or both.

In the first seven topics, the Focusing In, Finding Out, and Following Through phases contain a variety of suggested approaches and activities to help focus on important thinking processes. These activities may be completed individually, in small groups, or with the class as a whole. You will be involved in a range of reading, viewing, research, and writing activities, including personal response journal writing and reviewing personally selected readings and visual material. You will also be responding to, creating, and conducting questionnaires and surveys, working in groups, visiting the library and other information areas, and designing and carrying out independent study projects.

Descriptions of the key learning activities you will be using are found in the "Notes on Key Learning Activities" section at the end of the text. You may wish to refer to these notes if you are unfamiliar with any suggested activity or if you are looking for ways in which you may vary its use.

It is important to understand that the suggested approaches are only that; you may wish to alter them or devise your own, as you work toward your goal of developing your thinking patterns and sharpening your overall thinking processes. In fact, once you get used to the three-stage process, you should adapt the suggested activities or design your own, either as a group or individually, or combining both. In the last three topics, this "scaffolding" gradually has been withdrawn. You are asked to take over the direction of your own learning and thinking by applying and adapting approaches and skills learned in working through the earlier topics.

It is hoped you will enjoy exploring the selected topics in this text. As you work through them, keep in mind that the ultimate intent is to help you develop skill in thinking through the ideas and issues you will meet in your everyday life.

TOPIC
one

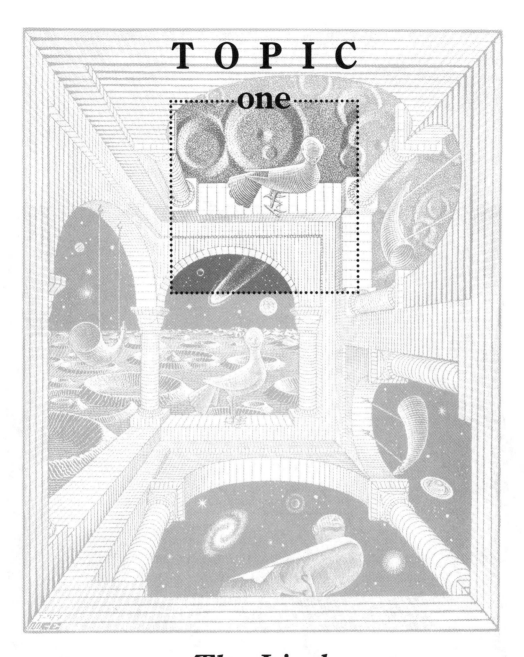

The Lively
(and Sometimes Deadly)
Art of Conversation

FOCUSING IN

How effective are you as a conversationalist? How aware are you of your conversation "image" or of what elements create it? More and more research indicates that effective communication in conversation depends on the interaction of a range of elements. The material collected here explores the interaction of the three key elements of conversation: listening signals, speaking signals, and body language signals.

Before exploring the art of effective conversation from the perspectives of various people who have studied it, you should reflect on your own experience to determine your initial reaction to this topic. For example, the idea itself may have already triggered some kind of personal response, particularly if your latest conversational experience has been an intimate chat with a close friend, or a bitter disagreement with someone you dislike.

SUGGESTED APPROACH
Step 1

Read the statements contained in the "Opinionnaire" on the following page. Each one is taken from articles you will be reading on this topic.

Complete the "Opinionnaire" in order to determine your initial perspective on the topic of effective conversation. (Write the numbers 1 to 10 vertically down the page in your notebook or journal. Beside each one, write the number that represents the extent to which you agree with each statement.)

Opinionnaire

	Strongly Agree	Agree	No Opinion	Disagree	Strongly Disagree
1. Conversation is not as random as it may seem. It is a highly structured, carefully followed set of rules.	5	4	3	2	1
2. Virtually the same conversation rules seem to be followed by members of all societies.	5	4	3	2	1
3. The problem in conversation is often the listener, not the speaker. Most of us listen selectively, hearing only those things we want to hear or which reinforce our own opinions.	5	4	3	2	1
4. The average person spends 50 to 80 percent of the day listening, but hears only half of what is said and understands only a quarter of that.	5	4	3	2	1
5. Women seem to be more adept at listening than men.	5	4	3	2	1
6. To be a good listener you must adopt an effective listening posture or body language.	5	4	3	2	1
7. The sexes may use the same language, but the meaning is different to the male and female ear.	5	4	3	2	1

	Strongly Agree	Agree	No Opinion	Disagree	Strongly Disagree
8. Body language (the way we move and gesture when we talk) goes a long way in explaining why we communicate so well, or poorly, with others, including people from other cultures.	5	4	3	2	1
9. Proving ourselves right underlies so much of our communications today. The average person is listening to his or her own conversation.	5	4	3	2	1
10. Men and women often fail to communicate because they have different styles of conversation.	5	4	3	2	1

Step 2

For each of the 10 items write a sentence that states the reason for your response. For example:

1. I strongly agree with this statement because . . .

Step 3

Determine the class response. Having worked through these statements to determine your own initial reactions, you may wish to compare them with those of the class as a whole. On a piece of paper recopy the number for each of your responses. When you have completed the task, indicate by an M or F at the top of the page whether you are a male or female responder. While the overall results for each item are being tabulated by one or two people, the rest of the class could speculate on the results. To what extent might male and female responses differ? Why?

When the results of the class opinion poll are available, they should be examined and evaluated in order to determine overall initial responses to the topic. As a whole, or in groups, the class should speculate on reasons for the collective opinions revealed by the poll.

Step 4

Write a journal entry in which you reflect on your personal reaction to the ideas in the "Opinionnaire," to the group and class discussion, and to the following questions.

    a. Do you think your initial response was based on reason, or emotion, or a combination of both?

    b. How would you describe your level of information on the topic?

    c. What kind of a conversation "image" do you think you project when you are with others, in terms of your listening signals, your speaking signals, and your body language signals?

    d. Do you believe in such a thing as "chemistry" between people?

FINDING OUT

The following articles examine the art of conversation from a variety of perspectives. The writers refer to the work of a number of researchers who have analyzed the key components of conversation: the listening signals, speaking signals, and body language signals that we send and receive in talking with others. These researchers point out that many of the problems we have with communication, with sending or picking up each others' "signals," are caused by poor conversation skills and different conversation styles among individuals and cultures. They also describe practices and procedures that can be used to overcome these problems and help ensure that conversation is more lively than deadly.

As you examine this first topic, you will note the crucial link between information, perspective, and opinion. The more information you have on a topic, the broader your perspective becomes. The broader your perspective becomes, the more convincing your opinion becomes, both to yourself and to others. You will also develop skill in identifying main ideas, summarizing and outlining ideas and information, locating and organizing information, and selecting evidence to support opinion.

SUGGESTED APPROACH

This activity may be done either individually, in pairs, or in small groups.

Step 1

Take three pages in your notebook and title the first one *Speaking Signal Problems and Solutions*, the second one, *Listening Signal Problems and Solutions*, and the third one, *Body Language Signal Problems and Solutions*.

Step 2

Skim over the eight articles and divide them in an equitable way among individuals, pairs, or groups.

Step 3

Each individual, pair, or group reads the assigned article(s), pausing during or after each one to enter key points made about speaking, listening, or body language signals and solutions. (Note: Some articles focus on one area more than others.)

Step 4

When you have finished, highlight which information is new to you and to what extent you are convinced by it. (For example, consider the weight of evidence supplied and the "credentials" of the various authorities referred to in the articles.)

Step 5

Most of the researchers referred to in the articles indicate that sex, occupation, and status are important factors in determining conversational patterns. However, Emanuel Schegloff, the researcher extensively quoted in the second article, "The Art of Chit-chat," ". . . strenuously objects to his colleagues' efforts to use sex, occupation or status as a way to explain why conversations work out the way they do," citing other factors. Which researcher(s) would you side with? Why?

WHAT YOU HEAR ISN'T ALWAYS WHAT YOU GET

....

By Don Oldenburg

In Center Harbor, Maine, legend recalls the day 10 years ago when Walter Cronkite steered his boat into port. The avid sailor, as it's told, was amused to see in the distance a small crowd of people on shore waving their arms to greet him. He could barely make out their excited shouts of "Hello Walter ... Hello Walter."

As his boat sailed closer, the crowd grew larger, still yelling "Hello Walter ... Hello Walter." Pleased at the reception, Cronkite tipped his white captain's hat, waved back and even took a bow.

But before reaching dockside, Cronkite's boat abruptly jammed aground. The crowd stood silent. The veteran news anchor suddenly realized what they'd been shouting: "Low water ... low water."

Do we hear what we want to hear? Conventional wisdom says we do.

But science has discovered that, once beyond the ear's physical limitations, what we hear has less to do with choice than with psychological influences and processing that unconsciously and regularly steer communications aground.

In 1938 when Orson Welles broadcast his notorious radio version of H.G. Wells' *War Of The Worlds*, thousands of listeners panicked, believing it was a news bulletin detailing a Martian invasion – despite four announcements during the program that it was a dramatization. Ever since, the event has repeatedly been cited as evidence that listening is the weak link in interpersonal communications.

"We are guilty of tuning out, yielding to distractions, becoming over-emotional, faking attention or even dozing with our eyes open," says Robert Montgomery, author of *Listening Made Easy*, who for 31 years has labelled poor listening "a 20th-century epidemic."

Hear 50 Per Cent

The numerous books and courses on effective listening list alarming research results: that the average person spends 50 to 80 per cent of his day listening but hears only half of what is said, understands only a quarter of that, and remembers even less; that our attention span rarely lasts more than 45 seconds; that most people use only 25 per cent of their native ability for listening. But, they insist, you can vastly improve your listening ability by honing a few simple skills.

Recent investigations of listening seem to confirm all that. But there's nothing simple about improving how the brain processes what the ear transmits to it.

Consider the psychological mechanism called "selective listening." When consciously activated, it can help to clarify communications – but when left to its own devices, it can distort, misinterpret, even ignore messages.

Ruth Day, a Duke University psychologist who specializes in the study of perception, memory, comprehension and language, says the human mind is an active processor of information and not a passive receiver.

In general, she says, the speech signal that gets into our ears and up into our brains is usually degraded in some way – by mis-speaking, by the person listening, by noises blotting out sound."

That, says Day, is when the mental processor kicks in to perform what scientists call the phonemic restoration effect. "The many layers of language enable you to fill in what you were unable to get ... and more often than not allow you to interpret what actually was said," says Day.

People Add Words

Phonemic restoration, experts say, fills gaps in most of our everyday conversations. While enabling the mind to piece together what it heard – or what it thought it heard – it also provides an opportunity to jumble the communique, to make sense of nonsense and vice versa. In a demonstration of auditory perception devised by Richard Warren at the University of Wisconsin and later conducted by Day at Yale, audiences were asked to write down as much as they could remember from a long list of words she read. Most people easily recalled hearing some of the words, like "slumber," "rest," "yawn," "pillow" and "snore." But usually about three-quarters of each test group was certain Day had mentioned "sleep." She hadn't.

Yet in actively constructing our perception of ambiguous events, the mind sometimes paints the message with its own prejudices or hidden agenda. "The problem is . . . when you are trying to actively construct a meaning, you very often have to infer things about messages that aren't explicit," says George Ledger, associate professor of psychology at Hollins College near Roanoke, Va. "And by trying to infer those things, you often are led astray by your own inferences."

Ledger says studies in which subjects listen to several simple declarative sentences, such as "The turtle is on the log," "The log is in the stream," "The cabin is by the stream," "The man is in the cabin," often leave people convinced they heard another sentence: "The man sees the turtle." He says inference-laden ambiguities like that are standard fare in political speeches. . . .

Day says a biased misinterpretation usually involves other factors, such as an unclear or too-rapid signal or a worn-out listener, but "the listeners could have these various needs or wants – that they want to hear it only one way, or they believe something is so and it therefore biases their perception. It is called 'mental set' and they hear certain things and not other things."

Bob Bookman takes his cue on selective listening from something TV's Archie Bunker once said to his wife Edith: "The problem with our communication is I speak in English and you listen in dingbat."

A consultant who has taught corporate managers and naval officers listening skills, Bookman sees the primary influence in selective listening to be conflict. Whether discussing with a spouse which partner should be changing the baby in the morning, making a corporate proposal or negotiating a nuclear test-ban treaty, "proving ourselves right underlies so much of our communications today," says the president of Bookman Resources Inc. in Arlington, Va. "Most of us do listen in dingbat – the average person is listening to his own conversation."

Relevancy strongly influences what we hear, according to Anne Treisman, a psychologist at the University of California in Berkeley, renowned for her research on motivation and perception. She says experiments have shown that the selective listening process monitors meaning as we listen.

At a . . . party, says Treisman, you may pick up your own name mentioned in a conversation across the room, but have no idea of the name of the person introduced to you a moment before. "It's an effective filtering system that shuts out things we are not currently attending to. Nevertheless something in our brains keeps a lookout for things that are important.

"People still don't agree what effect attention has . . . I think it can shut down and prevent us from completely hearing and understanding. But there are people who think the brain is aware of everything that goes on whether we are paying attention or not."

To further complicate listening is the fact that we are poor judges of whether we've understood a message. "When you get information, you construct a meaning for it," says Ledger. "After a period of time, you reconstruct that message – but you reconstruct it through a filter of your own attitudes so it is no longer the same message.

"After the first few reconstructions, a solid version will emerge and you will view it as an accurate reproduction of what you heard. But it seldom is."

As Ruth Day says, "The problem, in most instances, is that the head works much faster than the mouth and the ear."

▫

THE ART OF CHIT-CHAT

....

By Anne C. Roark

Imagine yourself walking down the street. You see a friend and call to him, but he apparently does not hear you. You call out again. This time, he turns around and says, "Oh, hi. I didn't hear you call the first time."

You might wonder how he knew you had hailed him more than once if he did not hear you in the first place. Was he lying to you?

The answer, according to Emanuel A. Schegloff, a 49-year-old sociologist at the University of California, Los Angeles, is neither. It is quite likely, Schegloff says, that your friend did not hear you the first time, but it is equally likely that he knew there had been a first time.

Something in your voice – pitch, volume, placing or placement of words – would have informed him that what he heard was not the first thing that had been said to him.

Such changes in tone and inflection, the patterns of words and their timing, are the subject of a relatively young scholarly discipline known as conversation analysis.

Founded by Schegloff and a colleague at the University of California about two decades ago, the field has focused on the talk in real conversations.

Linguists and rhetoricians have long theorized about the formal structure and use of language. But, until recently, there was no systematic attempt to understand how people actually speak to one another – the elaborate exchanges of information and feelings, the give and take, the starts and stops, the often unintelligible utterances that make up ordinary conversation. . . .

Conversation, even chit-chat, is not as random or disorderly as it may seem. It is a highly structured enterprise that relies on a complex and almost inviolate set of rules and highly regularized practices.

When people talk to one another, they ordinarily talk one at a time, one after the other. When everyone tries to speak at once or when no one speaks at all, there is an immediate effort to restore "order." Someone stops talking. Someone steps in to fill the silence.

Sometimes the order goes awry – a silence may continue for too long, or the simultaneous talk may not cease quickly enough. People begin to fidget; they look at the floor; they shift in their seats. Or they become competitive. Their voices become louder and higher pitched. These, Schegloff says, are "special states" of conversation that are invariably and quickly resolved in favor of normality – one speaker at a time.

But how do people actually know what is too much? How do they know when their turn is up?

"The assumption before was that talk was very personal, very idiosyncratic," says Deirdre Boden, one of the organizers of a recent California conference entitled Talk And Social Structure.

But now, says Boden, even expressions such as "eh" or "well," once thought to be individual errors, are no longer viewed as mistakes at all but as intentional expressions or manifestations of the rules of ordinary conversation.

"What is so remarkable," she adds, "is that people follow these rules without ever being taught them – indeed, without even knowing . . . that they exist." Moreover, according to a group of conversation analysts at the University of Texas, "virtually the same rules" seem to be followed by members of all societies.

In addition to maintaining order, Schegloff has found, an important function of the conversational rules is avoiding unpleasantness.

"That is what the introduction of 'ah' or 'well' is all about," Schegloff says. "Think about what you do when you ask someone to do something for you or to go someplace with you. If you are afraid the answer may be no, you will fill your conversations with 'ahhs' and 'hmms.' You may even restart your sentences several times over before actually launching into what it is you really want to say," avoiding eliciting an undesired response.

Schegloff, considered one of the dominant forces in the field of conversation study, strenuously objects to his colleagues' efforts to use sex, occupation or status as a way to explain why conversations work the way they do. Who the participants are or where they are, he argues, is often irrelevant to basic conversation analysis.

Practical Uses

"If, for example, we say that one speaker is interrupting another speaker just because he is male and she is female, then we may miss the fine details of what happened in the conversation that may have caused the interruption to occur.

"There is still a great deal of basic information about talk that we simply do not yet understand," he says.

Nonetheless, some conversation analysts seem to be taking on questions with obvious practical applications.

Turning the art of old-fashioned rhetoric into a science, a number of conversation analysts have demonstrated quite precisely how politicians manipulate the rules of conversation to cause audiences to applaud at specific moments.

Other researchers have shown scientifically how such manipulation can force even experienced news reporters to ask certain kinds of questions of politicians, while causing them to steer clear of others.

What is behind the concerns of many researchers, they say, is the intriguing question of who dominates conversation.

IS ANYONE LISTENING?

By Gregg Levoy

Person One: "I was watching a program on television last night about Jean Dore, the mayor of Montreal, and . . ."

Person Two: "Oh, have you been to Montreal? I went there a few years ago and we stayed at the Bonaventure Hotel, and we took a carriage ride around Mount Royal. Now, what were you saying?". . .

. . . Few people know how to listen, says Eric Reitz, director of the Centre for Family Enrichment near San Francisco. Done properly, he says, the listener gets "that 'aha' experience" and the speaker gets what author Robert Heinlein referred to in his book, *Stranger In a Strange Land*, as "grokked – profoundly understood."

Done properly, the listener can re-create for the speaker "the intent, the meaning, the emotion behind what was said, not just the words," says Reitz. "Listening is hearing more deeply than the speaker hears himself."

What It Involves

But listening is the most difficult step in communication, he says, and women do tend to be somewhat more adept at it than men. "Men are more blocked about emotions, and since emotions are the essence of communication, men have a more difficult time listening for and expressing them."

Nonetheless, listening is also a collaborative process, and there is much that each partner can do to remedy the situation and help each other. One place to start is understanding what good listening really involves.

According to Florence Wolff, a University of Dayton communications professor who has literally written the book about it, called *Perspective Listening* (Holt, Rinehart & Winston, 1983), claims that 70 per cent of our time is spent communicating; reading, writing, speaking and listening. Of that time, 9 per cent is taken up by reading, 16 per cent writing, 32 per cent speaking, and 45 per cent listening – poorly.

"We spend all of our school years learning how to read; 13 years of education for 9 per cent of our communication skills. But we don't have anything for listening. We're terrible listeners, and it takes a toll on our relations, our politics and our businesses, says Wolff.

In the business world, Wolff points out, such a problem has even been quantified. The Sperry Corp. in New York, she says, found that, "with 87,000 employees, if each one made a $10 mistake due to not listening, misunderstanding, taking a wrong number or a wrong order, they would lose $1 billion a year. Businesses are beginning to realize that good listening means business dollars. . . ."

When adults are tested for listening skills, says Wolff, they routinely hear between 25 and 50 per cent of what was said, and that's under test conditions, immediately after listening to someone.

Listening, she says, is generally regarded as a passive activity.

But if you're listening well, you're working pretty hard at it. If you're relaxed after half an hour of listening, you probably weren't really listening.

Six things occur in rapid succession when we're listening to someone, says Wolff, and it

is very different from merely "hearing" someone.

Hearing, the first step, is a physiological thing; listening is an emotional and intellectual one. We hear a lot of things that we don't really listen to: the strains of traffic, the humming of a fan or radiator – all quite different from actually listening.

The second step is selection, choosing what we want to perceive, blocking out the rest. Then comes assimilation, assigning meaning to the sound ("That's the sound of a . . ."").

After that is organization, the brain racing to put information somewhere, into a previously designed category. Stage five is retention. And finally "covert response," the internal thought about the sound or information which immediately precedes a verbal response, Wolff says.

Mostly, our brains work to get in the way, says Sally Webb, past president of the International Listening Association, and a communications professor at the University of Wisconsin, Eau Claire. "We have terrible habits."

The first is faking it, she says. Some people have mastered the art of looking at you and nodding. It only looks like listening. She says you can usually tell when someone is programmed like that: They forget to react.

Poor listeners also neglect proper listening posture: That is, sitting up straight and looking at the speaker. When the eyes are elsewhere, says Webb, so is the mind.

Part of this problem, Wolff says, is that we're "*Sesame Street* listeners." We're addicted to entertainment, says Webb.

"No speaker can reasonably compete with television. It's too much stimulus, the pace is too fast, there are too many jokes, it's too edited and jazzed up."

Distraction, too, is one of the bugbears of good listening. The average room, says Wolff, contains 43 decibels of sound, all competing for the average *Sesame Street* attention span. There are also internal distractions: You're hungry, you just got a parking ticket.

It all sounds so mundane, but the results of not listening are far from trivial. Wolff points to the high rate of suicide among teenagers and young adults as one social problem directly related to not listening and to the isolation that that brings about in people who really need to be heard. . . .

Trigger-words

Reitz suggests doing the following when you find yourself distracted from listening: Stop the conversation, admit that you're distracted (or defensive) and ask for a moment to recoup your attention.

There are also semantic distractions, as Wolff calls them. These are trigger-words that send the blood rising: abortion, nuclear, gay, communism. They become the focus of attention, instead of what the person is saying about any of those things, and the mind shuts down.

Don't just listen to the verbiage, says Webb. Notice, also, the emotional content behind it, the inflection, eye contact, pitch, tone, speed and body language – so that you can actually "see" what somebody means.

"Listening is focusing," she says, "That's why drinkers are usually terrible listeners."

A good exercise to enhance listening, perhaps especially when one is emotional, Webb stresses, is what she calls "re-creating" the speakers' communication. Listening to it, then repeating it, emotions and all.

"But when a speaker's message is re-created, he or she feels more connected to the listener, to themselves, and to the communication."

Also, when the speaker feels genuinely heard and understood, he or she will be more inclined to do the same when it's [his or her] turn to listen.

Listening, says Wolff, is caring. It is an act of love at the best, and a courtesy at the least.

DEFUSING VERBAL ATTACKS IS POSSIBLE IF YOU UNDERSTAND WHAT'S BEING SAID

....

By David Streitfeld

Forget the old cliche, says psycholinguist Suzette Haden Elgin. Words can hurt you. . . .

Verbal Abuse

Most verbal abusers are men and most of their victims are women, but this isn't just a sexist or domestic matter. At home, the attacker can be your spouse, parents or child; at work, it could be your co-workers or your boss; and in the professional world, it could be anyone from a doctor or lawyer to a government worker or teacher – anyone who outranks you in knowledge or status. From the health care worker's "You're not the ONLY patient I have" to the salesman's "If you REALLY cared about your family, you wouldn't buy a cheap car," verbal abuse is almost everywhere. . . .

Sucker Punch

For example, when someone says, "if you REALLY loved me, you'd lose weight," what that actually implies is, "You don't really love me," says Elgin. "But the victim responds to the wrong part of the sentence – the second part, the bait – and the result is a big row, which is what the abuser wanted. It's a sucker punch."

Her recommendation: Ignore the bait and respond to the presupposition with something neutral, such as: "When did you start thinking I didn't really love you?". . .

"English is a language in which at least 65 per cent of the meaning is carried by things other than the words – by the melodic patterns, the stresses," says Elgin. "The most basic example of this is a sentence like, 'What are we having for dinner, mother?' as opposed to, 'What are we having for dinner – MOTHER?' I think I've managed to identify a set of melodic patterns that are always attacks."

Among these attacks, with the stresses indicated by capitalization:

"Don't you even CARE about . . . (your children, your grades, world hunger, our marriage, etc.)?"

The presupposition here is that you don't care, and that therefore you are despicable. You are expected to argue, to say "of COURSE I care," and jump into a fight. Elgin's advice is to say "no," which in her analysis would lead to a dialogue like this:

"Don't you even CARE ABOUT NUCLEAR DISARMAMENT?"

"No."

"NO! I don't believe you SAID that! Only a CREEP would say a thing like that!"

"I'm sorry – are we talking about disarmament or are we talking about creeps?"

- "EVen a WOMan should be able to understand THAT book!"

The presupposition here, of course, is not only that women are inferior, but also that the book doesn't require much brainpower to understand. The attacker expects the victim to take this as a personal attack and be forced to defend herself.

The better response, Elgin says: "When did you start thinking women are inferior?" This removes the argument from the personal level and puts the attacker on the spot.

- "YOU'RE only DOing that to get atTENtion, you know!"

This sentence is designed to pick a fight. If the victim responds to the bait with, "I am not pretending! I really am sick!," the attacker has the chance to say you aren't sick and to wrangle over your symptoms.

"The only reason anyone says this with these stresses is to cause a row," says Elgin.

Her approach: "Say in a neutral voice and without sarcasm, 'It's so kind of you to be so understanding.' You're accepting that it refers to you but you're denying it's an insult."

Dennis Becker, president of The Speech Improvement Co., a Boston communications consulting firm, generally gives Elgin's methods a favorable rating.

"She can oversimplify what needs to be done, and in some cases doesn't go far enough, but, on balance, her approach does help," he says. "Any time we can get people to be more self-critical or self-evaluative, we're doing them a service."

Women in Emergency Medicine, a national society of emergency room physicians based in Palo Alto, Calif., is giving Elgin its 1986 Leadership Award. She taught the doctors linguistic techniques for dealing with frightened patients who say, "If you REALLY cared whether I was in pain, you'd give me something FOR it."

"Patients don't want an explanation of why they can't have a pill," says Elgin. "They want reassurance." She counselled the doctors to respond with an acknowledgement of the patient's suffering: "Of course I care you're in pain."

The difference between physical and verbal abuse is equivalent to that between an immediate illness and working in a building set on a toxic waste dump, Elgin says.

"Damage from the second may not show up for a very long time, but it's just as dangerous as the first, and will make you just as sick."

MAN – WOMAN TALK

Why We Should Also Listen Between the Lines

....

By Deborah Tannen

Riding home in a car, a woman asks, "Are you thirsty? Would you like to stop for a drink?" The man answers, "No," and they do not stop.

The man is later surprised to learn that the woman is displeased: She wanted to stop. He wonders why she didn't just tell him what she wanted.

The woman is disgruntled, not because she didn't get her way but because she felt her opinion wasn't sought and wasn't considered.

When she asked, "Would you like to stop?" she did not expect a yes-no answer. She expected a counter-question: "I don't know. Would you like to?"

She could then respond, "Well, I'd kind of like to. How tired are you?"

The woman must realize that when he answers "yes" or "no," he is not making a non-negotiable demand. If she has other ideas, he expects she will state them without being invited to do so.

A woman who led workshops with a male colleague was distressed because he did all the talking. When anyone asked a question, he answered before she had a chance to speak.

She blamed him for dominating her.

One common way of understanding this situation would be to suggest that men are chauvinists and think nothing of interrupting women. Another would be to look for psychological motives in one or both parties: She is passive; he is narcissistic.

But another, more elegant explanation is possible: a linguistic one.

Linguistics could tell us that these two individuals have different timing habits for when they take turns. She expects a slightly longer pause between speaking turns than he does.

So while she was waiting for what seemed to her the proper pause, he became restless. The appropriate pause to him had come and gone.

To avoid what he thought would be an uncomfortable silence and the appearance that neither of them had anything to say, the man began to answer.

The linguistic solution worked in this case. No therapy was needed, no consciousness-raising other than linguistic.

The woman pushed herself to begin speaking just a bit sooner than seemed polite to her. The miraculous result was that she found herself doing much of the talking, and her colleague was as pleased as she was.

Another example: A man fixes himself a snack and is about to eat it when he notices that his wife looks hurt. He asks what's wrong and is told, "You didn't offer me any."

"I'm sorry," he says, "I didn't know you were hungry. Here, have this."

She declines: "You didn't make it for me."

He is confused, because he regards the snack as a matter of food: the message. But she is concerned with the metamessage: Does he think of her as she would think of him?

Yet another example is a conversation in which a man asks a woman, "How was your day?"

She responds with a 20-minute answer, full of details about whom she met, what was said and what she thought – regardless of whether she spent her day at home with the children or in an executive office.

Then she asks him, "How was your day?" and he responds, "Same old rat race."

Conversations like this lead women to complain that men don't tell them anything and lead men to complain that they don't understand what women want.

This practical approach to language is part of a new trend in linguistics. It analyzes mechanisms, such as turn-taking, that are the gears of conversation.

Other linguistic signals include shifts in pitch, loudness, pacing, tone of voice, and intonation, and linguistic devices such as questions, story-telling and relative indirectness.

Linguists are concerned with linking the surface level of talk – what people say and how they say it – with the semantics (the meaning derived) and pragmatics (what people are seeking to do or show by speaking in that way at that time).

This has brought the discipline into the arena of human interaction and real-world communication problems, and it offers a genuinely new way of understanding human interaction.

The application of linguistics to real-world communication problems is received with mixed emotions within the discipline. Many contemporary linguists see the study of the mechanisms of conversation as basic to the work of linguistics.

They applaud the fact that applying linguistic analysis to these mechanisms means that linguistics can play a role not only in elucidating how language works, but also in grappling with the real-world problems caused by miscommunication.

But there are many other linguists who are uneasy about this development. Some feel certain that it stretches the scope of the field so far as to weaken it.

Modern linguistics has been heralded as the science of language, and many linguists feel it is crucial to maintain both the rigorous methods of scientific investigation and the concomitant severe limitations on appropriate data.

Turning the lens of linguistics onto real-world language has meant broadening the scope of investigation beyond the sentence to spates of language as large as people produce.

And the study of discourse – the most popular new subdiscipline in linguistics – entails studying language in its natural settings: language in education, doctor-patient communication, language and the law, public negotiations, and the most common, most encompassing form of discourse: everyday conversation.

Included in all these contexts is the issue that is perhaps the most widely appealing outside of the discipline, but also particularly controversial within it – male-female differences in language use.

Issues of male-female communication strike at the heart of everyone's everyday experience, at home and at work. . . .

For example, a frequent complaint of women about men is that they don't listen to them. Men frequently protest, "I was listening!"

The question of listenership reflects the core of relationships: "Are you listening?" means "Are you interested?" which means "Do you love me?" The questions, "Are you listening?" and "Are you interested?" lie at the center of most conversations, including, for example, job interviews and business negotiations.

There may be instances in which people actually are not listening, but these are far fewer than people think.

A linguistic approach suggests that many of these misunderstandings can be traced to habits for displaying listenership.

For example, research has shown that, on the average, women give more frequent overt signs of listening: "mhm," "uhuh," "yeah," head nods, changing facial expressions.

Expecting the same show of responsiveness, women see men who listen quietly and attentively as not really listening at all, like the spectre of silence on a telephone line that causes one to inquire, "Are you still there?"

Conversely, a man who expects a woman to show she's listening simply by fixing her eyes on his face, feels she is over-reacting when she keeps up a steady stream of "mhms" and "uhuhs."

Whereas women tend to say "yeah" to

mean "I'm listening and following," men tend to say it to mean "I agree." So part of the reason women offer more of these listening noises, according to anthropologists Daniel Maltz and Ruth Borker, is that women are listening more often than men are agreeing.

Maltz and Borker report extensive research that shows that men and women develop assumptions about the role of language in close relationships from their childhood friends.

Little girls play with other girls, and the center of their social life is a best friend with whom they share secrets. It is the telling of secrets that makes them best friends.

Boys, in contrast, tend to play in groups, so their talk is less likely to be private. Rather, it is competitive talk about who is best at what, or performance talk that places the speaker at center stage, like Othello telling about his travels.

What makes boys friends is not what they say to each other but what they do together. So when a man is close to a woman, doing things together makes them close; nothing is missing for him if they don't talk about personal details. But she is missing what, for her, is the definitive element in intimacy.

Neither of these styles is right or wrong; they are just different. The frustration that both feel comes from the conviction that his or her own way is logical and self-evident.

When viewed as culturally learned habits of conversation, differences do not go away, but they need not be interpreted as evidence of individual pathology ("He is not in touch with his feelings") or individual failure ("He doesn't love me") or a joint failure ("This is a bad relationship – we don't communicate"). . . .

. . . Whenever linguistic habits differ, each person is likely to make the other feel manipulated simply in an attempt to get comfortable in the situation.

For a nonverbal analog, imagine two people who have slightly different senses of the appropriate distance between conversants. The one who feels comfortable standing farther away keeps backing off to adjust the space, but the conversational partner who expects to stand closer keeps advancing to close up the space, so they move together down the hall until one is pinned against a wall.

The key to a linguistic approach is that neither one nor the other must bear the blame for being manipulative. Rather, the culprit is the difference in their styles.

MEN, WOMEN SPEAK TWO LANGUAGES, EXPERT SAYS

By Helen Bullock

"I didn't know you felt like that."

"You didn't ask me how I felt."

"How did I know you wanted to be asked?"

"You're insensitive."

"You're overreacting."

You all recognize the familiar domestic wrangle between men and women played out in the drawing rooms of the nation. . . .

All the fuss is caused by two things: a man and a woman. What's at the heart of their problem, according to California consultant Dr. John Gray, is the sexes' inability to speak the same language. They may use the same words but the meaning is different to a male or female ear.

"Unless such differences are acknowledged, men and women don't work well together," Gray said. "The product of lack of communication is always the same: resentment, frustration and a falling off of enthusiasm and productivity."

Gray, who has taught seminars and been a therapist for 15 years, helps men and women understand what they've always suspected, even in these days of equality and androgyny: Men and women are different.

In order to deal successfully with the opposite sex, you must talk in a language that's clearly understood, that informs, flatters and respects them. . . .

Often men and women's conflicting priorities are revealed through language. Men are proud of what they *do*: they have a need to have concrete accomplishments they can walk people around.

Women also need to build on their accomplishments but are equally concerned about how they relate to people and what state their working relationships are in. It's unlikely a woman boss will be happy with a project if the working relationships are lousy.

Though both sexes suffer from stress on the job, "women tend to open up under pressure and need to talk and men withdraw and grow silent," Gray said.

"Talking is important to women in a way it isn't to men. Under a great deal of pressure, a woman may need to spill her problems out, talk them through. If she does it in front of a man, he wants to jump in and immediately solve them. 'Okay, here's what you do' approach.

"Women are irritated by this; they need the catharsis of speech. They're irritated by the instant Mr. Fix-it."

Gray says in addition to the social conditioning we hear so much about, science is discovering more physiological differences between the sexes. For example, "just recently, brain pictures revealed women have more connecting tissue between the right and left hemisphere of the brain," he said.

"It means women can switch more easily and quickly from the logical left side to the creative right side. It's why they easily think about several different problems or situations at the same time.

"Men are prone to over-focus on one problem at a time. They have total awareness of one work problem and block out other work or personal problems, while women have all these related and unrelated things going around at the same time.

"The pressures on women can be much greater than on men because they feel the weight of several problems at once."

Despite the frustrations of an increasingly co-ed workplace at every level, including the highest, the advantages work for everybody.

"Women have already humanized the workplace," Gray said in an interview from his California headquarters. "The so-called 'feminine' factors of good communications skills, assertiveness rather than aggression and cooperation rather than competition, are big improvements in the quality of working life.

"They de-stress men and make it more comfortable in the office. Also, if men are conscious of their emotional selves during the day, it builds a bridge to their personal life at the end of the day. Men don't have to shut down one personality and find another before they go home."

Gray says the answer to many of the workplace battles of the sexes is to support each other's complementary differences and borrow from each, too. Common ground is usually found in the middle. It's not a question of right or wrong, just different.

In business, of course, it's always a question of effectiveness. Fifty years ago, the all-male model, in a predominantly male business world, in an almost exclusively male executive world, worked just fine.

Today, its effectiveness is dulled by the social impact and changes fostered by working and succeeding women. A new style is still struggling to be born out of conflicting differences and modes of operation, and again it won't be a question of right or wrong. Just a way of handling, acknowledging and working with the differences until they spell s-u-c-c-e-s-s.

DESMOND MORRIS: THE GURU OF BODY WATCHERS

··

By Kathy Hacker

So here you sit, in Desmond Morris' considerable presence, and suddenly you're feeling strangely self-conscious and sort of . . . exposed.

Has he noticed the telltale way your arms are folded across your chest, or your left foot bouncing up and down like a yo-yo? Did he see you raise your hand to your mouth or twist your hair and, from that, deduce certain things about you, the real you?

Through these innocent little gestures and postures have you revealed yourself as insecure or aggressive, anxious or annoyed, deceitful, repressed or (horrors) nerdy?

Relax. For the moment, at least, Morris is too busy talking about bodies to indulge in watching yours or anyone else's.

That is not to say he wouldn't love to.

A broad-shouldered, barrel-chested Briton with narrow black eyes and a wit as dry as unbuttered toast, he has been a tireless observer of the human form for more than two decades, devoting untold hours to pondering the true meaning of some 3,000 mannerisms, from the Eyebrow Flash (you're pleasantly surprised) and the Eyebrow Shrug (you're unpleasantly surprised) to the tightly clasped Thigh-Thigh Cross (ah, feeling a bit defensive, are you?). Indeed, on an ordinary day, he could size you up handily. . . .

"It was my dream," . . . Morris says grandly . . . "to make a complete tour of the human body, bit by bit, and cover every action associated with every part."

[With his recent book *Body Watching: A Field Guide to the Human Species*] he has very nearly done it, mapping the human physique from hair follicles to tootsies and, along the way, attempting to explain why we are the way we are and do the things we do:

- Why males have heavier jaws and facial hair (they create a more aggressive and hostile visage for enemies).
- Why we cover our yawning mouths (in ancient times, folks believed that the soul could escape through the gaping orifice and an evil spirit could enter).

It is a typically fascinating Morrisian mix of fact and speculation, possibilities and probabilities. It is the stuff of best-sellers. It is also grist for endless quibbling among evolution theorists, who seldom agree about anything with anybody and with Desmond Morris in particular – this despite the upgrading of his credentials to Oxford research fellow.

He tells you that body-watching is hard work.

"This is not casual observation," he stresses. "This is analytical observation that very often involves measuring how many times a single movement occurs. One must also study the way that gesture or posture changes as one moves from group to group and place to place . . . You end up with an enormous amount of material."

Although Morris has been around the world twice, he admits to doing some of his body-watching in front of the TV set.

Talk shows, he says, are show-cases for body language at its most bizarre.

With no script to guide them, guests understandably get the jitters. "They know their bodies are going to be giving off signals. So over and over again, you see this celebrity sitting on the sofa and the top half of his body is relaxed and smiling, while the bottom half is twitching.

"Maybe his foot is bouncing. Maybe he's tapping it on the floor. Up top, he looks like he's having a marvelous time and he'd like to stay there forever. But his foot is saying, 'I wanna get out.' "

The Nose Touch is also much in evidence on talk shows, particularly after someone has been asked a difficult question.

Morris interprets it as a sign of "a split

between the state of mind and the state of body. There's a sort of deception going on. Though outwardly the person is calm, the brain is seething. It is churning and saying, 'Shall I tell the truth or not?'

"When he does give an answer, it may well be an honest one. You can't be sure he lied, but you can be sure he was worried."

Which brings up a salient question about body-watching: How reliable are the signals? Morris replies that they are quite dependable enough to satisfy a statistician.

Yet having said that, he tells the story of an unusual photograph that he kept in his office for months.

It showed a man standing in an empty New York street with his arms stretched as wide as they would go and his fingers cupped into outward-facing palms, with thumbs pointed up.

The picture plagued Morris. He'd never before seen such a posture, and as the months went by, he cooked up a series of intriguing explanations that, nonetheless, didn't quite fit. Finally, he pulled out a magnifying lens and scoured the print.

The man was carrying a sheet of glass.

BODY LANGUAGE IS KEY TO SUCCESS: THERAPIST

Give therapist Derek Balmer 30 seconds and he'll tell you exactly how you relate to the people around you.

The way your eyes move when you talk, the tone of your voice, your breathing patterns and changes in the color of your skin all are subtle forms of body language, he says.

These non-verbal signals go a long way to explaining why you get along so well – or so poorly – with a lover, a business partner or a casual acquaintance.

"Twenty per cent of information is verbal; 80 per cent of it is non-verbal," Balmer says.

"Without rapport, you cut off 80 per cent of communications.". . .

Balmer . . . is one of Canada's leading practitioners of neuro-linguistic programming [NLP]. . . .

NLP begins with the premise that people use their senses in ways that are as distinctive as their fingerprints. Of particular importance is the extent to which they rely on sight, hearing and touch and how that sensory information is conveyed to their minds.

People who are dominated by vision often paint imaginary pictures when asked to recall something that has happened in the past. Kinesthetic or "feeling" people pay more attention to emotions than images. Auditory people "tune in" to sounds easily, even to the point of being able to recreate the sounds of a symphony orchestra in their minds.

Put two different types of people together in a marriage and the potential for poor communication is almost limitless, Balmer says. Take the case of a kinesthetic husband and a visual wife and a classic irritant such as eating crackers in bed.

"Crackers in bed would be entirely offensive to someone who highly values comfort and relaxation," he says. "A visual person would hardly notice, and certainly not with the same degree of discomfort as the kinesthetic."

The same kind of mismatched communication that helps poison personal relationships can stand in the way of business success. Balmer taught a sales course using NLP techniques last year for people in real estate and has a course on negotiations in the works for lawyers.

In both cases the goals are to teach people how to establish rapport with clients or colleagues and exchange information with them comfortably.

"Business applications are mind-boggling," says Balmer. "It seems to me that half the trouble as I wander around business today is straight miscommunication at a very elementary level."

FOLLOWING THROUGH

Now that you have explored the art of conversation from other perspectives as well as your own, re-examine your original opinion.

SUGGESTED APPROACH

Step 1

Look back over your individual and class responses to the "Opinionnaire" and re-read your journal entry. To what extent has your opinion changed or deepened?

Step 2

Write either a final journal entry or describe an episode that develops or supports your new perspective.

SOME FURTHER FOLLOW-THROUGH SUGGESTIONS

Some of these suggestions may be done as independent study
activities, either individually or in small groups, or as whole class
activities.

• Re-read your initial journal entry on your own conversation "image" and
  use it to write a profile of your conversational skills – an analysis of your
  own listening, speaking, and body language signals. Include ideas of how
  you might improve your conversational abilities.

• Do some "people watching" to verify or disprove some of the key ideas
  in these articles, particularly the idea of different conversation patterns
  between men and women. Make a list of the elements you will be
  looking for beforehand so that you will know what to focus on as you are
  watching.

• Pair yourself with a class member of the opposite sex and tape a five- to
  ten-minute conversation on a mutually acceptable topic. Afterward, listen
  to the conversation and assess the extent to which it "proves" or
  "disproves" the researchers' findings concerning different male-female
  conversational patterns.

• Watch television newscasts, talk shows, quiz shows, and televised
  parliamentary debates to verify or disprove some of the key ideas in
  these articles.

• Create a series of questions based on some of the important ideas
  expressed in these articles, and conduct an opinion poll to determine the
  validity of the ideas.

• Make a videotape that demonstrates the "do's and don't's" of effective
  conversation.

TOPIC

two

Getting a Job

··

FOCUSING IN

There is an old saying that first impressions are lasting impressions, and nowhere is this more evident than when seeking employment. A negative first impression usually results in the early rejection of a job applicant.

Usually the first impression we create with a prospective employer is achieved through a completed job application form or a résumé. One of the best ways to explore the importance of first impressions is to role-play, to look at your application or résumé from the perspective of the potential employer.

SUGGESTED APPROACH

Step 1

Read the following job advertisement. From the perspective of the employer who placed the ad, read the two responses (résumés and accompanying letters) and reflect on the different overall impression each one creates and why.

In determining your initial response, consider the following:

a. aspects of the application that led to your overall impression;
b. elements in your own personality that affected your impression;
c. qualities you would want in the people you hired if you were running your own business;

d.   qualities you would list as being important in the person or company that employed you;

e.   your own experiences(s), or others you have heard of, in applying for employment.

Westdale Trust

Our current retail expansion has created opportunities in Westdale for qualified customer-oriented

Tellers

Providing personable, enthusiastic, and efficient customer service, you will manage your own cash and be responsible for the promotion and selling of a wide range of retail banking products. Part-time and full-time positions available.

Send your résumé to:

Branch Manager
1372 Laclie Street
Westdale, Nova Scotia
B7X 3R6

Derek Cheung
69 Kingswood Place
Westdale, Nova Scotia
B3T 1M2

Branch Manager
1372 Laclie Street
Westdale, Nova Scotia
B7X 3R6

Dear Sir/Madame,

I would like to apply for the position of a Bank Teller.

In my high-school career I have studied math, computing, and other useful subjects. My average mark in high school was a B+. Although I will graduate from Caledon Business and Technical Institute in January, 1991, I plan to go on to college to earn my business degree.

Enclosed is my résumé. I draw your attention to my recent work experience at Atlantic Currency Service Ltd. At that time I gained experience in bookkeeping and using the computer.

You may also contact Ms. Rochester, my math teacher at Caledon, 3208 Midland Avenue, Westdale, Nova Scotia, B1S 1C1, (902) 496-6695 and Carol Williams, owner of Atlantic Currency Service Ltd., 47 John Street, Westdale, B1T 1X4 (902) 473-3798 for my references.

I'm looking forward to working in your branch as a Bank Teller. I am available for an interview at your convenience. Thank you for considering me.

Sincerely yours,

Derek Cheung
Derek Cheung

Derek Cheung
69 Kingswood Place
Westdale, Nova Scotia
B3T 1M2
(902) 498-2438

EDUCATION

1987 – Present

Caledon Business and Technical Institute
Area of specialty: Data Processing

EMPLOYMENT BACKGROUND

1988 – Present

Worked at Atlantic Currency Service as a Foreign Money Exchange Teller. My duties included taking care of customers, selling traveller's cheques, cash balancing.

ACTIVITIES AND INTERESTS

My hobbies include computing, reading, music, tennis, skiing, cycling, and lacrosse.

REFERENCES

Available upon request.

68 Greenbriar Crescent
Westdale, Nova Scotia
B2R 1R6
November 10, 1991

1372 Laclie Street
Westdale, Nova Scotia
B7X 3R6

Attn: Branch Manager

Dear Sir/Madame,

I am applying for the part-time Teller's position you have advertised in the newspaper. My name is Jackie Shafer and I'm a graduate from Westdale Secondary School. I feel I have the qualifications for the position. I get along well with people and I've had experience handling money. I have enclosed a résumé along with this letter of application. Please contact the following people as my references.

Harry Chung	1354 Ellesmere Road	476-2149
Julie Cousins	44 Citizen Road	496-2136
Janet Bregg	51 Brookside Avenue	487-3342

If you have any further questions about my letter of application, please contact me at the above address. I look forward to hearing from you.

Sincerely,

Jackie Shafer

Jackie Shafer

Jackie A. Shafer
68 Greenbriar Crescent
Westdale, Nova Scotia
B2R 1R6
483-1918

EDUCATION:

Westdale Secondary School
38 Crawford Road, Westdale
493-1628
Specialty Area: Business
September 1987 – January 1991

WORK EXPERIENCE:

Henderson Car Sales
1900 Glendale Road, Westdale
493-2608
Night Cashier: My duties included handling money, customer service, typing, and answering the phone.
Manager: Tom MacPhedron
May/89 – July/90

Langstaff Leasing
230 Park Street, Westdale
495-2796
Filing Clerk, Accounts Payable: My duties included filing gas cards and typing cheques.
Supervisor: Linda Smith
Jan/89 – April/89

Parkway Systems Canada
715 Miller Road, Westdale
491-9452
Filing Clerk: My duties included working with microfiche, filing, typing, and inputting materials into the computer.
Supervisor: Donna Jasper
Oct/88 – Jan/89

INTERESTS:
I enjoy sports, reading, and working with people.

Step 2

Assume the role of the branch manager. (a) As the prospective employer, consider your initial impressions of each job applicant that you formed from reading their letters and résumés. (b) Write a brief memo to yourself listing the strengths of each person, the weaknesses of each person, and questions you will ask each of them during a job interview. (c) From the information provided by the letters and résumés, which person presents a better first impression?

Step 3

Working in small groups, complete the following tasks.

a. Compare responses to the two résumés by comparing the memos written in Step 2.
b. Identify the different factors or criteria the various "employers" were apparently using to make their decisions.
c. Assess the usefulness of identifying criteria when making decisions.

FINDING OUT

The material in this section examines the subject of getting a job from three perspectives: the job seeker, the prospective employer, and the professional agencies that help people find work. The articles that follow identify the key methods used by successful job seekers and the various qualities employers are looking for in prospective employees. They also offer tips for producing a high-quality résumé and for having a successful interview, the two essential elements in landing a job.

In reading this material, you will develop skill in finding similarities and differences among a variety of ideas and perspectives. You will also develop skill in predicting and speculating on potential outcomes, in formulating questions of inquiry, and in identifying and applying criteria as an important method of assessing or justifying an opinion, an action, or a decision.

Suggested Approach

This activity is best done in small groups.

Step 1

Each group should read the material that follows and identify (a) the key employee qualities identified by prospective employers, (b) the key elements of a successful résumé, and (c) the key elements of a successful interview.

Step 2

Each group should report its findings to the rest of the class and a master list of criteria should be generated for each of the three areas noted in Step 1. This master list should reflect the frequency that specific methods, qualities, and elements were mentioned in the various articles.

Step 3

As a class, prioritize these criteria in each of the areas by voting on their order of importance.

Step 4

Compare these prioritized checklists with the checklists you generated from your perspective as prospective employers in the Focusing In section. Note similarities and differences between perspectives. How do you account for them?

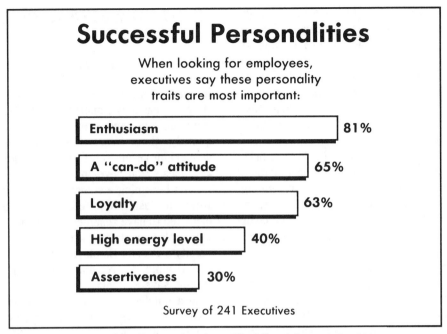

Successful Personalities

When looking for employees, executives say these personality traits are most important:

Enthusiasm	81%
A "can-do" attitude	65%
Loyalty	63%
High energy level	40%
Assertiveness	30%

Survey of 241 Executives

Adapted from *Psychology Today*, taken from *The Liberal*, January 6, 1989.

APPLICANTS JUDGED ON THEIR POTENTIAL

....

By Janis Foord

To many students, interviews for career jobs are scary prospects. . . .

Employers are mysterious beings, many say, their needs and expectations unknown. "What are they looking for?"

I decided to put that question to employers in a variety of fields, including banking, television, retail management and computers. Some are personnel professionals who recruit on campus, others are managers who interview in their offices. All have extensive experience with young workers.

When talking to young people, they say, they're looking for clues. They look for potential rather than experience, personality rather than a proven track record, and for what one employer called, "the correct fit."

That's not to say that skills, training and expertise aren't important. "Marks deliver a clear message," observed another employer. But in the end result, personal qualities and attributes tip the scale.

Consistently, I heard the same themes: initiative, communication, and interpersonal skills. In all fields, it seems, self-starters who talk and listen well and who get on well with others, take preference.

The world of broadcast journalism is a case in point. Studies in political science, English, history and economics provide good basic training, but without initiative and a tenacious curiosity, it's hard to get to first base. How can you persuade employers that you have those qualities?

"There's always a way," says Susanne Boyce, senior producer of *Midday*, CBC's noon-hour current affairs show. "I had someone call me and say, 'I'm meeting with you next week and I don't want to screw up the interview. But I haven't seen your show lately. Where can I get some tapes?'

"That gave me the idea that he would

be a good researcher. He knew where to go for the information. In our business, I need people who think ahead. You're looking at initiative."

Imagination is another big seller, says Boyce. "I really like it when people come in with ideas. I don't even care if they're achievable. What's interesting is to see how their minds work."

In the more structured banking world, imagination is less important than ambition, drive, and again, initiative. Those recruiting for the retail side of banking stress interpersonal skills, while commercial bankers favor advanced business training and some entrepreneurial experience.

A desire to be of service is a must. Volunteer work and extra-curricular activities noted on a résumé indicate "strong service skills and dedication," said one bank executive.

Gerald Nicholls, personnel manager for the Toronto region of The Hudson's Bay Co., interviews business students for management trainee positions. He looks for confident, well-rounded people. "Someone who can look you in the eye."

What kind of people do well in retail sales and management? "People who like change, who don't require a lot of structure, who have a high energy level and a desire to get ahead," says Nicholls.

Even in computer research and development, one of the most scientific sectors of the workplace, academic standing takes second place to "self-discipline and, (you guessed it) initiative," according to one vice-president in the computer industry.

"I interviewed one fellow who had built himself a submarine. He got the job on the spot. I didn't care what his marks were," he recalled.

HOW TO WRITE A RÉSUMÉ

....

By Allyson Latta

In today's competitive job market, the résumé is an increasingly important tool. People are changing jobs, and even careers, more frequently than ever. And employers are demanding résumés for job categories – such as trades – that never needed them before.

"It's becoming a standard job-hunting tool, where it wasn't required before. People are expected to have résumés," says Susan Reitsma, a placement counselor at Carleton University's Canada Employment Centre.

A résumé is a résumé is a résumé. Right? Wrong, says Reitsma.

In a nutshell, a proper one should outline "what I want, the skills I have, and where I've demonstrated them."

But for many people that's easier said than done. Job-seekers often have difficulty assessing their own goals and related skills.

That's why about 20 Ottawa firms now offer résumé services, ranging from basic wordprocessing to personalized consultation. . . .

Patrick Langston, owner of Career Advancement Consultants, says not everyone needs professional advice.

"But some people don't have either the skills or confidence to market themselves," he says. "They don't know what's blowing their own horn, or what's being modest."

Reitsma believes there are benefits to preparing your own résumé, even if you later have someone else critique it.

First, job-seekers best know their own aspirations, related skills and the kind of work environment they're comfortable with. Writing the résumé increases their chances of job satisfaction.

And the process of résumé-writing is good organizational preparation for the anticipated interview.

A résumé, says one counsellor, is not a legal document. "It's not a biography and it's not a confession."

The key is marketing, say experts. Think of the résumé as an advertisement. Take the time to know the product – which is you – and the buyers who are the potential employers.

No one résumé format is appropriate for every job-seeker, or every employer.

Résumés are a lot like dating, according to Richard Nelson Bolles, author of what many people consider the job-seeker's bible: *What Color is Your Parachute?*

"There is no man who is liked by all the women he dates. There is no woman who is liked by all the men she dates. Some employers like résumés; some hate them," he writes.

Though Bolles questions the effectiveness of résumés compared to other job-search techniques, he identifies their four-fold potential. They're a self-inventory for the job-seeker, an extended calling card for an interview, an agenda for that interview, and a memory jogger for those doing the hiring.

Today's trend is toward résumés that are shorter, more professional-looking, better print quality, and containing less personal information. They are less a chronological list of positions and duties than a functional description of achievements, and "transferable skills" gained in one position that can be applied to another.

Many include an introductory statement, career objective or goal that can be altered slightly to suit the position applied for.

Improved wordprocessing and printing technology now allow consumers to produce a professional look, select from a variety of typefaces and formats, and personalize résumés.

It's not necessary to spend a fortune, says Reitsma, but it is important to use a clean, readable typeface, high quality photocopying, and bond paper – preferably white, buff or grey.

Employment counsellors warn against gimmicks, such as humor, photographs, or even colored paper that might trigger bias in the employer. Such frills are occasionally appropriate for those seeking graphic arts or marketing positions.

"You want to stand out, but stand out gracefully and with class," says DeShaw.

Reitsma says many people wrongly dismiss experience they've acquired through activities other than paid employment: volunteer work, community activities, hobbies, sports, travel.

And as with any type of advertising, don't be false.

"The person will have to go through the interview and perform on the job as well," says Reitsma. "If they're putting information on the résumé that isn't true, it will show up eventually, and you'll have to live up to your exaggerations."

Always proofread your résumé. Reitsma says the "dumbest" mistakes she's seen include spelling errors, or leaving one's name off the document.

There's scads of free information available on résumé preparation.

An estimated 150 books provide guidelines and sample formats, many available at the local library. And free job-search seminars, including information on résumé preparation, are offered by the four area Canada Employment Centres, as well as the Women's Career Counselling Service outreach program.

DO

- Make your résumé clear, concise, complete and correct.
- Carefully assess your goals and related skills, including those acquired through volunteer work or hobbies.
- Research the employer, both organization and individual.
- Target your résumé as much as possible using devices such as career objective.
- Use a format emphasizing relevant skills

and achievements, rather than a chronological list of positions and duties.

- Use high-quality type, paper and photocopying.
- Leave plenty of "white space" to allow
easy reading, and room for notes by
interviewer.
- Sum up, in the case of a long employment
history, several old positions in one paragraph focusing on achievements.
- Put your name on every page.
- Proofread your résumé carefully for spelling and accuracy, and have someone else
check it too.

DON'T

- Exceed two or three pages.
- Include anything, such as preparation
date, that dates the résumé.
- Abbreviate, keep it formal.
- Include salary requirements. You might
price yourself too low or too high.
- Try to ham it up with humor, photographs, colored paper, unless you're confident such devices will be well-received.
- Use sentences filled with "I, me, my."
- Include personal information such as sex,
health, height, weight, or age unless it's
relevant to the position.
- Emphasize weaknesses or areas of
improvement.
- Include reference names or letters, but
mention these are available on request.
- Mislead, or include details that can trap
you in the interview.

HOW TO PERFECT A RÉSUMÉ AND GET ON THE SHORT LIST

....

By Gary Dessler

In his new book, *Hot Tips, Sneaky Tricks And Last Ditch Tactics*, Jeff Speck makes some points about the job search process for new grads that are well worth learning.

For example, when a firm is preparing for interviews, three or four people usually sort through résumés, so you've got to be sure not to give any of them a reason to screen you out.

The résumé sort is a first cut, a search for rejectables, so you've got to make sure that your résumé is perfect – or see the job go to someone who has taken more care.

Each reviewer develops a way to cut 200 résumés to a viable 20 or so, but here, as described by Speck, are the steps one big firm uses:

- Eliminate the losers.

   These people are not really losers, of course; they just gave so little thought to their résumés that it's easy to reject them. At this stage you'll reach the reject pile by making obvious résumé mistakes. Misspellings are inexcusable, as are grammatical or stylistic errors.

   Similarly, check for punctuation or cap-italization mistakes. Be careful: Some of the worst culprits are professional résumé preparers, who may not have the vested interest you do in making sure your résumé is perfect and grammatically sound.

- Comparisons.

   At this point, the standards start tough-ening up. You will, of course, be compared with other candidates in terms of academic standing, previous work, activities and probable interest in the job.

Unless you are careful to adapt your experience and goals and accomplishments to the job and industry at hand, the likelihood is you'll be screened out right now.

Furthermore, résumés produced on a dot matrix printer or those done without careful layout on a typewriter will probably be next to fall.

- Personal preferences.

Your screener is down to 20 or so résumés, all apparently well-qualified and all with perfect résumés. The next cut (to get down to the five who will be invited) may be based on the question: "Whom do I like here?"

To make the cut, you may need some extra feature that will set you apart.

The safe approach, says Speck, is to list something unusual or otherwise interesting under your extracurricular activities or job experience that will set you apart.

Worthwhile things – starting a [school] club, coaching a team – are good examples. So are fun activities. (One candidate held a job as Goofy at Disney World one summer and got lots of interviews.)

Nothing special to list here? A personal paragraph might help, but remember that your aim is to distinguish yourself. Listing mundane points like "enjoy tennis, skiing" or "play touch football" or "enjoy fine dining" will probably do more harm than good.

Strong personal interests might include "play jai-alai," "write and perform jazz music" or "ski instructor."

ATTITUDE IMPORTANT IN FINDING JOB

By Janis Foord

"I'm willing to hire people right out of school if they've got the gumption and they're willing to try," says Andy White, publisher of D. A. Publishing Corporation. "It gets down to whether a person impresses me with their attitudes and the questions they ask. Whether they seem intelligent and want to learn."

White's attitude is typical of employers in industries of all sorts. Personality, eagerness, willingness are all qualities employers are looking for. How does White find them in a single interview? "I like to hear people talk," he says. "If someone sits there and gives me one-word answers, they're out of the picture right away."

Such comments don't auger well for young workers like Helen, a shy 21-year-old who has been looking for clerical work for several months. "When I'm with my friends, I don't have any trouble talking," Helen says. "But put me in an interview, and I freeze up. I really don't know how to sell myself."

Interviews are sales opportunities. And, with a little planning and practice, even quiet people like Helen can learn to make the most of them.

For the most part, interviews follow a pattern. Initially, there will be a few minutes of "easy" talk to help you relax. Discussion might then move to the technical aspects of the job in question and your ability to handle them. Next, employers usually want to discuss your personal information in an attempt to learn about your attitudes and values. In the final stages, the interview may be turned over to you with, "Do you have any questions?"

No one part of an interview is more important than any other. At each stage you, the job seeker, will be called upon to openly discuss yourself and your suitability for the job.

Professional career counsellors offer the following tips to help you prepare for positive interviews:

- Consider the interview a two-sided exchange of information. Learn to say to yourself, with conviction, "Sure, it's them deciding if they want to hire me, but it's also me deciding if I want to work here."

- Treat interviews as a challenge and a learning experience. Say to yourself, "I'm here to learn about this field. If there's a job for me, great. And even if there's not, I'll learn something new."

- Ask a couple of friends to help you, one to ask you questions, and another to observe your answers. Use a tape recorder for these sessions and work to become aware of what you say and how you say it.

- When objections like, "I'm concerned about the fact that you've never worked in this field before," are raised in an interview, remind yourself that the interviewer is not saying, "You won't do," but rather, "I need more information."

- Before an interview, compile a list of all the questions you want answered. Such questions should revolve around the job and its responsibilities and future opportunities. Leave questions about salary, benefits and holidays for a second interview.

    Interest, above all, is valued by employers like White. "A lot can be said for someone who walks in with a pad full of questions," he says. "It shows forethought and thoroughness."

PITFALLS TO AVOID WHEN TRYING FOR JOB

There are certain traits every employer looks for in a prospective employee. Ironically, a candidate may often unwittingly emphasize the things an employer doesn't want to hear or insert a few blunders on a résumé, say executives for two recruiting firms.

In an interview, there are four "I ams" that should be communicated, regardless of the position sought, said Mitchell Berger, an official with Howard-Sloan Associates Inc:

- "I am not a clock watcher," or, I do what it takes to get the job done regardless of time.

- "I am a self-starter."

- "I am a team player."

- "I am an initiator," or, "I originate ideas and think beyond what's expected of me."

    On the other hand, Berger said, an employer is likely to see a red flag upon hearing certain responses:

- "I really need this job." What you should be doing, he said, is emphasizing why the company needs you.

- "This is a good career move for me." Instead, explain why employing you would be good for the company.

- "This is one of three positions I'm considering." Don't play hard to get with potential employers.

- "I want better experience." Why would a company want you with bad experience?

- "I think this is what I want to do." Companies are looking for people who know what they want to do.

- "I have no questions to ask." If you're interested in the job, you should have many questions.

Berger recommended memorizing the four "I ams" and developing a manner of expressing them which is comfortable.

Hiring decisions are based on a combination of chemistry and face-to-face discussions, said Berger. Too many job seekers concentrate on their résumés and neglect to prepare for an interview. The résumé is just a door opener.

To get that door open, however, [you] should pay attention to what goes on your résumé and in your cover letter, said Dale Winston, president of Battalia and Associates in New York.

The company offered the following pointers:

- Don't be informal.
- Don't use colored paper such as orange, brown or gray for your résumé.
- Don't include a picture.
- Don't use gimmicks.
- Avoid hyping your language.
- Leave out personal information. No one is interested in your children's names, where or when you graduated high school or your religion.
- Don't send too much material. Don't send your current company's annual report or turn your résumé into a book-length project. If a search firm or personnel official wants that sort of information, they'll ask for it.

STYLE IS IMPORTANT FOR JOB INTERVIEWS

By Dr. Arnold Rincover

Looking for a job can be an excruciating experience. Our happiness, self-esteem, family relationships – not to mention food – are often so closely tied to having a job that being unemployed can cause severe depression, helplessness and anxiety.

Fortunately, research has shown that the job interview itself can influence the hiring process even more than one's experience and we can improve job interviewing skills. So, help is available.

There are several things that one can do to improve the chances of getting the job. Some have to do with style (how you say it), and some have to do with content (what you say).

In terms of style, it is important, first, to look at the interviewer much of the time, not down at the desk or over his shoulder. Looking a person in the eye conveys confidence, self-esteem, control. Second, it is important to be lively, not emotionally flat – vary the pacing, loudness and emotional tone of your voice – as it displays interest, as well as being at ease in difficult interpersonal situations.

Third, it is helpful to speak fluently; eliminate "er," "uh," "well," and the like, because it suggests you might be unsure of yourself, easily swayed and dominated by others.

Finally, it is essential to smile. Smiling is so important because it tells so much – how comfortable you are socially; how non-threatening you are, even in a very competitive situation; how you might get along with co-workers. Smiling can take the sting out of a conflict and put others at ease.

These components of style are crucial, because the interviewer will assume that the style shown here is the same style that will be shown in the workplace. Therefore, if any elements of style are difficult for an applicant, they must be practised and rehearsed before the interview.

In terms of content, several questions must be answered. Many of these questions will not, however, be asked directly by the interviewer, so the applicant must know what the real questions are, and initiate topics of conversation that will answer them.

The "real" questions one is evaluated on are, is this person enthusiastic about the job, competent to do the job, eager to learn, able to get along with others, able to work independently, ambitious, with a good track record in previous jobs?

Interviewers are not likely to ask, "Are you enthusiastic?" or "Do you get along well with others?" but they are going to evaluate the applicant on it. Knowing this, it is wise to bring up experiences that ensure a positive answer. "I really enjoyed that job at the GM plant because I was able to help others as well as do my own job;" "Since I just graduated from school, I don't have any direct job experience – but this work interests me so much that I took correspondence courses, got books on it, and learned a lot on my own time."

These statements show enthusiasm for the job, as well as other positive characteristics (confidence, helping others, eagerness to learn). Such statements should be planned to cover each of the areas that an applicant will be evaluated on.

In addition to covering the questions that may not be asked, there are a few other content-related skills that help. First, make positive statements about past experiences, training, or education – facts about one's previous responsibilities; enjoyment of past jobs, challenges, or supervisory duties; information about educational and training accomplishments; special competencies or skills, indications of reliability and conscientiousness ("I only missed one day of work in the last two years.").

It is also important to ask questions, as it shows that you are interested in the job, and it helps you to find out if in fact the job is appropriate and appealing to you.

These skills do not, of course, insure that you will get any job you want. They do, however, increase the chances of success on virtually any job interview. Moreover, several U.S. studies have shown that such skills can be taught, and most people who receive such training do subsequently get a job.

FOLLOWING THROUGH

This final phase of the topic contains suggested activities to help you to apply the criteria identified in the previous phase. It also provides material that presents another perspective on the subject – the growing trend in business and industry toward psychological testing of prospective employees. It asks you to predict what effects this trend might have on the whole job picture.

SUGGESTED APPROACH

Step 1

Write a résumé (or revise it if you have already completed one) in which you incorporate all the key criteria that make an effective résumé. (Don't forget the importance of the visual as well as the written impact of the résumé.)

Step 2

Using role-playing techniques, conduct mock job interviews, again applying criteria you identified earlier. Evaluate the interviews, from the perspective of the applicant and the potential employer, using the checklist of ranked criteria you created earlier.

Step 3

Read the following articles that describe the trend among companies to supplement résumés and interviews with additional methods of finding the right person for the job.

Step 4

As a class or in small groups discuss the appropriateness of these other methods of employee selection compared to, or in addition to, the traditional résumé and interview.

FIRMS PROBING PSYCHE OF WOULD-BE EMPLOYEES WITH CONTROVERSIAL TESTS

....

By Kathy English

Résumés and references alone won't get you a job in today's high stakes job market. Revealing your innermost thoughts, fears and fantasies might, though.

Human rights legislation prohibits prospective employers from questioning you about your age, marital status, religion and racial background. But the law doesn't prevent employers from probing your psyche.

Consider these questions put recently to several candidates for a middle-management job in a well-respected multinational corporation. In a lengthy series of psychological tests, the applicants were asked to indicate whether they agreed or disagreed with these statements.

- You feel guilty about certain thoughts and feelings you have.
- You would love to make a citizen's arrest of someone honking a horn needlessly or disturbing the peace.
- You are aware of your own capacity for violence and viciousness.
- You fall in love easily and naturally.
- You are at times capable of mystical experience and wide horizons of future possibilities pass through your mind.
- You have fantasized about things you would not want to share with other people.

Bizarre? Nobody's business? You don't have to answer questions like these, of course. But then you might not get the job either.

And whether you're job hunting or moving up the corporate ladder, chances are you'll encounter psychological tests with questions like these as employers increasingly search for alternatives to job interviews to place the right people in the right jobs.

"Firms today want to be absolutely certain they find the best person for the job because hiring mistakes can be very costly," said Ross Finlay, executive director of the Personnel Association of Ontario. "There's still faith in the gut feeling of the interviewer, but firms are looking for other kinds of assessments to provide more balance."

Psychological tests that purport to assess intelligence, personality, attitudes, values and interests are used routinely by all types of business and industry throughout Canada. The premise of testing is to compare a job applicant's answers to various questions about [herself] with "norms" established by those who've done the tests previously.

There are no "right" or "wrong" answers to such questions. Testers are interested only in patterns to compare to others who've proven to be a success on the job.

"The questions taken by themselves can lead you to scratch your head in wonderment, but the full results, compared to others who've tested before can lead you to believe certain things about an individual," said Michael Thomas, president of the executive search firm Westcott, Thomas and Associates Ltd.

There's even a growing use of handwriting analysis as a tool to determine job suitability.

Look Inside

Both these methods have the same goal – to help employers discover the *real* person beneath the dress-for-success pinstripes and interview rhetoric.

"Employers want to know who a person really is. They want to be able to look inside his head," said Phil Daniels, a registered psychologist and partner in the management consulting firm of Stevenson, Kellogg, Ernst and Whinney.

"In the selection process, everyone wishes they had a crystal ball to tell them how someone is going to perform on the job," added Claudia Verburgh, who works with Daniels in the firms' management assessment centre, a "business simulator" which tests employees' skills by observing them in mock management situations.

Daniels warns that any employment testing should not usurp a company's interviewing and screening process.

"We tend to take ourselves too seriously sometimes and have a tendency to think our tools are the end all and be all, so some companies take them too seriously," he said. "Many tests are used too frequently and too indiscriminately without any discussion of what they can really offer."

Human rights legislation prohibits employers from demanding that job applicants undergo any tests that are not job-related. But, the Ontario Human Rights Commission has never dealt with any cases of alleged discrimination based on psychological job testing or handwriting analysis.

Michael Gage, executive director of the commission, said he suspects such tests have "slipped into the culture" without anyone really bothering to question them.

"Nothing precludes anyone from challenging that kind of testing," he said. "I suspect the issue will come up sometime in the future."

Gage said the essence of the code is that any testing must be a "legitimate and reasonable" predictor of work performance.

"The issue is whether a test is getting at something that's a bona fide requirement for the job," he said.

Whether psychological testing or handwriting analysis are legitimate or reasonable is a source of controversy – especially among those who administer the tests.

In Europe, where more than 50 per cent of firms use handwriting analysis in hiring, psychological tests are considered unreliable. In Canada, where psychological tests have been used since World War II, handwriting analysis is looked at with suspicion.

"Europeans view psychological tests as some kind of black magic. Here handwriting analysis is seen in the same way," said Thomas.

Handwriting analysis is becoming more acceptable in Canada now, especially in British Columbia where municipal governments, banks and major corporations have utilized it. In Chilliwack, graphology has been used 14 times in the past three years to hire upper management civic employees.

A clue to whether firms might use the practice to assess potential employees is if they ask for a handwritten job application.

Daniels believes more firms are considering handwriting analysts because "the whole thing is pretty sexy."

"These people promise to take something from someone and tell you what's in their mind," he said. "My problem with it is how do you explain to someone that they didn't get the job because of the way they dotted their i's and crossed their t's."

Graphologists believe a person's handwriting can reveal their character and personality. Employers use it to help determine traits that could lead to success on the job.

"You look for qualities such as intelligence, intuitiveness, ambition and emotional stability," said Toronto graphologist Edith Leslie, who suggests her clients use psychological tests as well as handwriting analysis.

"A psychological test can paint a picture of a person but the person can guess what the test is after and answer accordingly," she said. "With handwriting analysis you can't hide who you really are."

Gordon Brittain, the owner of a Metro chemical engineering company called Thermidaire Corp., is a graphologist who has used handwriting analysis as a hiring tool for 15 years.

"You look at handwriting to see the depth of

a person's emotional state, whether they're serious or flippant and how they might react to different people already working in the organization," said Brittain, who has never had a prospective employee object to handwriting analysis.

He provides graphology service to several "major firms" and predicts graphology will eventually be used in Canada as routinely as psychological testing.

"It's no different than hiring a psychologist and it tells so much about the person without going to the expense of psychological tests."

Psychologists vehemently oppose that view. The American Psychological Association has gone so far as to release a statement condemning handwriting analysis as being totally without substance.

"Handwriting analysis tells you how a person writes and that's it," said Michael Godkewitsch, an industrial psychologist who worked at Imperial Oil for 10 years and now runs his own consulting firm. "Scientifically, it's a complete dead end and people who flog it are charlatans."

Godkewitsch said there is no comparison between psychology and graphology. Psychology is a science based on scientific data amassed in a scientific way, he said.

"There's nothing magical or secretive about psychology. It's as reliable a scientific pursuit as building a bridge," he said. "The fact that it deals with people doesn't make it any more secretive."

Godkewitsch believes psychological testing makes one of the best predictions of job success there is if it is related to skills needed for the job. It's much more objective than interviews or references, he said.

But, he admits the possibility for abuse is enormous because many commonly used tests have not been properly validated with results of people who've proven to be successful on the job. Like anything else, there are good tests and bad tests, he stressed.

'No Validity'

Godkewitsch tells of a major insurance firm . . . that has used the same psychological test for prospective employees for the past 25 years. Another psychologist recently correlated job performance appraisals of the firm's employees with original test results and found no relation between the two.

"The test had no validity at all. The bottom line is that it's useless," he said.

Studies indicate that a person whose test answers are similar to those of someone who has been successful in the same type of a job will probably also succeed, said Michael Thomas of Westcott Thomas.

For example, if a firm wants to hire a dynamic person with loads of leadership ability, they look for test results similar to those of dynamic leaders.

"If the results show an applicant walks like a duck, quacks like a duck and thinks like a duck, then there's a good chance you've got a duck," he said. "These tests allow you to compare an applicant to the other ducks."

Whether the tests are a valid measure of job performance is a controversial question even among psychologists.

"That's the $64,000 question," said Daniels when asked about the validity of psychological testing. "At best we can say they have a success rate of about 50 per cent."

Although he is a registered psychologist with a doctorate in psychology, Daniels considers himself somewhat of a renegade and questions the reliability of many commonly used tests.

He particularly questions "quickie" personality tests that require job applicants to indicate how they see themselves and how others see them.

A personality profile doesn't necessarily indicate how someone is going to do on the job, he said. For example, a psychological profile might indicate an individual has a tendency toward such negative traits as procrastination or impulsiveness. But, said Daniels, that doesn't mean they'll act impulsively or procrastinate on the job.

From the job seeker's point of view, testing can be irritating and intimidating. Most applicants don't know what the tests are after and have no idea how to respond to commonly posed statements such as:

- You have contempt for what might be called conformist society.
- You have impeccable good manners and people time and time again comment on your courteous behavior.
- It irritates you when others treat life as nothing more than a game.
- You believe in being completely honest at all times.

"Psychological tests are psychological torture," said a Toronto executive who was so angry with the results of a psychological assessment carried out when he was up for a promotion that he complained to the company's board chairperson.

Often, job applicants will be interviewed and then put through a series of tests. If they don't get the job they never learn what the test results indicated.

Hedge Bets

"You go away and don't get the job and wonder whether they found out something really horrible about you," said Verburgh, of Stevenson, Kellogg, Ernst and Whinney.

Employers use the tests to "hedge their bets," said Thomas. They want all the proof they can amass in advance that an applicant is the right one for the job.

Consultant Ed Van Wyck, former president of F.G. Bradley, a division of Schneiders, used psychological testing extensively to hire employees at all levels.

"You're talking to a believer from the corporate world," he said. "Testing really did

help reduce failures in hiring every time I've used it," he said.

Anyone involved with psychological testing agrees companies must take strong measures to ascertain the tests they use prove anything of value. That means thoroughly checking out the tests and testers.

"There are a lot of unscrupulous individuals flogging tests that are cheap to use and promising to put the right people in the job," said Godkewitsch. "Often those tests are totally invalid – worthless.

"Business must be skeptical," he said.

□

GRAPHOLOGY TESTS UNRELIABLE ASSESSMENTS

The article, *Firms Probing Psyche of Would-be Employees with Controversial Tests* . . . noted that, while psychological tests are viewed with suspicion in Europe, handwriting analysis (graphology) is viewed with considerable suspicion in Canada. This would lead one to believe that the usefulness of a particular approach to selecting employees is a matter of opinion, and that there are simply differences in opinion between Europeans and North Americans.

The reliability and validity of any selection tool, however, is empirically testable. For example, we can look at the association between scores on a selection test and later indices of job performance. Where this has been done, graphology has not fared well at all.

Not only do graphologists typically demonstrate poor agreement in their interpretation of the same writing sample, such analyses have been shown repeatedly to have a near zero association with later performance on the job. On the other hand, psychological tests of knowledge, skills and abilities have been shown to be excellent predictors of success in a wide range of jobs.

It is on this basis that the American Psychological Association has condemned handwriting analysis as being totally without substance. Likewise, graphology fails to meet the minimal guidelines for educational and psychological testing as established by the Canadian Psychological Association.

It is quite likely that handwriting analysis will lose favor among laypersons as employers become increasingly accountable to Canadian human rights bodies for the selection tools they use.

RICK D. HACKETT
Member of the Executive
The Industrial-Organizational
Psychology Section
of The Canadian
Psychological Association

RECRUITING QUACKERY?

Now that psychologists and handwriting experts are on the job recruitment scene in Canada, boning up for an interview may never be the same.

Last week, it was reported that job seekers nowadays are often forced to take psychological tests and expose the inner workings of their minds to the scrutiny of science.

Some are even asked to submit handwriting samples for analysis by a graphologist before they get a crack at the job.

True, employers are entitled to hire the best-qualified people.

But sometimes the psychological questions seem marginal, if not downright nosy.

Try agreeing or disagreeing with these statements, if you can:

"You fall in love easily and naturally," or, "You have fantasized about things you would not want to share with other people."

Can people no longer have a secret fantasy or two? And what proof is there that if the answer is yes, or no, that they'd perform better at work?

One expert quoted recently by *The Star*'s Kathy English says answers to test questions can be compared usefully to those given by someone who's succeeded at the same type of job.

"If the results show an applicant walks like a duck, quacks like a duck and thinks like a duck, then there's a good chance you've got a duck," he says. "These tests allow you to compare an applicant to the other ducks."

That may be fine for the pond, but it doesn't seem to have much to do with dignity in the job market.

SOME FURTHER FOLLOW-THROUGH SUGGESTIONS

Some of these suggestions may be done as independent study activities, either individually or in small groups, or as whole class activities.

- Select a job or an area of work that interests you and find out what criteria employers in this area apply to prospective employees. This may include interviews with those who work in the field, both employers and employees.

- Research future job trends by examining information from Statistics Canada and other sources of data in your resource centre. Derive a list of general criteria that will be necessary for "tomorrow's worker."

- Find out about starting your own business, what help is available for the young entrepreneur, and what the criteria are for ensuring your success.

- Set up a "Careers' Day" for your class or school and invite various community employers and working people to talk about their companies and their jobs.

- In small groups, select various local companies to research. Include interviews with both management and employees.

- Produce a videotape of the "Do's and Don't's of Getting a Job." (This could be scripted or improvised.)

- Find out more about the growing trend toward the use of job selection tools such as psychological tests and graphology to evaluate potential employees.

TOPIC

three

*The Drinking
and Driving Problem*

FOCUSING IN

Drinking and driving is a major social problem costing thousands of lives and billions of dollars in damage and follow-up health care. We all have different levels of interest in the issue and various opinions on dealing with it, depending on our personal levels of involvement and awareness.

SUGGESTED APPROACH
Step 1

Responding to the following Questionnaire will help you focus on your present level of information and your attitude toward drinking and driving. In your notebook or journal, write the statement that best describes your level of information and your level of concern.

Questionnaire

1. My level of information about the issue could be rated as:

high – I feel well-informed. I could write an essay or discuss the issue at some length.

medium – I could write a couple of pages or discuss the issue for a few minutes.

low – I could write a paragraph or have a brief dialogue with someone.

minimal – I could write a sentence or two or make one or two remarks about it.

2. My level of concern about the issue is:

high – I feel personally affected by the drinking and driving problem.

medium – I'm generally interested in the issue; I think it's a serious problem that needs attention.

low – I'm indifferent about the issue; I'm not really interested one way or the other.

negative – I'm tired of hearing about the issue.

3. Right now, if I were asked what should be done about the drinking and driving problem, I would say . . .

Step 2

Examine the following two advertisements. Determine which has the greater impact on you personally and why.

Step 3

Think about your responses to the ads and to the questionnaire. In your journal sum up your initial reactions to the issue, reflecting on the reasons for them. You may wish to illustrate your reactions with an anecdote, a brief personal account, or even another anti-drinking and driving advertisement.

Step 4

Now that you have determined your own level of response to the drinking and driving issue, you may wish to reflect on it further with others. As a class or in groups jot down three or four questions about the drinking and driving issue that came to mind as you thought about the issue or that you feel need to be asked about the drinking and driving issue in society. As a class or in groups, you might wish to use these questions to review initial reactions.

"Dad, you've got to help me."

"Sandy, what's wrong? Are you hurt?"

"No, Dad, I'm fine."

"Where are you?"

"At Pat's. We all came over here to celebrate after the game."

"It's almost 12:30. Isn't it time you called it a night?"

"That's just it. Remember you always told me if I was out never to drive with anyone who's had too much to drink? And not to be afraid to call you if I had no other way of getting home? Well, tonight I'm taking you at your word."

"Stay right there. I'm coming to pick you up."

"Thanks, Dad. Oh, and something else."

"Shoot."

"Are you angry with me?"

"Angry? No, Sandy. Not on your life."

Seagram

We believe in moderation and we've been saying so since 1934

How much alcohol can you safely handle? Write for a free chart on drinking limits.
P.O. Box 847, Station H, Montreal, Quebec. H3G 2M8

Not all impaired drivers are picked up by the police.

WHAT YOU SHOULD KNOW ABOUT DRINKING AND DRIVING BEFORE YOU MIX THEM.

A lcohol is a Drug which takes effect in just 20 minutes. It takes hours to wear off.

O ne or two drinks may make you feel good. Feeling good <u>will</u> create a false sense of confidence. Alcohol, in fact, slows down reaction time and affects your judgement. That can be deadly when you're in control of a ton or more of moving metal and glass.

D riving a car looks easy, but it means doing all sorts of things at once. It's not just handling controls while judging speed and distance — it's anticipating what other people will do. It's being ready for something unexpected.

C ars in front will stop suddenly. Pedestrians and cyclists will appear without warning.

Y oung drivers pride themselves on their quick reflexes — but, even after a few drinks, young drivers are <u>three</u> times more likely to have an accident.

T hese things happen all the time — and it's your future and other people's lives at stake. We promise you that a car crash is a living nightmare that stays with you.

Mixing a drink with a drive is deadly.

**There are alternatives: Designated Drivers
Public Transportation
Taxis**

Make the Right Choice!!! Lives depend on it.

A MESSAGE FROM DURHAM, HALTON, PEEL, YORK AND METROPOLITAN TORONTO POLICE FORCES

CO-SPONSORED BY:

Bank of Montreal

Telemedia Procom Inc.   McLaren, Morris and Todd Limited   Bergman Graphics Ltd.

Courtesy of the Metropolitan Toronto Police Department

FINDING OUT

The following material examines the toll of drinking and driving from a number of perspectives: the victims, their relatives and friends, the offenders, their community, and society at large.

As you are reading and viewing this material, be aware of the extent to which an emotionally charged issue is affected by the point of view, the perspective, from which it is being seen. Also, notice how the selection and organization of the information, and even the choice of words and images are brought together to create an overall tone that strongly affects the reader's or viewer's overall reaction.

In trying to deal with drinking and driving, or any other massive social problem such as this, we need to see it from as wide a perspective as possible, because of the incredible emotional force it generates. Any plan of action to deal with drinking and driving must recognize and incorporate all of the dimensions of the problem, including the potential consequences of any proposed plan. To engage in problem solving, you must develop skill in the following areas: defining the scope of the problem, formulating questions of inquiry, generating hypotheses, exploring possibilities, setting goals and objectives, planning strategies for solving the problem, and setting and applying criteria to assess potential solutions.

SUGGESTED APPROACH
Step 1

As you are reading the articles, interact with the ideas and their emotional force by jotting down your "inner voice dialogue," that is, what inner discussion is going on in your own mind. What you are creating is a learning log, a running description of how you are interacting with what you are reading. The following focusing suggestions may help you with your inner dialogue, but feel free to respond to anything else that comes to mind.

Focusing Suggestions

- What important ideas are being voiced?

- How is the selection of information being affected by the point of view or perspective from which the material is being written?

- What are the emotional effect(s) of the article(s) on you?

- What major patterns are emerging as you reflect on what you have been writing?

- How is the information adding to or changing your perceptions and/or your emotional response to the drinking and driving problem?

Step 2

After reading the material, use your learning log entries to work through the following in small groups.

  a. Compare reactions to each of the articles.
  b. Note common patterns of ideas among the articles.
  c. Examine the problem from the point of view of the victim(s), the driver(s), all those associated with each of them, and from society in general.
  d. Have each person review his or her initial reaction on the Questionnaire and explain any change in his or her thinking on the drinking and driving problem as a result of having read and viewed this material.

Step 3

Reflect on what you have learned about the drinking and driving problem and on the extent to which your initial emotional reaction has changed, by writing an entry in your response journal.

DEATH OF A YOUNG MAN

....

By Robert Collins

There were only a few lines in the morning newspapers about Jeff Collum's death. That year in Canada it was just one of some 2700 attributable to drunken driving. But the loss of this loved boy on the brink of manhood sent out shock waves that engulfed all whose lives he had touched. This is the story of those other victims of the accident – those who live to grieve, to remember, and to regret.

Larry Scott couldn't believe his eyes. It was almost midnight on July 20, 1981, and the 29-year-old appliance repairman was driving north from Toronto on six-lane Highway 400. He glanced idly to his left at the three lanes of southbound traffic across the median – and saw another motorist's tail-lights *going north* straight into the oncoming cars.

"He's driving the wrong way!" cried Scott incredulously as he turned towards his fiancée, Kim Shugan. On the other side of the median, a brown Pontiac Firebird was moving at a steady 100 km/h clip, its driver apparently oblivious to everything around him. Traffic was light, but soon a southbound car bore down on him in the same lane.

"He's going to hit!" Scott shouted. But at the last moment the southbound car veered away. The Firebird neither swerved nor slowed.

Scott eased his half-tonne truck alongside, flashing his lights (his horn wasn't working), waving, trying in vain to catch the attention of the other driver. For several seconds – a lifetime, it seemed, to Larry and Kim – the two vehicles drove in tandem with only the shin-high median between them. Suddenly another southbound car loomed in front of the Firebird – and the young couple knew something terrible was about to happen.

Throughout most of that Monday afternoon and evening, the Firebird's driver had been celebrating a new job. Robert Benmergui, 25, mustached and bespectacled, with a shag of dark hair, had just been promoted from senior sales representative to manager of a branch in a television sales and rental chain in Metropolitan Toronto. Jubilant, he drove from his east-end store to share the news with friends in a neighbourhood bar. There the owner, also a friend, began pouring Grand Marnier as fast as Benmergui could drain his glass.

By dinnertime, befuddled but still festive, Benmergui led the way to a nearby hotel dining room. After that, his evening became a blur. By 10:45 p.m., Benmergui was, as he admitted long after, "in terrible condition." Sensing that he was unfit to drive, he went to the front desk and asked for a room. "We have no vacancies," the desk clerk said.

So Benmergui got behind the wheel of his Firebird again. First he drove a co-worker to her home in King City, 35 kilometres north, and about 11:45 p.m. he turned back to Toronto, probably down a secondary road. Somewhere along the way he ignored a no-entry sign and blundered north into the three southbound lanes of Highway 400.

Moments earlier, Jeffrey Collum, 19, had pulled his small blue Toyota Corolla onto the highway from Canada's Wonderland, a theme park, and headed south towards Toronto. A slightly built youth with neat, light-brown hair framing a wide smile, he had just finished the late shift at a restaurant. The summer job was going well.

So was the rest of his life. He was in love with 18-year-old Jennifer Meen, the girl he hoped to marry. He got along well with his parents, Howard and Helen, with whom he lived. Jeff's amiable nature helped him to see their point of view, even if he didn't always agree with it. To them he was "everything anybody could want in a son."

Parental pride aside, Jeffrey *did* seem gifted. A YMCA counselling test had rated his mental ability in the "superior range." He played cello in the Earl Haig Secondary School orchestra, was a budding poet, showed a natural bent for black-and-white photography, read omnivorously and handled his father's eight-metre sailboat with aplomb.

In a few weeks he and his closest pal, Glenn Hefford, would move into an apartment and start university in Waterloo, 110 kilometres west of Toronto. Jeff was enrolled in environmental studies. He was on the threshold of adulthood, with everything to live for.

He was also a good driver. He'd taken driver training at age 17 and always drove responsibly. He had been under way probably four minutes when he entered a shallow depression, a mere dip in the road, but enough to mask, until the last terrible split second, the unbelievable sight of Benmergui's headlights closing in. He had no time to react. Afterwards, police found no skid marks. The two cars crashed head on at normal highway speed. Jeff Collum died instantly.

The story ran briefly on an inner page of *The Toronto Star* the next day. In *The Globe and Mail* it was melded with another traffic death on page nine of the classifieds. Traffic accidents, even deaths, are too commonplace to be big news in a major city. But Jeff Collum's death, like a pebble in a pool, sent out ever widening ripples of pain – touching, marking, changing irrevocably the lives of family, friends and total strangers.

"It's Not Fair!"

As Larry Scott and Kim Shugan watched, helpless and horrified, the two cars met with a sickening crash. Flying glass clattered onto Scott's truck. He pulled over, then ran across the highway with a flashlight, Kim at his heels. A quick glance showed that the Firebird driver was semiconscious. "Better go back to the truck. I'm afraid the other one is dead," Scott told Kim, and began waving off approaching motorists with his flashlight.

About a kilometre to the north, Const. Brad Dunbar, 25, of the Ontario Provincial Police had just pulled a driver over for a minor infraction. A passing motorist yelled, "Bad accident down the road!" Dunbar was on the scene one minute later, at 12:04 a.m. In less than three years with the OPP, the constable had attended six or seven "fatals" – more than some police officers see in a lifetime. But frequency makes a highway death no easier to accept, and Dunbar wasn't mentally prepared for this one.

The moment he saw the Toyota, he knew it was more than just a "bad accident." The driver was crushed, bleeding and still. Dunbar steeled himself and checked for breathing and pulse. None.

Then he peered into the Firebird. It smelled of alcohol. Its driver muttered, "I wanta get out," but his doors were jammed. Soon firemen arrived to pry them open.

More police came to record accident details and to handle the traffic as onlookers paused to gape. Dunbar left the scene at 1:32 a.m., drove to York-Finch General Hospital, ten minutes away, and took a brief statement from Robert Benmergui. Glassy-eyed, still reeking of alcohol, just out of X ray with a fractured hip and chest lacerations, Benmergui seemed to remember nothing.

Dunbar went off duty at 4 a.m. He was learning, as all policemen must, not to take the day's work home, but it was easier said than done. *It's not fair!* he thought. *A young guy like that, totally innocent and, bang! He's gone.*

By that time, two Metro Toronto police officers had completed their own ordeal; breaking the news at the Collums' home in suburban Willowdale. Howard and Helen were holidaying at the family cottage on an island in Georgian Bay, 275 kilometres north. Jeff's sister, Melanie, 26, was home alone when the knock came. At first she thought her brother had forgotten his keys. Then the policemen were at the door. "Is this the home of Jeffrey Collum?" they asked. "We're very sorry . . . there's been a fatality. . . ."

The words were explicit enough. But Melanie's mind refused to grasp them. She heard "northbound car" and cried, "That's impossible. Jeff would have been in the southbound lane!" She tried to make sense of it, but there was none. Just the reality: Jeff – the one in all her family she felt closest to – was dead.

The family cottage had no telephone. Melanie phoned the mainland marina and asked them to take a message across. At the policemen's insistence she invited a girlfriend to stay with her; one officer volunteered to fetch her. She phoned her older brother at his apartment across town. "Are you sure you're not dreaming?" Philip, 28, cried in disbelief. He came to her immediately. The police went away. Then Melanie, to keep from thinking, began cleaning house. *There will be people here tomorrow. Better make it look respectable.* She worked furiously through the night. By 7 a.m. the place was clean.

Always Signed "xo"

Helen Collum, 54, an elementary-school teacher, dark and dynamic, and Howard, 57, a retired architect and town planner, a lean and gentle man, had weathered other bad times. Twenty-seven years before, their firstborn, Danny, had died of cancer at age 3½. Philip and Jeff were both plagued by allergies. Melanie, a child of the free-wheeling '60s, had left home at 16. But Jeff was a kind of pet for Philip and Melanie (known to their parents as "The Big Kids" and to Jeff as "The Bickits"). In his teens he hardly ever had harsh words with his parents. He'd sit back, Helen used to say, "like a little Buddha," patient and benign while his high-spirited family seethed around him. He was, his cousin Susan Buckley said, "almost a perfect person."

A week before the accident, Jeff had spent a long weekend with his parents at the cottage. Aboard the boat one day he'd laughed him-

self to tears when Helen, who gets seasick, hammed up her affliction like a swooning silent-movie heroine. On the Tuesday morning he'd kissed her good-by, and rode across to the mainland with his father. *The roles are reversed,* Howard had thought. *I used to leave the kids here to go to work in the city. Now Jeff's leaving.*

One week later, deep in this cool blustery night of July 21, the Collums awoke to the drone of a motor-boat approaching their island dock. It was a disturbing sound. No one would be out joyriding on such a night. Howard went down to see if they needed help. It was a friend from the marina.

"I've got bad news," he said. "It's Jeffrey . . . killed in an accident!"

On her neighbouring island, Susan Buckley heard Howard's anguished cry. From her bedroom Helen heard it too, and instantly knew that something had happened to one of the children. She was a worrying kind of mother, but she had always reassured herself: *We lost Danny; lightning never strikes twice in the same place.*

But it had.

Moving like robots, they pulled clothes on, returned to the mainland in tears and phoned Melanie.

Around 5 a.m., after waiting for fog to clear, the Collums began the interminable drive to Toronto. At a service station along the way Helen went to the washroom and heard a radio newscaster say, "Another traffic fatality on the 400. Nineteen-year-old Jeffrey Collum . . ."

In the city, they stood in the hospital with Philip and Melanie, hands clasped to fortify themselves for the awful task, and formally identified what was left of Jeffrey. He had died of massive brain damage and multiple fractures, lacerations and bruising of the face, chest, spinal cord, arms, legs and internal organs. (Philip and Melanie would have to identify him again for the coroner the next day.) Then they went home. Close friends came to share their grief. One was Jennifer Meen.

For Jennifer, a brown-haired girl with a sweet and usually merry face, the news came while she was getting ready for work. Since they'd met 2½ years before, she and Jeff had been almost inseparable. They loved movies, music and ice cream. They exchanged funny, affectionate notes and cards, always signed "xo" followed by a drawing of a heart. Their lives were full of little anniversaries. One of the rare times good-natured Jeff snapped at his mother was when she had chided him for neglecting his homework while phoning Jennifer to plan an "anniversary."

Jennifer didn't hear the phone that morning. Suddenly her father was at the bathroom door. "Jenny! God-awful news!" he blurted.

She thought, *Oh, my God, it's the dog, he's been run over!"* "No, please don't tell me!" she cried.

But her father, overwhelmed by his own distress, went on: "It was a drunk driver . . . he was coming home from work . . . he was killed instantly . . . Philip just called. . . ."

Philip? Then she realized. "Jeff?"

"Yes," her father said, realizing he hadn't made it clear, and reaching out to her. But Jennifer shrank back like a small wounded creature, thinking wildly, *It can't be.* Her closest girlfriend, Joanne Storey, came quickly. Together they spent the day with Jeff's family.

The Collums moved purposefully through the grim rituals of death. They insisted on reading the autopsy report and realized that, had Jeffrey survived, there would have been little left of his glowing intelligent self. They chose an open coffin, with his photo beside it.

"We want young people to see what used to be Jeff Collum," Helen said. "We want them to know what can happen to a nineteen-year-old on a summer's evening."

The day after the accident the Collums discovered a poem in their son's room. In June he had driven alone to the cottage for a solitary weekend with camera, typewriter, books, stereo and the family dog. He snapped pictures of glorious sunsets from the family's favourite vantage point. And there he wrote a long poem entitled "Shores of Eternity."

At the funeral, family friend Mary Sue McCarthy, a professor in the faculty of education at York University, read it aloud. When she came to the final lines it was as though Jeffrey was calling out to all of them:

. . . There was any man
Standing at the edge
Of any shoal.
He was a dark
Isolated
Indeterminate figure
Entirely
Alone.
I snapped the evening's last
picture
And I thought
As he blended with the
background
Disappeared
Completely
I thought
This man
Could be me.

After the service, subdued friends flocked to the Collum home. Helen and Howard encouraged them to visit Jeff's upstairs room. It told much about him: a clutter of souvenirs, records, plants in wild profusion and three tiers of bookshelves. On his desk was a list of things to do. A copy of *The Girl in a Swing*, Richard Adams' haunting story of love and the supernatural, lay open. In a corner sat Racky, a worn stuffed raccoon that his father had given him when he was a baby. Helen had found a new one, which she'd planned to give him as a joke after high-school graduation.

The young friends took turns going in to sit quietly and remember. Afterwards, Susan Buckley told Helen, "I could feel his presence."

But Jeff Collum was gone. It was over. Or was it? As the survivors began to pick up the pieces of their lives, they realized that the memories, the emptiness, the pain, might never be gone.

"A Fragile Line"

When Robert Benmergui came to his senses in hospital, he couldn't believe he had killed another human being. He began hyperventilating so badly from fright that he had to be sedated. Soon he was home, however, with nursing care and a walker, realizing his physical injuries were the least of his troubles.

One week after the accident and five days after Jeff Collum's funeral, Constable Dunbar came to interview him again. Benmergui was to be charged with criminal negligence causing death, the most serious of drinking-and-driving charges under the Criminal Code. He could be imprisoned for life. After advising him of his rights, and questioning him further about the accident, Dunbar asked, "How do you feel right now?"

"Terrible! I'm very depressed."

As Dunbar left he felt almost sorry for Benmergui. Then he reminded himself, *Whoa! He's the one who did it, and he's still alive!*

Throughout that cruel summer the Collums were now alone with their grief, but their sorrow was leavened with a growing rage. Helen regarded Robert Benmergui "the way some people feel about cockroaches." Howard had "an animal feeling of wanting revenge." They asked a police friend to run Benmergui's name through the computers, but found nothing on his record more incriminating than parking tickets. They sought out every detail of the accident and tracked Jeff's smashed car to a pound, took photos and discovered to their disgust that the tape deck had been stolen.

Philip went back to summer school, still grappling with the loss of a brother who, in a sense, he had just rediscovered. Two days before the accident, he dropped by his parents' home to find Jeff out front, vigorously ripping up a flower bed and replacing it with fresh petunias. "I'm tired of half-dead flowers!" he said. The brothers talked that day as they hadn't done in a while. They played records and realized they shared the same taste in music. That night Philip, who was going through a bad patch in his life – allergies, financial problems, a yearning for a career in art or music – thought with pleasure, *He's my best friend!*

Melanie returned to her summer teaching job. Jeff's death became a turning point in her life. She felt now that as each of us is "walking a fragile line between life and death, we want our life to have meaning." She resolved to turn this awful loss into something positive. Never again would she take her life for granted.

When Jennifer Meen heard that the wrecked Toyota could be seen, she also had to go. Her friend Joanne Storey went along for company. "I have to know exactly what I'm dealing with." Jennifer explained. "If I don't, I'll always wonder."

She planned to look from a distance but, once on the scene, she climbed the high fence and ran to the car. She stared at the dark-blue seats with their stains of dried blood, reached out to touch them – and recoiled in horror. *Real blood!* Then she realized she'd cut her hand climbing the fence.

The Collums gave Jennifer a key to their house. "Come anytime," they urged. Often she let herself in, sat quietly in Jeff's room, played music, had her private cry and slipped out again.

She thought of cancelling her university plans but went on to the University of Western Ontario in the autumn to study psychology. The first year was bad. No one in residence could appreciate her sorrow. But her family was a comfort and at least one classmate understood. He wrote her a poem that read, in part:

> Though the sun sets, it still
>   shines.
> Though it rains, it's still dry.
> Though the winds blow, it's
>   still calm.
> This I'm sure you know
> This I'm sure you know . . .

But for the next two years, Jennifer could not date or form a close friendship with another young man.

A sense of loss hung over Earl Haig Secondary School when its students reconvened in the autumn of 1981. Grace Halasz, Jeff's guidance counsellor, felt especially bereft. Through Grade XIII she had helped him struggle with course difficulties and his nagging allergies. One June day he came to her office unannounced and, unself-conscious in front of other adults, presented his thank-you: a bunch of wild flowers.

In November, at Earl Haig's annual commencement exercises, the program carried a remembrance of Jeff, with a reprint of "Shores of Eternity" and notice of a scholarship fund established in his name.

Jeff's presence clung to the classmates who had moved on. Nineteen-year-old Glenn Hefford was particularly desolate. He and Jeff had been best friends since meeting in the cello section of the school band in Grade VII. One summer they drove to Newfoundland. They had gone camping together, played tennis and planned to take the same course at university.

Glenn thought he could handle death; at 13 he'd lost his father. The fact of Jeff's passing did not sink in until after the funeral. Then memories began to haunt him. He, too, went to the pound to face the ruined car before going to Waterloo, taking the apartment they had booked and starting university.

But nothing was right anymore. And by the second semester it was clear Glenn had lost his freshman year. He returned to Toronto and took a job as a runner for a department store.

One Tragic Slip

Although the Benmergui case would eventually plod into criminal court, the Collums launched a $100,000 civil suit, not for the money but to make a point. "It's our way of saying, 'This shouldn't have been,'" says Helen.

The Collums discovered that some 2700 Canadians had died in alcohol-related accidents in 1981 alone; that, on average, someone is injured or killed in a traffic accident involving a drinker every 30 minutes; that penalties for drunk drivers are often light and inconsistent.

They learned of other young victims who, unlike Jeff, had survived – but barely. One young woman was confined to a wheelchair for life while the drinking driver who put her there received a $100 fine. Another woman and her fiancé were killed; their killer got a three-month license suspension and served a five-month sentence on weekends.

"That's socially acceptable *homicide!*" Helen exclaims angrily.

While Robert Benmergui did not consider his act socially acceptable, he felt he was in part a victim of a society that makes partying almost mandatory.

"Everyone I know has been driving when they shouldn't have been, at least once," he said. "In the corporate world it's a joke: You go to meetings, they bring in the bar, you stay for two hours, and what happens? They send drinking drivers out on the road!"

To friends and family, Benmergui was one of those "good" citizens who'd made just one tragic slip. The second oldest of two sons and three daughters, he had taken rabbinical studies at a private school in New Jersey. He dropped out after two years, returned to Toronto and went into sales. By the winter of 1982 he was in charge of 14 employees and was earning about $30,000 a year. His boss termed him an "excellent" worker.

But Benmergui was tormented by guilt, and spent sleepless nights reflecting on the enormity of his mistake, and the reckoning still to come. He drove and redrove the stretch of Highway 400, trying to understand where he'd gone wrong. He prayed for forgiveness and almost daily discussed the accident with his father, Elias, a man he revered. One day he said, "Dad, if I were the judge, there would be no sentence. I've already paid."

But, of course, he had not.

Nearly ten months after the accident, the preliminary inquiry into the death of Jeffrey Collum finally convened on May 12, 1982. In the provincial courthouse in Newmarket, 40 kilometres north of Toronto, Robert Benmergui, a subdued figure in tan suit and tinted glasses, took his place beside defence lawyer Robert Holden. Head down, he avoided the Collum family's eyes. Howard and Helen sat close together, clutching each other's hands for comfort. Jennifer Meen was with them.

They felt like spectators at their own tragedy. They were not asked to testify. From now on, Jeff's champion would be Crown Attorney Larry Owen, ten years a public prosecutor. Yet even his role was, inevitably, tilted towards punishing the offender, rather than seeking solace or redress for the victims. "In the language of the court, Jeff wasn't our beautiful son who was just beginning his life," Helen said later. "He was the 'victim' with a small *v!*"

Although the defence pleaded not guilty and elected for trial by jury, the case seemed clear-cut. Benmergui's blood alcohol reading that night was .24 milligrams; .08 milligrams is the "impaired" level.

Witnesses, including Larry Scott, Kim Shu-gan, Constable Dunbar and an ambulance attendant, told what they had seen. A toxicologist explained that a blood alcohol count of .24 milligrams is roughly equivalent to ten standard drinks or ten bottles of beer. Benmergui chose not to make a statement. The judge remanded him for trial at a later date.

With autumn, Helen was back in her classrooms again – a partial release from the continuing pressure and anguish. Howard, with no such outlet, remained inconsolable. Since his retirement, he and Jeff had become especially close. He had often driven his son to class and looked forward to his company after school. Now the empty house was almost unbearable.

Late in 1982, before the case went to trial, the defence changed its plea to guilty. Benmergui told his lawyer that he didn't want to "go on causing people pain."

Now the crucial issue was: What sentence would he receive? Crown Attorney Owen told the Collums he would ask for the most they could reasonably expect: two years less a day – meaning Benmergui would go to a provincial correctional centre, if convicted, rather than a federal penitentiary. It seemed little in view of the crime and of the maximum life sentence available under the law.

But the courts tend to reserve higher penalties for the worst crimes committed by the worst offenders. In a legal sense, Benmergui was not the "worst" offender: no criminal record and no previous driving convictions.

When the players in this private drama next gathered in the courthouse on January 13, 1983, the room was almost empty. Helen and Howard sat alone, limp and weary, holding hands, tears coursing down their faces. Benmergui sat slumped with his head in his hands. His parents were ranged behind him. *Something like a wedding – bride's side, groom's side,* Helen thought ironically.

The defence submitted letters attesting to Benmergui's good character. Elias Benmergui told the court that his son was a good boy. Robert's employer reaffirmed that he was an excellent worker, normally a moderate drinker and a responsible man.

A formal presentence report from the Ontario government probation and parole office was, the defence stated, "one of the best I've seen." No report was invited on the state of the surviving Collums.

After citing lengthy precedents to reinforce its position, the defence asked for a prison term of six to nine months. Robert Benmergui, when invited to speak, stammered, "Regardless of whatever the sentence is, I'm deeply sorry to everybody concerned. I can't say . . ." His voice trailed away.

As Judge D. R. Shearer recessed 15 minutes to reach his decision, the Collums heard a woman wail from the Benmergui side of the room, "They can't take him away! It was *only* an accident!" Helen had been on the verge of crossing over to speak to the other family. Now, any compassion she might have felt for them evaporated.

In his summation, Judge Shearer cited Benmergui's background and clean record, noting that his parents had been devastated by the accident. "One can only conjecture, of course, concerning the plight of the family of the deceased youngster," he continued, "and one might be inclined to conjecture that their devastation is worse." The accused had learned his lesson, Shearer added, and seemed truly remorseful. He sentenced Robert Benmergui to 12 months in prison. There was no license suspension.

The Collums felt angry and cheated. Jeff had been murdered, they felt, and this was all his life was worth in the eyes of the court. Constable Brad Dunbar called it "an insult to the Collums, an insult to me. It's almost a waste of time when you see how much damage he [Benmergui] did, how much work went into getting a good conviction and then he gets his wrist slapped."

"I Think of Him Every Day"

Benmergui entered Mimico Correctional Centre, a prison on the southwestern outskirts of Metropolitan Toronto. He found it difficult but he was treated well.

After a while, as a community service and a form of rehabilitation, he began working with children with cerebral palsy. He also participated in radio programs against drinking and driving as the anonymous voice of the drunk driver.

After 66 days he was transferred to Madeira House, a treatment centre for convicted impaired drivers that is primarily funded by the Ontario Ministry of Correctional Services. He spent 92 days there. Thus, although he had killed another man, Benmergui served only 43 percent of his sentence in any form, and less than 20 percent of it in an actual prison.

At Madeira, Robert Benmergui grappled with the reality of what he had done. "We try to tap into the heavy burden of guilt they carry," said Ramsay Kane, a therapist with a long career in social work. "The program not only straightens out a drunken driver, but also other kinks in his life."

There were times when Benmergui was deeply remorseful – and times when he claimed that he was a victim of society. "Our counsellors never told us anything about this in high school," he'd say. "All you ever got was the coach laughing because everybody was going out for a beer after the game!"

But Kane and his staff refused to allow such a cop-out. "Don't expect me to say you're not responsible, because you *are*," Kane told Benmergui and the others. "It's not 'just one of those things,' and I'm not going to take the guilt from your shoulders." Neither does Madeira House tell its inmates to never drink again.

"Drinking is a privilege," Kane emphasized. "If you are going to drink, you must assume responsibility for it."

Once a week Benmergui sat down with

other inmates and parolees, their wives or girlfriends, police and probation officers, and victims of impaired driving. While they did not match up victims and offenders – such as Benmergui and the Collums – the sessions were an emotional wringer.

Throughout his stay Benmergui repeatedly said he wanted to communicate with the Collums. An opportunity came for an indirect message. Journalism students from the University of Western Ontario were making a video on drinking and driving. The Collums and Benmergui were interviewed separately.

"I want them to know that I *really* care," Benmergui said on camera. "I want them to know that I never meant any of this to happen. And I want them to know that I think of him too, all the time, every day."

"Sure he's sorry – maybe," said Howard Collum when he heard Benmergui's emotional statement. "And if he doesn't think about it every day, then he *is* damned. Because *we* do, hourly!"

The Collums, meanwhile, joined PRIDE (People to Reduce Impaired Driving Everywhere).* Founded in 1981, PRIDE is a voluntary group whose goals include raising the drinking age to 21; lowering the legal blood alcohol level for "impaired" from .08 to .05; impounding the vehicles of impaired drivers for various periods of time; better rights for victims; and banning life-style advertising of alcoholic beverages – the kind showing young people having a wonderful time with their booze and motor vehicles.

PRIDE was the battleground Helen needed to vent her outrage, sorrow and enormous energy. Her speeches brought tears to listeners' eyes. "Someone has taken the sunshine from my life," she often began. "I will not suffer in silence."

Howard initially disliked "going public," but

he became an eloquent advocate of a better deal for victims – and for taxpayers. "Our values are skewed," he says. "We spend thousands of dollars on prosecutions, but little public money is channelled into support of those who suffer the offense."

By 1984 Benmergui was a free man in the eyes of the law – yet his life had been turned upside down. His father died of a heart attack later that year – Benmergui believes it was partially brought on by stress resulting from the accident. His mother suffered a nervous collapse, from which she has recovered.

Benmergui still drinks, but never when he is driving. He is lucky to *have* a license to drive, in fact; had his case come up later, he might still be in jail.

In response to the public outcry, the courts are getting tougher. Less than two years after Benmergui's case was closed, an Ontario man was given 21 months on an identical charge. The Crown appealed and, in a landmark decision, the appeal judge *increased* the sentence to three years.

In late 1987 another Ontario driver, with more than twice the legal limit of alcohol in his blood, killed a 19-year-old. He was sentenced to four years and lost his license for ten years. In British Columbia an appeal in a similar case increased the original two-year sentence to five years, with a license suspension of 20 years.

In Ontario, which has about one third of the motorists in Canada, the rate of drinking drivers involved in crashes per 1000 licensed drivers decreased by 49 percent between 1980 and 1986. But for Helen and Howard Collum, the fight is far from over. In the province, 17,723 drinking drivers had accidents in 1986, and 28 percent of drivers involved in *fatal* crashes had been drinking.

So, Helen still spends up to 30 hours a week after school and on weekends, working for PRIDE on the speaking circuit and with victims. Howard computerizes PRIDE's mailing

*Not to be confused with the National Parents' Resource Institute for Drug Education Inc., also known as PRIDE.

lists and attends to myriad behind-the-scene jobs. As a team they have twice visited Mimico Correctional Centre for informal talks with the drunk-driver inmates.

The elder Collums, according to their son Philip, will never get over the loss of Jeffrey, but they are coping in their distinct ways. Helen quotes the German philosopher Friedrich Nietzsche: "That which does not kill me makes me stronger." And she adds, bleakly, "This young man's death has made me a very confident person."

"My response has been different," Howard says. "I say, 'What doesn't kill me may just wound me.' My wounds may never heal."

Their anger at Robert Benmergui has abated only a little; more truly, it has simply widened to include all others who drink and kill on the highways. "Many people think I'm too vindictive," Helen says. "But anger is the fuel that keeps us going."

In 1987, after interminable postponements, the Collums settled their civil suit out of court for $35,000, plus $1500 for each surviving child. They have made their point. Money could not bring the sunshine back to Helen's life. Howard still weeps on the anniversary of Jeffrey's death.

The ripples of this young man's life and death still reach into many other lives. Mary Sue McCarthy reads "Shores of Eternity" to students in her course on adolescence. Jennifer Meen, now a probation officer, has been in a relationship for three years, but keeps mementos of Jeff. She still has the comic card he gave her the day he got his driver's license: "I've got this dumb dog that jumps all over people and nuzzles them and pants real hard in their faces. I want you to come over and see him but call first – and give me time to get into my dog suit."

Constable Brad Dunbar cannot forget the case. "A year or two afterwards, my younger brother started working at Wonderland. And all I wanted was to make sure he got home every night."

Kim Shugan Scott still sees, in her nightmares, the crash she and Larry witnessed that night. They won't have even one drink if they're getting behind the wheel. Neither will Glenn Hefford, now a computer programmer, or his wife, the former Joanne Storey.

Melanie Collum, now a potter in Guelph, Ont., still flinches at the sound of a knock late at night. Tears come suddenly, unexpectedly, as she thinks of her brother. Yet neither she nor Philip nor Jennifer Meen feel vindictive towards Robert Benmergui. All are curious about him, and both young women express a hesitant desire to meet him and see what kind of a person he is.

"He never intended to kill Jeff," Jennifer says. "And I know he's living with it."

Over lunch one day Benmergui sits red-eyed, miserable, not touching the food, breaking down again and again. He has been sick for two days at the thought of the interview, he says, but wants to try to explain his feelings.

"I'd like to do something; my problem is to figure out something positive," Benmergui says. "It's not like giving back. I can't give back. You can't pay for it. You know how many people I've hurt, don't you?"

He begins again: "I *will* do something. I definitely will do something! I wasn't a bad guy, you know. I didn't mean it to happen. I'd really like to touch the Collums and tell them that, you know, to touch them . . . I would speak to them if they would want to talk to me. . . ."

He lives now in northern Ontario, where he buries himself in his work with another TV-store chain. "Nobody will ever understand," he says, "how I agonize. It gets worse, it doesn't get better. What I've been through in the last years, I don't wish on anybody."

Maybe his message will stop someone else from driving while drunk. Those drinking drivers might heed another message: Robert will never entirely escape his burden. The ultimate truth is that no ocean of tears, no depth of contrition, no lifetime of tireless effort will bring Jeff Collum back.

"It seems so long since I've seen him," muses Jennifer. "He would be twenty-six now."

.....

WHEN TEENS DRINK AND DRIVE . . .

....

By Leslie Fruman

Seventeen years old and full of life a few months ago, John Leahy today is slumped motionless in a chair at Sunnybrook Medical Centre.

Essential fluids are pumped into his body through plastic tubes taped carefully to his skin; bandages mitten his hands to stop him from unconsciously ripping out the delicate, life-giving tubes.

No one knows what he is thinking as a group of high school students gathers around him to listen to his father Paul tell about the night last June when his son had "a couple of beers too many" and got into his van to drive some buddies home from a party.

And no one really knows – not the nurses on the ward, not the doctors who have treated him, and not his heartbroken parents who wait anxiously for some sign of their son's old life – if John will ever recover from the accident on that warm spring night when a pole crashed through the window of the van and struck his head, after he'd smashed his vehicle into a tree.

Statistics show that teenagers who drink are more at risk than adults when they mix drinking and driving. The combination of an inexperienced driver who is also an inexperienced drinker can lead to hazardous, sometimes fatal accidents.

Drivers aged 16 to 24 make up 16.8 per cent of all licensed drivers in Ontario, and they account for a staggering number of accidents that involve alcohol; 51.1 per cent of all drinking-driving collisions, and more than 40 per cent of all traffic fatalities involve this group of drivers, according to statistics from the Ministry of the Attorney General's Drinking-Driving Countermeasures office.

As the Christmas season gets underway, the temptations are out there. Post-exam parties, Christmas bashes and boozy get-togethers over the holidays are an invitation for teens to enter into the potentially fatal mistake of having a few drinks for the road. But students from Unionville High School who met Leahy at Sunnybrook recently will think twice.

Immobilized Teen

As part of their health program, they came to Sunnybrook to participate in a program developed by the hospital, called PARTY (Prevent Alcohol Related Trauma Among Youth). When they marched up to the ward to meet John and his parents, they weren't prepared for what they saw. They stared incredulously at the immobilized teen, who is roughly the same age as them. Though his eyes fluttered occasionally, his face remained expressionless. His father pulled out pictures taken of John months before the accident that show a happy, well-groomed youth, ready for life. The head injuries John suffered as a result of the crash have left him unable to comprehend what is going on around him. He can't go home because he requires too much medical care. His parents don't know if he'll ever go home. What would have been a bright future has been drastically displaced.

"He was so full of life," says Paul Leahy. "He had so much to live for. There weren't enough hours in the day for him."

Leahy pauses.

"Look, don't let this happen to any of you.

Just don't let it happen," he says, staring intensely into each student's eyes.

The program developed by emergency nurse Judy Radford at Sunnybrook is designed to give young people a first-hand view of some of the consequences of drinking and driving. Medical staff and social workers at the hospital participate, along with a paramedic and patients who volunteer to tell their stories to the spellbound students. Any misconceptions the students may have had about drinking and driving are quickly eliminated.

Showing a slide presentation of multiple-vehicle accidents, paramedic Ken Murray points to trapped drivers and bloodied passengers.

"I've never been trapped in a car myself," says Murray, showing a slide of a trapped woman. "But you can see by the terror in this woman's face, that it's not any fun."

The room is hushed as the images sink in, and then the students have questions about the people they have seen in the pictures. Did they live? Will they get better?

The answer is usually no.

A social worker tells the students about his job at the hospital. "Often people who have been involved in accidents don't remember what happened," says Chris Aslett, a social worker at Sunnybrook. "You can imagine how difficult it is to be reminded of what happened. Either you're a victim, or you're responsible for the accident. You might have caused your best friend to be killed. Try living with that for the rest of your life."

Aslett appeals to the young people to think long and hard before getting into a car after having a few drinks.

"As teenagers, you're just getting used to your growing independence. If you're involved in an accident, you can watch all your independence be taken away. You could become completely dependent on the legal system, the welfare system, the hospital system. You may never be able to work again, or if you're responsible for harming another person, you might be required to support that person for the rest of your life. Insurance doesn't usually cover what it costs to repay a person you've hurt and he may sue you. You could be paying for the accident for the rest of your life.

"As you meet people in the wards, think about their families. Imagine that you could have been the one who put them here. Think about it."

Dr. Peter Lane, an emergency physician at Sunnybrook, explains to the students that though most people have an image of someone who is drunk as being someone who is acting silly and falling down, this isn't an accurate description.

"After you have your first drink, your ability to make decisions, your judgment, is affected," says Lane. "You may not even realize this. One or two drinks can take you beyond the legal limit of alcohol (.08 milligrams – or 80 milligrams of alcohol in 100 millilitres of blood) in your blood; and police can impound your car if you have .05 milligrams of alcohol in your blood. If you're going to be driving, you shouldn't drink at all."

Of all the trauma patients coming through the emergency doors at Sunnybrook, the majority have head and spinal cord injuries, Lane says.

Peer Pressure

"Head injuries have a subtle effect," says Lane. "You don't think as well, you don't do as well in school. You may have a seizure disorder from a head injury that will be with you for the rest of your life. It will affect your relationships with your friends and family."

The students from Unionville High School felt differently by the end of the day than they had when they arrived.

"You know, you go to parties and everyone is drinking, and bragging about drinking and you wonder, what are you supposed to do? There's peer pressure, definitely," says Sean Gonsalves.

"But man, after seeing this, there's no question. Do you really have to get blasted to have a good time?"

While drinking is not foreign to these students, many say driving will be out of the question for them after they've had something to drink.

"You just don't drive to the party in the first place," says Gonsalves. "That's all there is to it."

Nadine Williams says she doesn't drink, but she still worries about drinking and driving.

"I don't do it, but I have to be afraid when I'm out at night. Who knows if the other guy on the road is drunk?," says the Grade 11 student.

Effie Miranda was hit hard by what she saw.

"When I saw those kids, I couldn't believe it," says the Grade 12 student. "Every time you go to a party you're faced with a situation where someone you know is drinking and probably someone is driving too. I'm just going to say no from now on. I'm not getting into a car with someone who has been drinking. There's no way."

BLAME DENIED IN MODEL'S CRASH SUIT

By Jack Lakey

The driver of a car involved in an accident that left a fashion model a quadriplegic has denied admitting responsibility for the collision to the other driver.

"The guy's not only a drunk, he's a liar," Roger Simpson said of testimony heard Wednesday in the Supreme Court of Ontario from Michael Kasubeck, who was driving a 1976 Malibu that slammed into the rear of Simpson's car in dense fog.

Kasubeck had testified that after his car collided with a borrowed, 1979 Lada Simpson had been driving, Simpson "told me he was sorry, that he shouldn't have been stopped in the driving lane."

Simpson, 30, told court yesterday he exchanged words with Kasubeck immediately after the collision, but vehemently denied apologizing or saying he had been stopped in the driving lane.

He said he was more concerned about his girlfriend, Wendy Crawford, who was unable to move, and didn't want to talk to Kasubeck.

Simpson also testified that Kasubeck appeared drunk at the time. Kasubeck, 25, earlier testified he had drank between six and nine bottles of beer the night of the accident, but felt sober and capable of driving.

Acquitted on Charges

Kasubeck was charged with impaired driving and criminal negligence causing bodily harm stemming from the accident, but was acquitted on both charges at a trial in October, 1984, due to a technicality.

Crawford was being driven by Simpson to Pearson International Airport from her Cambridge home early on July 5, 1984, to fly to Tokyo for her first international modelling assignment, when the accident occurred.

The accident crushed two vertebrae in her neck and left her a quadriplegic, paralyzed from the neck down.

Crawford, 24, is suing Kasubeck and insurers for Simpson and John Hillman, the owner of the car in which she was riding, for damages totalling more than $5 million.

She has already agreed to a $700,000 out-of-court settlement from the Town and Country Tavern in London, where Kasubeck had been drinking before the accident.

Mr. Justice Nicholson McRae is determining liability in the civil trial, and deciding the amount of damages to be awarded to Crawford.

Simpson angrily clashed several times with Crawford's lawyer, Laurie Mandel, who grilled him over inconsistencies between his testimony yesterday and earlier evidence he gave at Kasubeck's 1984 trial.

"What are you getting at, that I lied?" Simpson said at one point to Mandel, his voice breaking.

Simpson said he set out early on July 5 to take Crawford to the airport, but fog became so dense on Highway 401 he decided to pull off at an exit ramp leading to a gas station.

Seconds before, he had been driving so slowly the car stalled, Simpson said. He had just got it re-started and was easing onto the exit ramp at a slow speed when the car was rear-ended.

The trial continues.

HOTEL MUST PAY $1 MILLION TO TEEN HURT BY DRUNK DRIVER

....
By Rick Haliechuk

A Peterborough-area hotel must pay nearly $1 million in damages to a teenage girl disabled for life when hit by a driver who had been drinking at the hotel just before the accident.

The Ship and Shore Tavern in Lakefield, and Kevin Billings, the drunk driver, are equally responsible for the crash which paralyzed 14-year-old Melissa Hague and killed her mother Jacqueline in October, 1983, the Supreme Court of Ontario ruled yesterday [April 27, 1989].

"If tavern owners are allowed to sell intoxicating beverages, they must accept as a price of doing business, a duty to attempt to keep the highways free of drunk drivers," Mr. Justice Thomas Granger ruled.

Billings of Tory Hill was convicted of criminal negligence causing death in 1984 and sentenced to 2½ years in jail.

Damages of $1.89 million were agreed to before a lengthy trial last fall and yesterday's judgment [April 27, 1989] determined the hotel and Billings must each pay half of the settlement.

Most of the money goes to Melissa Hague, now a paraplegic, and other, lesser amounts go to her father and twin sister. The Hagues live in Buckhorn, near Peterborough.

The accident occurred at 10:45 p.m. on the night of Oct. 28, 1983, when Billings drove across the centre line on Highway 28 south of Lakefield and plowed into the Hague vehicle.

Evidence at last fall's trial disclosed that Billings, now 30, and two others had spent the entire day drinking beer and whisky, and smoking marijuana as they cruised the back roads of the Haliburton area.

The judge said the trio had consumed 50 pints of beer, a 26-ounce bottle of rye whisky and had smoked a substantial amount of marijuana by the time they arrived at the Oasis Tavern in Bancroft, north of Lakefield, at about 7:15 p.m.

But after serving Billings and one of the others one beer each, hotel staff concluded they were drunk and cut them off.

At 8:00 p.m., as the hotel staff at the tavern watched out the window, Billings headed south toward Lakefield "and eventual disaster for the Hague family," the judge said.

Granger criticized the Oasis staff for not calling a nearby Ontario Provincial Police detachment, but he said the trial evidence did not establish that the staff's failure to act led directly to the accident.

By 9:00 p.m., the trio had arrived at the

Ship and Shore Tavern in Lakefield, where Billings had four pints of beer over the next 90 minutes, Granger said.

The judge said if the staff at the first tavern were able to notice Billings' intoxication earlier, then so should the staff at the second hotel.

But apparently because the staff was busy with many other customers, "the Ship and Shore Hotel continued to supply alcohol to an intoxicated person," the judge said.

▢

SON'S DRUNK DRIVING ACCIDENT STRAINED FAMILY, STUDENTS TOLD

By Royson James

"Tell them it ain't worth it."

That's the painful message Anita Farmer delivered to 150 students at a mock drunk-driving trial in Markham yesterday.

It came from her 20-year-old son, Dan – more than two years after he sped his car off a concession road near Barrie, killing a passenger, damaging his brain and ruining the lives of his family.

He was driving while impaired.

Since the 1985 accident, Dan's older brother has run away from home "unable to come to grips" with the tragedy, Farmer said. His younger brother lives with the hurtful remarks at school from those who can't forgive Dan for the fatal accident. And his father suffered a heart attack under the strain.

"These are the fringe people," Farmer told the students. "Their lives are unalterably changed. You never go back and it (the pain) goes on and on."

The day-long event was sponsored by the York Region board of education, the Addiction Research Foundation and Students Against Drunk Driving. Students leaving the Markham Theatre said the message got through.

"That was scary," said 17-year-old Melinda Preston of Aurora, following Farmer's talk. "I'm not going to drink and drive. I wouldn't want that to happen to my family and friends."

David Foster, 17, of St. Andrew's College in Aurora, said he started out the day not convinced about the dangers of impaired driving.

"Now I am," he said.

Farmer, from Stroud, just south of Barrie, spared no detail in relating her son's future – "imprisoned in a body that doesn't work anymore."

He is disabled for life and must live with the thought that his actions resulted in someone's death. Last month, Farmer said, he was admitted to the psychiatric ward of a London, Ont. hospital because of a suicide attempt.

"Imagine an 18-year-old man in diapers," she told the hushed audience. "Imagine him rolling around on a gym mat on the floor like a toddler?"

Earlier in the day, a mock trial student jury found one of their peers guilty of impaired driving causing death and prescribed a sentence of three years.

Kelly Cluett, 18, had practised the role of the accused since last October, but yesterday said she wasn't prepared for the overwhelming sense of guilt she would face – even in a mock trial.

"Even for that short time, it was horrible; it changed me," Cluett said.

Cluett, president of the SADD chapter at the Markham District School, said the three-year term her peers handed down was not enough.

SADD was started in September, 1981, by students in Massachusetts. Last year, Attorney-General Ian Scott officially formed SADD Ontario for this province's students.

FOLLOWING THROUGH

Society has attempted to deal with the drinking and driving problem in many ways. Examine the following material to gain a further perspective on the variety and effectiveness of methods of dealing with this serious social problem.

SUGGESTED APPROACH

Step 1

This should be done individually.

Read the material, considering the following:
   a. what you think are the best methods or combinations of methods, and
   b. what unexpected consequences can result from "solutions" that don't anticipate unexpected outcomes.

Step 2

This may be done in groups or individually.

Compare the various methods that society used to deal with the problem and rank them in terms of their effectiveness. Don't forget to include possible adverse outcomes which, in effect, could worsen the problem or cause others.

Step 3

This may be done in groups or individually.

From the following list of criteria, select two or three that you feel could be used to judge the potential effectiveness of any possible plan for dealing with the problem. Remember that workable solutions tend to be based on criteria that incorporate a number of perspectives.
   • it must reduce the problem to a considerable degree
   • it must eliminate the problem

- it must not create another problem of an equal magnitude
- it must not create other problems
- it must be cost efficient
- it must be feasible
- it must be humane
- it must be ethical
- it must be enforceable
- it must not trample on individual rights
- your choice

Step 4

This may be done in groups or individually.

Using your established criteria as a guide, work out a tentative plan for dealing with the drinking and driving problem. You might wish to focus on one particular target group, such as teenage drivers. Write down the details, including potential consequences.

COURT RULES NO JAIL FOR DRUNK DRIVERS TAKING TREATMENT

....

By Rick Haliechuk

A repeat drunk driver can avoid going to jail if he takes an alcoholism treatment program that makes it probable he'll never drink and drive again, Ontario's highest court says.

In a 2-1 judgment, the Court of Appeal yesterday dismissed the crown's appeal for jail terms for two men given conditional discharges for drinking and driving offences, although each had a long record of convictions.

And for the first time, the court has set down factors a trial judge should consider when deciding to grant such a discharge to a person.

Laurence Douglas Ashberry, 35, and Malcolm James Mills, 37, could have been jailed for up to five years.

'Public Interest'

The Criminal Code permits a trial judge to grant a conditional discharge as an alternative to jail if the accused agrees to take treatment for alcoholism. If the person completes the treatment program to the court's satisfaction, the conviction won't be entered on his record.

If a trial judge is satisfied that a treatment program would guarantee the accused would never drink and drive again, "then obviously a discharge would be in the public interest," said Mr. Justice David Griffiths.

Griffiths, supported by Madam Justice Hilda McKinlay, set down these factors for trial judges to consider:

- Circumstances of the offence.
- Motivation of the offender.
- Availability of treatment programs.
- Probability that the treatment will work.
- Criminal record of the accused.

The death or injury of a person caused by the offender's drunkeness will generally mean no conditional discharge, but a bad driving record should not, by itself, work against the accused, the court said.

In dissent, Ontario Associate Chief Justice Charles Dubin agreed with the need for trial judges to consider several factors when sentencing a drunk driver.

But the paramount consideration "must be that the discharge is not contrary to the public interest," he said.

Ashberry was arrested by York Region police in February, 1987, after being seen driving a car erratically. His blood alcohol level was more than 2½ times the legal limit.

The trial judge was told that Ashberry had a long criminal record, including six previous drinking and driving convictions, plus convictions for indecent assault, theft, and break and enter.

When he was arrested in York Region, he was on a temporary absence pass from prison where he was serving two years for dangerous driving and a concurrent 12-month sentence for impaired driving.

At the time he was sentenced, Ashberry was taking an alcoholism treatment program in Windsor.

Mills also had six prior drinking and driving convictions when he was found by police sitting behind the wheel of his car, which was in a ditch. His blood alcohol level was twice the legal limit.

Four months later, he was found by the police in similar circumstances.

NOT JAILING DRUNK DRIVERS IN TREATMENT CALLED 'ABSURD'

By Rick Haliechuk

The head of a group fighting drunk driving has condemned an Ontario court ruling that repeat offenders may avoid jail by taking treatment.

"It doesn't make any sense to us," John Bates, president of People to Reduce Impaired Driving Everywhere, said in an interview yesterday.

"What it says, really, is that being a drunk is an excuse for drinking and driving," he said. "It treats people who enter alcohol programs separately from others."

On Monday, the Ontario Court of Appeal ruled in a 2-1 decision that a trial judge could grant a repeat drunk driver a conditional discharge if it's probable he won't drink and drive again.

Drunk drivers with two or more convictions may get conditional discharges if they agree to enter treatment programs for alcohol or drug addiction.

Normally, drunk drivers get a minimum of two weeks in jail on the second offence and longer terms on further convictions.

The court was dealing with the crown's appeal of conditional discharges granted two men who each had six previous drinking-driving convictions.

Both were given long terms of probation, but if they successfully complete the treatment programs, the convictions won't go on their records.

Mr. Justice David Griffiths and Madam Justice Hilda McKinlay concluded a trial judge could grant a discharge if satisfied the treatment program is likely to succeed.

Bates called the judgment ridiculous and suggested the procedure is open to abuse by devious accused who will say they are addicted and need treatment.

Repeat offenders make up 30 per cent of drunk-driving convictions, he said.

Susan Ficek, the crown lawyer who argued the appeal, said the crown wanted significant jail sentences for Laurence Douglas Ashberry and Malcolm James Mills.

Ficek said the decision will be reviewed by senior officials in the attorney-general's ministry, who will decide whether to appeal to the Supreme Court of Canada.

SOME DRUNK DRIVERS ARE EXECUTED

Dear Ann Landers: For many years I have read your blasts against drunk drivers. I say more power to you. Your statement that a drunk driver who kills someone is a murderer and should be treated like one is right on the button. A neighbor whose daughter was killed by a drunk driver had 100 copies of that column made and sent them to judges all over the country.

The Minnesota Licensed Beverage Association put out some interesting facts that you might want to share with your readers. It tells how drunk drivers are dealt with in other countries. Here they are:

Australia: The names of convicted drunk drivers are published in the local newspapers under the heading: "Drunk and in jail."

South Africa: A drunk driver is given a 10-year prison term, a fine of $10,000 or both, depending on the circumstances.

Turkey: Drunk drivers are taken 20 miles out of town by the police and forced to walk back under escort.

Malaya: The drunk driver is jailed. If he is married his wife is jailed, too.

Norway: Three weeks in jail at hard labour and the drunk driver loses his licence for one year. A second offence within five years and the driving licence is revoked permanently.

Finland and Sweden: Automatic jail sentence for one year at hard labor.

England: One year in jail, one-year suspension of driver's licence and a fine of $250.

Russia: Driver's licence is revoked for life.

France: One year in jail, the loss of licence for three years and a fine of $1,000.

Poland: Jail and fine determined by the judge. All drunk drivers are forced to listen to a set of lectures on the effects of drunk driving on families and the community.

Bulgaria: A second conviction of drunk driving is the last. The punishment is execution.

El Salvador: Drunk drivers (first offence) are executed by a firing squad.

These sentences may seem extremely harsh but I'll bet they don't have many second offenders. Maybe if we cracked down harder on our inebriated citizens who jeopardize the lives of innocent people every day, we wouldn't have so many tragedies. What do you think, Ann? – **K.M. Madison, Wis.**

Dear Madison: I think you're on to something. As a reader in Hemet, Calif., wrote recently (he also sent the list), "The chances of a drunk hitting anything with a gun are rather remote, whereas with a car it is a relatively easy matter."

We need tougher laws, tougher judges and frequent, effective awareness campaigns to keep drunks out of the driver's seat.

We also must educate our young people about the hazards of driving while high on pot, speed, cocaine and the various drugs that are being used for recreation, escape, thrills and what have you.

When one considers that more people are killed in car accidents in the United States every year than died in Vietnam, and that approximately 60 per cent of those deaths were alcohol or drug related, it's high time we took this problem seriously. Wake up, America!

PRIME TIME TV SHOWS HAIL DESIGNATED DRIVERS

By Nikki Finke

Considered separately, they were two unremarkable bits of TV dialogue.

During the Nov. 16 episode of CBS' *Wiseguy*, Vinnie Terranova, played by Ken Wahl, was drinking with some friends at a blue-collar bar where an obviously inebriated man was preparing to leave. "Are you sure you can drive?" the worried bartender asked the slurring, stumbling stranger. "I better go take care of him," Wahl told his friends.

Meanwhile, on NBC during that same hour, the maitre d' on the upscale urban drama *Tattinger's* was concerned about whether a drunk patron was going to drive home. "They've got a limo," he was reassured.

A coincidence? Or another example of how TV shows are so unoriginal? Neither, actually.

Blame Jay Winsten, a Harvard PhD in molecular biology who has spent this year prodding the TV industry to expose the dangers of drinking and driving and to promote the designated driver program, especially during the holiday season when people are more apt to be around alcohol.

So far, 15 shows – including *Baby Boom* and *Hunter* on NBC, TV *101* on CBS and *Mr.*

Belvedere and *Who's The Boss?* on ABC – have either broadcast or made "definite commitments to lay in a few lines of dialogue" on the subject in forthcoming scripts because of Winsten's lobbying.

He also persuaded the three major networks to launch a prime-time public-service campaign promoting the "designated driver" program, which will continue through the holiday season.

"People are saying this is the first time since *Love Story* that Harvard and Hollywood have teamed up on anything," said Winsten, assistant dean at the Harvard school of public health and director of the university's centre of health communication, which is trying to use the media to motivate behavioral changes among the public on several health issues.

The decision by the Harvard Alcohol Project to focus its lobbying effort on the TV industry was made "because nothing can begin to rival prime-time entertainment programming in potential impact," Winsten said. "The case has been made that different economic and demographic groups closely follow particular programs and closely identify with particular characters, so there's a very powerful potential for the modelling of behavior within that."

Winsten's success is remarkable, considering not only that the networks derive considerable revenues from alcoholic beverage advertising, but also the sensitivity of producers and writers to any perceived infringement on their creative independence.

"People said to me, 'You're an outsider. They'll never accept you. They'll never listen to you'," recalled Winsten, who knew nothing about the TV industry when he started. "Well, thank God I didn't know how tough it was supposed to be. Because I might not have attempted it."

Winsten isn't the first crusader to try to wheedle at least a smidgen of air time on TV for a good cause. But he had some obvious advantages, not the least of which was the allure of his Harvard affiliation and the stature of his advisory board (which included former CBS president Frank Stanton and NBC commentator John Chancellor).

"Jay's crusade was one that we could do something about fairly easily, unlike a lot of other worthwhile causes," noted Grant Tinker, president of GTG Entertainment, who helped Winsten get in to see many of the 80 or so TV studio executives, producers, and writers that Winsten estimates he has met with over the past year.

"A producer or writer can very easily put this message in the mouth of a TV character in a social situation without preaching," Tinker added. "Considering the simplicity of it all, it's very hard for us to feel our independence is being challenged."

Bob Myman, executive producer of *Hooperman*, said his show will include some lines of dialogue about designated drivers "because it doesn't hurt us and it's smart."

But he also wondered if his colleagues realize they may be opening a Pandora's Box. "If any of the people really thought about it, they'd freak," he declared. "What do you do if everyone started hitting on you?"

Acknowledging that not every show can accommodate him, Winsten is nevertheless pleased with the response, attributing it to his low-key approach and modest goals. "I think people are going along with it because they don't feel pressure. I tell them we may go away sad but we never go away mad," Winsten said.

In fact, Winsten's request is not for entire scenes or episodes but for only five seconds of dialogue warning against drinking and driving or promoting the designated driver concept.

"The pitch is for each show to do it once or twice a season because to do it more would backfire," Winsten said.

TEEN LICENCE SUSPENSION PLAN IS "DISCRIMINATION"

....

By Eva Ferguson and Jim Cunningham

Alberta could be breaching the Constitution with a proposal to suspend the licence of any probationary driver caught with booze on his breath, says a legal expert.

Singling out a particular group under the law – 16 and 17-year-olds – could be considered discriminatory and contrary to the Constitution, said Kathleen Mahoney, University of Calgary law professor.

"The whole thing raises more questions than it does answers," said Mahoney.

Solicitor General Dick Fowler said Monday his department is considering a plan that would see probationary licences cancelled for probationary drivers caught with any amount of alcohol in their system – not just the .08 per cent of alcohol in the blood, which is the legal limit.

"A 16 or 17-year-old is not supposed to be drinking under any circumstances," the minister said.

"If they put themselves behind the wheel, then I believe probationary licence should be cancelled on them," said Fowler.

"The immediate lifting of a licence is a breach of Section 15, the equality section, because this group (probationary drivers) is being singled out for special treatment and that's discrimination," Mahoney said.

"A person is innocent until proven guilty and this reverses that approach because the person involved is being assumed guilty if their licence is taken away before their trial. The presumption of innocence is being put to the wayside."

Mahoney rejects Fowler's argument that a probationary licence could include any driver who has only driven for two years – not just 16- and 17-year-olds.

"It is obvious that most probationary drivers will be in this age group and the disproportionate impact of this legislation will fall on this age group," she says.

Bonnie Lowe, vice-chairman with Teenagers Against Drunk Driving (TADD) says she supports a harder line against drunk drivers, but the province's idea is unfair.

"I can't understand why they would discriminate against teenagers," said Lowe.

"Drinking and driving is not just our problem, it's everybody's problem."

The idea is being discussed by department officials and might not go to the government caucus for approval before next fall, Fowler said.

TEENS, POLICE CAMPAIGN FOR SAFE HOLIDAY

....

By Philip Mascoll

The Ontario Provincial Police in Whitby is displaying a grim reminder that Christmas is also the season of the drunk driver.

The Yuletide "decoration" in the front yard of the station house is a stark recreation of an auto crash instead of the usual Christmas tree and Nativity scene.

The twisted, shattered husk of a car sits in front of the detachment. It is surrounded by flashing lights, crime scene tape and a huge slogan board.

Facing drivers in the westbound lanes of Highway 401 and the busy Whitby GO Train station parking lot, the display immediately grabs the eyes of thousands of drivers.

It was prepared for the detachment by students of Whitby's Anderson Collegiate

Vocational Institute who are members of the school's group against drunk driving.

The group is called Anderson Against Drunk Driving (AADD).

OPP Sergeant Bob Foley said when the subject of a Christmas display at the station house came up, constable Bill Phillips suggested they go for the auto wreck and its impact, rather than the usual Yuletide scene.

Phillips sold the idea to staff adviser Diane Townsend and her group at the school, and they, along with art teacher Rein Reiart and his group of students, did the rest.

All nine members of AADD – there are 1,400 students in the school – are zealots when it comes to discouraging drinking and driving.

Julia Everist, 19, nearly lost a friend to drinking and driving over last year's Thanksgiving holiday. The friend and three other people were in the car involved in the accident.

"One ended up in a neck brace, another with a pin in his leg," Everist said.

The boy driving the car had left a party, where Everist was also a guest, just before the accident.

"Everyone was saying 'Why didn't you stop them from driving?' But the guy was 6 feet 3 inches. How do you do that?" Everist said.

"I felt this was a way to help. If we can show people that drinking and driving is wrong, change their minds when they are young, maybe we can get rid of the problem."

☐

SOBER PILL POSES DILEMMA

··

By Malcolm Brown

The good news is that scientists are now as sure as they can be that they have a drug which can make a drunk person (or at least a drunk rat) sober.

The bad is that moral considerations could prevent its ever going on sale. The ability to "switch off" the effects of alcohol might tempt people to drink to even greater excess.

The drug, known as Ro15-4513, was first synthesized by the Swiss pharmaceutical company Hoffman-La Roche several years ago, but development work was halted when the company decided the ethical problems of marketing it were too great.

Now a group of American researchers at the National Institute of Mental Health in Maryland has reported such remarkable results with the drug that the question of its manufacture is bound to be raised again.

The researchers report in the journal Science that rats which had passed out from intoxication were back on their feet and running around normally within two minutes of being injected with Ro15-4513, and that those injected with the drug before being given alcohol did not behave as though they were intoxicated.

Ro15-4513, which is a derivative of the benzo-diazepines – on which the Roche tranquilizers Librium and Valium are based – is said to have no dangerous side effects.

One of the problems with the drug is that while it seems to act on the brain, so modifying behavior, it does not affect the metabolism or the blood alcohol levels.

This raises some medico-legal problems. It would be quite possible, for instance, for a driver involved in a car accident to claim that, despite his high blood alcohol level, he was perfectly sober because he had taken a tablet of Ro15-4513.

☐

LEAVING THE SCENE

Strict laws against drunk driving may be causing an unwanted side effect. A new study by Purdue University researchers shows that after Ohio instituted a tough drunk-driving law making it more likely for offenders to be jailed and have their licenses suspended, the number of alcohol-related accidents fell by 20%. But at the same time, the number of hit-and-run incidents caused by intoxicated drivers rose by 8%. "The higher the penalty for drunk driving," says Purdue Economist John Umbeck, a co-author of the report, "the more there is to gain by leaving the scene."

The study, which analyzed 500,000 accidents in Ohio from January 1982 to June 1983, suggested that motorists facing severe punishment for drunk driving might be strongly inclined to cut out, especially if the penalty for fleeing the accident is scarcely harsher than that for causing it. One possible remedy: stiffen the laws against hit-and-run driving.

IGNITION DEVICE CALLED KEY TO STOPPING DRUNK DRIVERS

The key to combating drunk driving may lie in the ignition.

An American surgeon proposed yesterday that people who have lost their licences for impaired driving should be required to have their cars fitted with a breathalyzer device if they want to drive again. The device acts like an ignition key.

Dr. Donald Trunkey of Oregon said the device, which costs about $300, starts the engine when the driver blows into it – unless the alcohol level is too high. Trunkey spoke at a news conference at the World Congress of Surgery at the Metro Convention Centre.

DRUNK DRIVERS

You *Can* Do Something About The Tragedy

By Sidney Katz

Attempts to curb drunk driving have so far been conspicuously unsuccessful. Will the new federal laws, which provide stiffer penalties for convicted impaired drivers, turn the tide? Are effective anti-drunk driving strategies available? These are some of the questions writer Sidney Katz put to Evelyn Vingilis on behalf of *Leisure Ways* readers. Born in Toronto 36 years ago, Ms Vingilis earned a doctorate in psychology at York University and now heads the Ontario Addiction Research Foundation's drinking and driving research program. An authority in her field, she serves as a consultant to government and industry. Ms Vingilis is the author or co-author of more than 60 presentations and publications in her specialty.

LEISURE WAYS: *Why are all our efforts to reduce impaired driving deaths, injuries and property damage taking so long to produce results?*
EVELYN VINGILIS: Perhaps the underlying reason is that we have underestimated the complexity of the problem. The simple truth is that no quick or easy solution exists. We are a society of both dedicated drinkers and drivers. During a year, 12 million of us drive a combined total of 130 billion miles and consume 45 million gallons of alcohol. Drinking is socially approved behaviour, strongly resistant to change, and even though impaired driving is a criminal offence, it's clearly regarded as socially acceptable.

LW: *Will the new, stiffer penalties deter impaired drivers?*
EV: The new, tough laws will be helpful but the significant factor in deterrence is *not* the

punishment alone but the drinking driver's perception of his or her chances of being stopped by the police. At present, according to estimates by Transport Canada, the chance of getting caught while impaired is 1 in 350 to 1 in 500. It's been estimated that, each year on Canadian roads, at least 52 million episodes of undetected impaired driving take place.

To increase driver expectation of apprehension, we should increase our police manpower and use it to expand our roadside screening program. The fact that roadside random checking is being intensified should be widely publicized. Other helpful measures: train police to improve their ability to spot impaired drivers; simplify arrest procedures; and increase the proportion of convictions. As for the various kinds of penalties, in order of effectiveness, licence suspension seems to have some deterrent effect, providing the period of suspension does not extend beyond nine months. After that, the convicted driver will drive without a licence. Moderate fines also discourage impaired driving but, for reasons not wholly understood, jail sentences appear to be least effective.

LW: *Would greater attention to licensed premises and their patrons reduce the number of impaired drivers on the road?*

EV: They certainly can. One investigation showed that, of 9,745 motorists checked, 646 were found to be legally impaired. Members of this group were two or three times as likely to have had their last drink at a bar, club or tavern than in their own home or in the home of a friend or relative. These kinds of data suggest that a good case can be made for keeping certain high-risk premises under close scrutiny by police squads engaged in spot-checking.

LW: *What can bartenders, waiters and others who are involved in serving alcohol do to discourage drunk driving?*

EV: They should make certain not to serve patrons who are under the legal drinking age. They should also monitor their clientele, keeping their eyes open for customers who are getting drunk. They should be familiar with the initial stages of intoxication and possess the skill to tactfully stop serving patrons who have had enough to drink. Indeed, in some U.S. states, bartenders are required to attend an alcohol awareness program where such matters are taught.

The law is increasingly taking the view that owners of licensed premises are responsible for damages caused by patrons who leave their establishment in an impaired state. Recently, an Ontario court required a hotel owner to pay more than $1 million in damages – the result of a car crash caused by a patron who had been served alcohol to the point of extreme intoxication.

LW: *A significant amount of drinking takes place at private parties. What can a party-giver do to keep guests from driving home while drunk?*

EV: This is a productive area for preventing drunk driving, and here are some tips for hosts and hostesses who believe that a *real* friend does not allow a friend to get behind a wheel while bleary-eyed.

- Serve the drinks yourself; guests tend to drink more when there's a self-serve bar.

- Serve food – not just potato chips and snacks. A full stomach slows down the absorption of alcohol into the bloodstream. And guests who are eating aren't drinking.

- At the end of the party, if a guest is tipsy, arrange his transportation. Call a taxi, ask a friend to drive him, or provide him with a bed overnight. If necessary, hide your guest's car keys. One study showed that, in 70 per cent of the cases where friends have intervened, the intended impaired driving trip did not occur.

LW: *Because disproportionate numbers of young people are involved in drunk driving* *mishaps, should we pay special attention to this segment of the driving population?*

EV: I think so and there are several things that might be done. There's evidence that fewer youths are involved in alcohol-related accidents when the legal drinking and driving age is increased to 21 and when youthful beginning drivers are restricted to dawn-to-dusk driving.

Most kids want to have a car at night – the time when most partying and drinking occurs. In surveys we conducted in Ontario, we found that almost half the licensed high school drivers reported driving within an hour of having had two drinks. More than 10 per cent did this at least eight times in the past year. In that same period, more than 20 per cent reported being involved in at least one collision, almost 5 per cent after drinking. Impaired youth who get into accidents tend to have a much lower blood-alcohol concentration than older drivers. This suggests that they are less able to tolerate alcohol and that their lack of driving experience is also probably a factor. These facts should be emphasized in educational programs directed at youth.

LW: *Any other suggestions for creating awareness of the drunk driving problem among young people?*

EV: Working with other groups, the Addiction Research Foundation has been trying a new strategy – staging mock trials in high schools. An "impaired" student driver is charged with causing the death of another teenager. Students, judges, lawyers and police participate in his "trial."

Recently, an imaginative Ontario coroner pioneered a new way of impressing on youth the seriousness of driving after drinking. A 16-year-old youngster died after ramming his car into a parked bulldozer one night after a party. His blood-alcohol level was twice the legal limit. The coroner ordered that the inquest be held in the gymnasium of the high school the youth attended so that his fellow students could witness the proceedings.

The so-called "parent-youth" contract is another new strategy designed to prevent drunk-driving fatalities. Introduced by Students Against Drunk Driving (SADD), an agreement is drawn up between teenagers and their parents and stipulates that if the teen is tipsy when it's time to leave a party, he phones his parents and they'll provide transportation with no arguments, and no questions asked at the time. Such an episode, later, can be used to initiate a useful discussion on the perils of impaired driving.

LW: *Some people have proposed affixing a special brightly colored licence plate to the car owned by the convicted impaired driver. It's claimed that [the person is] less likely to repeat [the] offence because his [or her] distinctive plate would bring him [or her] under constant scrutiny from police and public.*

EV: There are flaws in this suggestion. The vehicle belonging to a convicted impaired driver may often be used by members of his [or her] family with faultless driving records. Again, the convicted drunk driver can easily find another vehicle to drive – one with an ordinary licence plate.

Here's a suggestion that has greater merit: Require all drivers to display, at all times, their driving licence, which can be placed in a transparent plastic pocket on the front windshield. The driving licence of the driver with a record of impairment can be color-coded, making it immediately recognizable by police. This measure would also make it more difficult to drive while your licence is under suspension because suspended licences would bear special identification.

LW: *The legal definition of impairment, under the federal Criminal Code, is .08 per cent, that is, 80 milligrams of alcohol per 100 millilitres of blood. Would there be fewer drunk driving deaths if it were reduced?*

EV: Opinions differ on this issue, as evidenced by the different standards of impairment adopted by various countries. In the U.S., the blood-alcohol level of .10 per cent is used; in

Finland, it's .05 per cent. Some experts say that even one drink, to some degree, affects the efficiency of the brain function that determines driving skill. But it would be impractical and unrealistic, I think, to make the detection of a small amount of alcohol in the blood an offence. However, I would like to see us move away from the concept of an arbitrarily set figure as the absolute measure of impairment. Ideally, everyone would be so well informed about the effects of alcohol on driving skills that they would be able to assess their own impairment level, whether they had one drink or more.

LW: *What are the prospects for reducing drunk driving deaths and injuries?*

EV: Impaired driving is such a deeply-rooted, complex problem that we can't expect a fast, dramatic improvement. However, there are reasons for regarding the future with guarded optimism. The public attitude toward impaired driving appears to be shifting. More people regard it as socially unacceptable behavior, as witness the emergence of several citizen anti-drunk driving groups.

The other day I was told of a father who came to his office, angrily sounding off to his fellow workers about the behavior of the police. His 17-year-old son had been picked up for impaired driving and detained for several hours. Instead of the sympathy that he obviously expected to receive from his colleagues, he was sharply lectured for his failure to alert his son to the dangers of drinking and driving. That's a sign of progress.

SOME FURTHER FOLLOW-THROUGH SUGGESTIONS

Some of these suggestions may be done as independent study activities, either individually or in small groups, or as whole class activities.

- If feasible within the school context, take steps to put your plan into effect.

- Organize a school drinking and driving awareness activity.

- Give a dramatic performance (either scripted or improvised) on one of the situations you read about in this material.

- Make a school poster composed of a poem surrounded by a collage of assorted visual material.

- Design a series of anti-drinking and driving advertisements.

- Write a story that illustrates the horror of drinking and driving.

- Write an essay, story, or poem on the subject for the school yearbook or local newspaper.

- Give a speech to the class or a larger group on the extent of the problem of drinking and driving in your own community, using local news items and data.

- Have a debate on the topic: Resolved that the drinking age should be raised to twenty-one **or** that the driving age should be raised to eighteen (if it is 16 in your province).

- Conduct a school survey on student attitudes toward drinking and driving and write a report on your findings. This might be presented to an interested group.

- Research the outcomes of the cases referred to in some of the previous articles. Do any of the outcomes surprise you? Why?

TOPIC four

*Putting Your Best
Voice Forward*

FOCUSING IN

Whether we are aware of it or not, we all have a distinct vocal image. In fact, the human voice is very much like a fingerprint; no two are identical. Each person's vocal image is the result of the combination of several factors: individual cultural, social, and personal experiences, individual geographical backgrounds, and, of course, individual sets of vocal cords. When someone we know telephones us, it is no wonder that we can identify the caller after only one or two words. Next to our face, our voice most closely identifies who we are to our friends and acquaintances.

But what are the qualities of a good vocal image? How do we put our best voice forward? If we do, will we all begin to sound alike? Take a moment to think about the vocal images of people you know and of people you see and hear on radio, on television, and in the movies. In your mind, which ones have good vocal images? Which ones have vocal image voices you consider to be poor? What qualities are you considering when you judge them?

The following story "Who Said We All Have to Talk Alike" demonstrates two opposing opinions on vocal image and the meaning of "best voice." It will help you focus on your own initial thinking on the subject.

SUGGESTED APPROACH

Step 1

After reading the story, draw a line down the middle of a piece of paper and write two headings at the top: Neffie's Position and Beryl's Position. List all the points you can think of that Neffie would use to support her position and all the points Beryl would use to support her position.

Step 2

This may be done in small groups or as a class discussion.

Determine which woman has the stronger position and why. Determine why the two women failed to solve their problem. Suggest other steps they might have taken to produce a workable compromise.

Step 3

Use your response journal to think about the idea of vocal image and vocal improvement. Do you side more with the Neffie Pike's perspective or with Beryl's? What is the place of dialects and accents in the world? Will we all eventually sound alike? Think about your own vocal image, about how others perceive you when you speak. Have you ever seen yourself in vocal action on videotape? Have you ever thought about the elements that strengthen or weaken your own vocal image? Would you change it if you could? What ultimately is a person's "best voice" – the natural voice or the cultivated voice? Do we have a number of "best voices," depending on the occasion and audience?

WHO SAID WE ALL HAVE TO TALK ALIKE

....

By Wilma Elizabeth McDaniel

True, she "talked different," but who would have guessed that the kind-hearted Neffie could be such a bad influence on the two young girls? Certainly not Neffie.

Who knows how Neffie Pike's speech pattern was formed? Her Ozark family had talked the same way for generations. They added an "r" to many words that did not contain that letter. In spite of this, or because of it, their speech was clear and colorful and to the point. Most people understood what they were talking about, exactly.

Neffie was her parents' daughter. She called a toilet, "torelet," and a woman, "worman," very comfortably. The teacher at the country school never attempted to change Neffie's manner of speaking. She said that Neffie had a fine imagination and should never allow anyone to squelch it. In fact, Neffie never really knew that she talked different from most other people.

People in the tiny community of Snowball really loved Neffie. She was a good neighbor, unfailingly cheerful and helpful. The appearance of her tall and bony figure at the door of a sickroom or a bereaved family meant comfort and succor. A great woman, everyone in Snowball agreed.

She would have probably lived her life out in the same lumber house if her husband had not died. In the months that followed his death she developed a restless feeling. Home chores, church and charity work did not seem to be enough to occupy her mind. She started to read big-town newspapers at the library in nearby Marshall, something new for her. She became especially interested in the out-of-state employment want ads. She mentioned to

neighbors, "They are a lot of good jobs out there in the world."

One day she came home from Marshall and stopped at old Grandma Meade's house. She sat down in a canebottom chair and announced, "I have got me a job in California. I am a selling my house and lot to a couple of retired people from Little Rock. They will be moving in the first of June."

Grandma Meade sat in shocked silence for several seconds, then said, "Honey, I do not believe it. I mean that I never in the world imagined that you would consider leaving Snowball. You and Lollis was so happy together here." Her voice trailed off, "Of course nobody could foretell the Lord would call him so young."

Neffie looked stonily at her and said with her usual clarity, "A widder worman is a free worman, especially if she don't have no children. She ought to be free to come and go like she pleases. After all, I am only fifty-one years old. I can do as much work as I ever did. This job is taking care of two little girls while their mother works at some high-paying job. She has already sent me a bus ticket. I would be a fool not to go. Everyone has been to California except me. I always hankered to see the state for myself. Now is my chance to see some of the rest of the world. It may sound foolish, but it will sort of be like having a dorter of my own and grandchildren. I aim to write you a long letter when I get settled down out there."

Neffie left for California on schedule. After two weeks Grandma Meade began to worry a bit. She said, "I thought that Neffie surely would have dropped us a line by now. The last thing she told me was that she would write me a long letter. Well, maybe she hasn't got settled down yet."

A month passed without any word from Neffie.

Bug Harrison was at Grandma Meade's house when Neffie returned the day after Snowball's big Fourth of July celebration.

Neffie put her suitcases down and began at

the beginning. "Grandma, you was so right about so many things. I knowed I was in trouble hock-deep, only one minute after I stepped off that bus in California. A purty young worman come forward to meet me and said she was Beryl. I busted out and told her, 'My, you are a purty worman, even purtier than your pitcher.' She kinda shrunk back and looked at me like I had used a cussword. She stood there holding her little girls' hands and asked me, where on earth did you hear a word like worman, was it a female worm of some kind? She said, 'Worman is woe-man,' like you say woh to a horse.

"Her remark nearly knocked me off my feet. I felt like a fool, and I didn't even know why. My stomach started churning. I durst not say anything to defend myself, because I hadn't done anything wrong.

"We started walking to Beryl's station wagon in the parking lot. I told her that I never was blessed with a dorter or son, either. That set her off again. She said that her children were at a very impressionable age, that I would have to watch my speech and learn the correct pronunciation of words. She did not want them picking up incorrect speech patterns and something she called coll-oke-ism, something I had, and didn't even realize. I decided to shut up and get in the car. The worman had already paid for my fare. I felt that I had to at least give her a few months' service, if I could stand the punishment at all.

"On our way to Beryl's house, she stopped at a drive-in restaurant and ordered cheeseburgers and milkshakes for all of us. I decided to just eat and listen.

"It was sure a pleasurable drive on to Beryl's home. We followed the same county highway for the entire seven miles. The road was lined on both sides with pams, tall with them fronds waving in the breeze. It reminded me of pitchers I have seen of The Holy Land, really touched my heart. I forgot myself again and said that I never had seen pams before

except in pitchers. Quick as a flash Beryl told me, 'They are pall-ms, not pams. There is an l in the word.' After that, I sure buttoned up my mouth. I just said yes or no to anything she asked me.

"Her house turned out to be a real nice place, bright and modern with every type of electrical gadget you could think of. There were four bedrooms, each with a bath. I was so tired and upset over Beryl's attitude that I begged off sitting up to visit with her and the little girls. I ran me a full tub of warm water and took me a long soaking bath. I fell into bed and went sound asleep. Worman, I plumb died away, slept all night without waking up. To show you how hard I slept, there was a fairly severe earthquake in the central part of California where Beryl lived. It even shook a few things off a living room shelf. I tell you, I wouldn't have heard Gabriel blow his horn that night.

"I woke up feeling relieved that it was Monday. Beryl left for work promptly at seven-thirty. That meant the girls and I had the house to ourselves. Worman, I am a telling you, they was two living dolls, Pat and Penny. I made them bran muffins for breakfast and scrambled some eggs. They ate until they nearly foundered. It seemed like they had never seen a bran muffin before, asked me if I would cook them the same thing each day.

"I told them I knew how to cook other good old homely dishes, too. Every day, I tried something new on them, biscuits and sausage and milk gravy, buttermilk pancakes, waffles, popovers, french toast, corn dodgers, fried mush. You name it, worman, I cooked it for those dolls. It wouldn't be no big deal for the kids here in Snowball, they was raised to eat like that, but it was hog heaven to Pat and Penny."

Grandma Meade had been listening intently, her eyes pinned on Neffie's face. Now she asked, "How did Beryl like your cooking?"

Neffie laughed heartily. She said, "To put it plain, she LOVED it. I can say that she never found any flaw in my cooking, only made one complaint connected with it. I boirled her a fine big cabbage and hamhock dinner and made cornbread for our supper one evening. When we started to sit down at the table, I said that it was a nice change to have a boirled dinner now and then. That set her off like a firecracker. She said, 'That is boil-ed, not boirled.' I decided to let that snide remark pass. I saw she started dishing up the food – she lit in on it like a starving hounddog. That showed what she thought of my cooking, didn't it? My cooking sure helped me get through them weeks as good as I did."

Bug Harrison broke in, "What were your duties during the day?"

Neffie said, "I was hired to take care of the two little girls. That is what I done. I cooked because people have to eat. I always have, always will. That didn't put no extra strain on me. The girls and I played the most of the day. They would sit on each arm of my chair and listen to me tell them about my life back in Arkansas. I didn't hold back nothing. I told them about haunted houses, ghosts, robbers, bank holdups, tornadoes, snakes, tarantulas, times when the river flooded and we had to float on a rooftop to save our lives. Lordy, worman, they just ate it up. They would listen to me with their eyes as big as saucers. I don't quite know why I done it, but I asked the girls not to tell their mother about my stories. They were as secretive as little private detectives until a week ago. They got so excited over one of my stories that they forgot theirselves. I was busy in the kitchen putting some homemade noodles into a pot of chicken broth. I heard Pat tell her mother, 'Mom, back in Arkansas where Neffie used to live, they are wormans that can tell fortunes for people. They can look right through your face and tell if you are telling the truth or a lie. They can rub your warts with skunk oirl and say some words and all the warts will fall off, never ever come back.' I figured I was in bad trouble, but I kept on dropping the noodles into the broth. I

was a hundred percent right about the trouble.

"Beryl blowed her stack. She marched right back to the kitchen with the girls at her heels. She stood in the door and said, 'I have been afraid of this very thing. Neffie, I just can't keep you on any longer.'

"At that point Pat and Penny throwed themselves down on the floor and started bawling like two young calves. Pat sobbed out real angry-like, 'Yes, you CAN keep Neffie! She is the best storyteller in the whole world and the best cooker. If she goes home to Arkansas, we won't never have no more biscuits and sausage and gravy.' The tears began to run down her little face.

"Beryl stood there with her face like a flintrock. It looked like she wanted to be nice to me, but that her duty come first with her. She drawed in her breath and said, 'Neffie, you are as good and kind and honest as you can be, exceptional, but your speech is totally unacceptable. My children are at a very impressionable age. I have tried to overlook it, but they are definitely being influenced in the wrong direction. They say dorter and orter with regularity. This pattern must be eradicated immediately. I shall be happy to pay your travelling expenses home. You can look on this trip out West as my vacation gift to you.' I could see that her mind was made up and she wasn't going to change it.

"I did think to ask her if she had some other babysitter in mind. I didn't want to run out and leave her in a bind without one. She said there was a young girl from the college who wanted day work, so she could attend night classes. She thought that would work out great. I got her point. The college girl would be different from me, more to suit Beryl.

"Well, to shorten my story, she bought me a big box of real expensive chocolates and put me on the bus with my paid ticket, just like she had promised. She and the girls stood there beside the bus waiting for it to pull out. Penny looked up at me and blew me a kiss. I heard her say as plain as plain could be, 'Neffie, you are a sweet worman.' Then I saw Beryl put her hand over Penny's mouth. Right then, the bus pulled out of the depot and I lost sight of them.

"Worman, I done a lot of thinking as that bus rolled along the highway. I would eat a chocolate and think over my experience with Beryl. Things kind of cleared up in my mind, like having blinders taken off my eyes. I saw I had really been ignorant of some things that other folks knowed. I didn't talk right to suit some of them, but that wasn't my fault. *I didn't know we was all supposed to talk the same way.* I thought people hadn't all talked the same since before God tore down their tower at Babel and confused all their tongues. Folks all over the world have talked different ever since then. I guess some of them like Beryl want to go back to pre-Babel days. Anyway, it was sure an eye-opener to me, hurt me, too. Beryl just plain separated herself from me. It was like she took a sharp knife and cut a melon in half, and throwed away the half that was me. You know what you do with a piece of melon you don't want. You throw it with the rinds into the garbage can. Worman, who said that we all have to talk alike? Can anyone tell me that?"

FINDING OUT

The following material explores the concept of vocal image and vocal improvement from both general and particular perspectives. For example, the first two articles "If There's No Communication It's Gobbledygook Not English" and "Varieties of Canadian English" examine vocal image and "best voice" from a general Canadian perspective. The next three articles describe various methods being used to help people improve their vocal image in order to put their best voices forward. You will find some of the remarks and suggestions made in these articles to be controversial, particularly in view of Neffie Pike's original question, "Who said we all have to talk alike?" The last two articles give specific advice on how to put your best voice forward when giving a speech.

As you work through the material on this topic, you will be developing skill in identifying and assessing bias, predicting outcomes, developing conscensus through selecting, sorting, and weighing information and evidence, and identifying and applying criteria.

SUGGESTED APPROACH

Step 1

This should be done individually.

Read the first two articles and identify the forces that are changing the face of English in Canada in the opinion of the writers. To what extent do their opinions and information reinforce or alter your original perspective on putting your best voice forward?

Step 2

This should be done as a class discussion or a small group discussion.

Based on what you have read and thought, speculate on the future of Canadian English. What kind of English do you think future generations will speak? Will there be any "best voice" English? If so, what do you think it will look and sound like?

Step 3

Read the next three articles which describe why and how people are working to improve their vocal image. Divide a piece of paper into three columns, and as you read, pause to write down any statements or points you agree with, statements or points you disagree with, and statements or points you hadn't thought of before or which you find memorable in some way.

Step 4

With a partner, read each other's list and use the information as a basis for comparing your positions on the whole issue of vocal improvement.

Step 5

This may be done individually, in pairs, or small groups.

Read the two articles on giving a prepared speech or presentation, and identify all the "do's and don'ts" mentioned.
   Based on the information given in the articles, design a criteria checklist that could be used to evaluate a speech or presentation.

IF THERE'S NO COMMUNICATION IT'S GOBBLEDYGOOK NOT ENGLISH

....

And Moses was fourscore years old, and Aaron fourscore and three years old when they spake unto Pharaoh.

You guessed it. This is from the King James Bible of 1611.

The latest version of the Bible (1952) puts it this way: *Now Moses was 80 years old, and Aaron 83 years old, when they spoke to Pharaoh.*

Changed words, same meaning.

Words are not all that change in language. Go to Alabama or Texas. Or listen to a recent immigrant from England, particularly if she speaks Cockney. In words, meanings and accents, in sounds and in their combinations, language changes. From place to place. Over time.

The different versions of the Bible give us Old English, Medieval English and modern English. Modern English has its own tossed salad: British, Australian ('Strine), the English vernacular spoken in the southern United States, South Asian English, among others. Not to mention, of course, our own Canajan! All dialects of world English.

But what is Canajan? The English spoken in the corporate offices or the variety spoken in the local bar? How about this? *The bare farmer had a braffus of brews and starnaked, and went alang for a marning walk in the slob.*

That's Newfoundland English. Its meaning is not exactly what you think. Here's a translation: "The broke sailor had a breakfast of hard biscuit pieces soaked overnight, warmed in the morning and eaten with boiled codfish and butter (all this contained in the word 'brews') and tea without milk or sugar, and went along for a morning walk in the soft snow."

You will see Shakespeare, Chaucer and Spencer here. Irish, Scots and native dialect as well. But principally, you hear the speech of a fishing people cut off from the mainland.

Canajan, then, is all these regional dialects. And much more.

Hey, how'zit goin', man? says the guy with hair standing on its end to his buddy walking down Yonge St.

A yuppie to a yuppie would sound different: Hi, how're you doin'?

At the church, the Minister greets us still differently: "How are you this beautiful morning?"

These are all what linguists call *sociolects*. This is how Canajan can reflect social class.

Have you listened to CHIN commercials lately? Or a francophone trying to respond to a reporter, in English? Or "Chinglish" spoken in Chinatown, or "Italish" on Via Italia? These are the latest Canajan linguistic variations entering the language. Canada's own unique patois.

As with pronunciation, so goes grammar. Who would be willing to bet that "I don't have nothing" is used more frequently than "I don't have anything" in eastern, central or western Canada? Or in the U.S., the U.K., Australia or New Zealand, for that matter? I for one wouldn't mind putting my money down on it.

So anything goes, eh?

Not quite. Just as in any social behavior, there is propriety in language usage, too. Imagine Juliet wooing Romeo with the words, "Where the heck are you, man," instead of "Wherefore art thou, Romeo!" Or an auctioneer selling off his priced ware at the pitch and the pace of a judge in a courtroom.

Not one variety of Canajan is "bad" or "wrong" English. Inappropriate for a given situation, maybe. Non-standard, too. But not sub-standard!

Bad English is what someone learning English as a second language speaks and writes. Bad English is what we have when one native speaker cannot understand another native speaker. "Colorless green ideas sleep furiously," is Noam Chomsky's example of gobbledygook. It is not English, because there is no communication.

All our Canadian varieties of English, from Newfoundland to Cabbagetown to Rosedale, constitute good English. Street jargon, CBC English and journalese also carry the proud label "good English." As do Black, South Asian and Chinese Canajan.

The speakers of non-standard English may be the Johns and the Janes down the street and not the Northrop Fryes and the Pierre Elliot Trudeaus. But the only language they have ever known is Canajan.

Canajan, then, is that which all its speakers – the poor and the rich, the literati and illiterate – have helped shape, through the years. With a borrowed word here (remember Sputnik), a changed sound there (should we say "ske-dule" or "she-dule?").

But how is it that we never hear or read these different accents or varieties on radio, television and the newspapers? Are we witnessing a linguistic elite controlling our lives here?

And are the John and Jane Does, and the Italish, Chinglish and other speakers willing to take it lying down?

VARIETIES OF CANADIAN ENGLISH

John Corneil gets teased at work for the way he talks.

No wonder. The registrar of collections for the Canadian Centre for Folk Culture at the National Museum of Man uses expressions such as "gumtuckies."

In Ottawa Valley dialect, that means rubber boots – "gum" for rubber and "tuckies" because you tuck your pants into them.

Cornell, who picked up the expression while growing up in Carleton Place near Ottawa, says he hasn't heard it outside the valley.

Speech Peculiarities

Gumtuckies is only one example of the peculiarities of speech that exist among the English-speaking residents of the valley. But, says Ottawa linguist Howard Woods, many expressions attributed exclusively to the valley are heard all over Canada.

Woods defines a dialect as the speech characteristics of a particular region. The characteristics include grammar, vocabulary and pronunciation. Languages are collections of dialects and everyone speaks a dialect, he says.

People pick up dialects when they are young by "subconsciously imitating people they want to identify with."

"There is no standard English that all English-speakers speak. Everybody speaks what somebody else considers a dialect."

Woods, head of the English program development division of the Public Service Commission's language program, studied spoken English in the Ottawa area while he was a doctoral student at the University of British Columbia. . . .

During his research and field work, Woods compiled a list of expressions people said were "Ottawa Valley talk." But many are heard in other parts of Canada, too, he said.

For example, he was told that substituting bring for take – as in "Bring it over to the neighbors" – is pure valley-speak. In fact, he says, it's a common grammatical error heard all over North America.

The remaining traces of dialects brought by 19th-century settlers are being swept away by modern communications and mass education,

Woods says. From the Ottawa River westward, English has become increasingly uniform and standardized.

"Some people might find it sad, but I'm afraid there's very little local color left in terms of language. Canada west of the Ottawa River is the largest land mass in the world where a language is so similar all over."

Variety in Newfoundland

He describes standard Canadian English as the English heard on radio and television and taught in Canadian schools. It is the English spoken by broadcasters, teachers, political leaders, business people and other influential leaders.

What linguistic variety is left is found mainly in Newfoundland, he said.

"There are several Newfoundland accents. In fact, there are a whole bunch of them. Each bay and outport has its own accent or dialect."

Local dialects have survived longer in Newfoundland, and to a lesser extent in Nova Scotia, because these areas were settled earlier than Ottawa and the West, he said. They were also relatively isolated for a long time.

SHE TEACHES CELEBRITIES HOW TO TALK

By Ivor Davis

She has never starred in a movie but in Hollywood Dr. Lillian Glass, a speech pathologist, is a superstar in her own right.

Glass helped Sheena Easton lose her Scottish accent for her television role as Sonny Crockett's wife on *Miami Vice*, showed Dustin Hoffman how to look and talk like a woman in *Tootsie* (1982) and taught Julio Iglesias to sing *To All The Girls*, instead of *Do Oll De Gels*.

But Glass considers her greatest achievement her ability to get deaf actress Marlee Matlin to speak at the Academy Awards ceremonies. . . . Matlin stood up in front of millions and said, "The nominees for best actor are . . . ."

"We worked every day for two hours a day for six months to get her to use vocal inflections that most deaf people cannot use," she says. "Saying such names as Marcello Mastroianni was a great achievement."

Dubbed Hollywood's first lady of speech, Glass polishes the vocal patterns of the famous, eradicates their unwanted accents and coaches them on how to most effectively use their voice with their body movements. She recently wrote *Talk To Win. Six Steps To A Successful Vocal Image.*

"These days," says Glass, "stars have no qualms about going to a plastic surgeon to fix a nose, chin, eyes or breasts. I consider what I do cosmetic surgery of the voice. The way you speak is often more important than the way you look. It's criminal, we teach our kids to read and write, but we don't teach them how to talk."

Glass has had phenomenal success with celebrity clients.

Dolly Parton, Bette Midler, Janet Leigh, Matt Lattanzi (Olivia Newton John's husband), Ben Vereen and Billy Crystal have tapped Glass' expertise. . . .

In addition to the celebrities Glass has helped, there are many with whom she would love to work, including Tom Selleck, Arnold Schwarzenegger, Sylvester Stallone, Michael Jackson . . . and Tom Cruise.

Here is what Glass would do for each of them:

Tom Selleck: "He has improved his high-pitched voice. In *Three Men And A Baby* he was warm for the first time. I think his *Magnum P.I.* role was not good for him in terms of showing his true colors. The man is adorable, warm and electric, but on the show he came across as a monotone, nerdy fellow."

Arnold Schwarzenegger: "Sure, he makes a lot of money and does well at the box office but he is one-dimensional and has a bad public image. . . . He needs a vocal overhaul from stomach muscles to throat.

"I worked with Schwarzenegger's colleague Dolph Lundgren, who could have fallen into the same rut. Lundgren can now play sensitive characters; he is not just a dummy-type person, but has a wide range of emotions."

Sylvester Stallone: "He is like Schwarzenegger. I know he had a speech problem as a kid and he has come a long way, but he needs to inflect his voice more, sound more enthusiastic. I did a poll that asked people to list the most annoying speech habits. Mumbling and monotone came out on top – that's Stallone.

"Voice work could change his dimension. He showed flashes of vocal warmth in his first *Rocky* (1976). Now there are just these plastic, vapid characters who are formula. I would like to see the real Stallone come out. I know he is warm, caring and sensitive.

"Stallone could be one of the finest actors in the world if he worked on his voice; no major overhaul, just voice inflections using different facial language. He could win an Oscar and be respected by Hollywood as not just another body."

Michael Jackson: "He is a fabulous singer, but still has that little girl's voice – much too breathy. . . ."

Tom Cruise: "He needs to show more animation. He is good-looking and the movie *Top Gun* (1986) got a lot of hype, but there is room for more emotion. He still mumbles. He has good body movement, but his vocal pattern needs to match it. . . ."

"Most people hate the way they sound," she says. "Yet when I ask them what it is they hate about their voices few can pinpoint it. I believe that whether you're a movie star or a sales[person] the voice is a mirror of the soul."

□

MANY PUT MONEY WHERE MOUTH IS AND LEARN PROPER SPOKEN ENGLISH

....

By Helen Bullock

In many business transactions, the accent is on slick marketing, or the accent is on the product, or the accent is on the price – but in some cases, the accent is on the accent, when the speaker is someone whose mother tongue is other than English.

Many of those who have a good command of the English language in written material and can form the words and understand its nuances, may sound ineffective if they have pronunciation problems.

The results on a professional level may be low sales, ineffective management, hampered business deals because of misunderstandings by clients, customers or staff, and a stalled career. On a personal level, they may feel socially isolated and frustrated by their inability to advance themselves through social contacts.

Some of those so plagued are putting their money where their mouth is in the pursuit of clearly comprehensible English.

Although there are language and speech courses that aim at eradicating accents, speech therapist Christine Gandy has come up with a different and popular approach. She calls her course Accent Adjustment and that's just what it is. Rather than attempting to erase the traces of the original mother tongue, she teaches her students to adjust their way of speaking to include more of the sounds commonly used and needed in English.

Although it will still be obvious to a listener that the speaker's first language is not English, the English itself will be clear, crisp and perfectly comprehensible.

Speech Therapist

Gandy, a speech therapist for 20 years, works with a curriculum designed by Christine Rickards, a linguist and speech pathologist at the University of Toronto, to which Gandy has added input based on her own knowledge and experience in working with accented English.

The demand for the course is growing, she said recently between classes in sorting out recalcitrant "Ts," "Ps" and "Ds," as more business people from diverse ethnic backgrounds seek to establish themselves in mainstream business life.

"Many of the people I teach are professionals in their area and have built a successful career in sales, or are engineers of great technological know-how who can't seem to sell their message, or are doctors or lawyers who deal with members of their own ethnic community. They all want to branch out into the larger community or move up the corporate ladder and they need to make themselves easily understood in the language of the larger community."

Gandy said it is easy to assume, if you have heavily accented speech, that you are not promoted or denied opportunities because of your cultural background, but "linguistic competence is one of the factors in promotion.

"It has nothing to do with discrimination. If you plan to move into management, you must be able to make yourself clearly understood on several levels, to those managers above you and to those employees below you.

Mix of Cultures

"It applies to native Canadians as well – inarticulate, mumbling Canadians who have difficulty expressing their ideas or clearly stating instructions don't get promoted either."

(Gandy, who takes a no-nonsense but understanding and sympathetic stand with her students, thinks Canada should hang on to its mix of languages and cultures that has caused it to be described as a "tossed salad" rather than the U.S.-style "melting pot," but she insists "we should be a crisp tossed salad," meaning we should all understand one another.)

Gandy says the majority of pronunciation problems are "the result of interference from speech patterns used in the mother tongue that are inappropriate in English.

"Some of the sounds we use in English aren't even part of the repertoire in other languages and require different placement of the speech muscles."

As examples, she offers the mixing of the sounds made by "D" and "T," as in "have a cup of dee."

"The only difference in the two sounds is that little puff of air that the 'T' requires," she said.

"That's very awkward for some cultures. One student actually said to me, 'You English need a lot of breath.'

" 'TH' is also a problem for many tongues, so we hear 'dis' and 'dat' for this and that and the 'wh' difficulty giving us 'vhy is it you vish to do this?' Those from Oriental cultures have the 'R'-'L' awkwardness."

In some cases, often depending on the job, the imperfections mean little. But, "if people have to strain to hear you, especially if you are dealing with clients by telephone, they won't stay clients for long.

"It's too frustrating and annoying."

Physical Placement

It's the actual physical placement of the speech muscles, tongue and lips that can or cannot make the sounds, Gandy said. That is why her course starts with the physical restructuring of speech sounds, vowels and consonants, not just mimicry from language tapes.

"The first six weeks (of the 10-week course) is instruction in making vowels and sounds; we get back to the physical sensation of making the sound," she explained.

"Many of my students know they sound different but they can't hear how or why. So we isolate the sounds first, then move into words and phrases and sentences. But that's a lot of retraining of speech muscles and respiratory control to undertake and you can't do it without dedication and practice."

All babies, Gandy said, can make every sound in every language at the "babble" stage of infant speech development.

As they become aware of clear sounds around them, they pick out the sounds common to their culture and discard the rest. Once a person is physically able to reproduce the language of the culture, it's not easy to retrain and change an ingrained habit.

"But because it is a motor pattern that's being altered, or adjusted, it's a matter of dogged practice, and it can be done," Gandy said encouragingly. "But it's like handing someone who can type a typewriter with the keys scrambled and expecting them to type at the same speed."

Pronunciation is one problem that perplexes other cultures; inflection is another.

"People from the Islands and some Eastern countries have a very different rhythm and intonation from standard English," Gandy said.

"That intonation is one of the things that makes words intelligible to us, and meaningful. If the inflection, emphasis or style of speaking is very different and therefore very distracting or even irritating, we don't hear the words or the message."

More than words are needed to convey a message, as anyone who has taken a speech improvement or public-speaking course discovers. Body language, pitch, stress and style, volume and rhythm transmit as much as the text.

"The intent and attitude of the speaker, or the perceived attitude, has to match the words," Gandy said, "or the message is lost."

Some cultures stand too close or too far back for Canadian tastes; some don't make eye contact (it's considered rude) although Canadians expect you to look them in the eye unless you've got something to hide; some speak too softly, lightly or loudly to suit the message for North American ears.

Match the Style

In addition to being able to make the sounds for clear English, you have to match the style to the speaking voice and the expectations of your audience.

"When the manner of speaking contradicts the message, it's just confusing and unsuccessful," Gandy said.

She emphasized, however, that she is not trying to make everyone speak as a native son (or daughter).

"I only want everyone to speak the language clearly so they can be understood without difficulty. It's a great barrier to the very educated and under-educated alike when they want to get on here."

THE MEDIUM IS THE MESSAGE

How You Speak Says A Lot About Who You Think You Are. Here: Some Straight Talk On Voicing The Right Image.

....

By Cynthia Brouse

Celia Sanches, a secretary for a Toronto bank, has such a sweet, soft voice that she is continually asked to repeat herself, especially on the telephone. She finds people's attention drifts when she speaks. "I'm not able to express all of what I want to say," says Sanches. "Now, rather than speak, I keep quiet."

Karyn Baker, a consultant with a non-profit mental health organization, was asked last June to act as master of ceremonies at her brother's wedding. "I'd never been to a wedding where a woman was the MC," admits Karyn. "I wasn't sure if I'd come across confidently and strong." She was already nervous about her speaking voice since she'd made a presentation at work and was told her speech was peppered with "um's" and "ah's."

Many [people] suffer setbacks – professionally and socially – because of voice problems. Their voices may be too soft or too loud, too fast or too slow, too high or too low. They may lack resonance, or their voices may be hoarse, squeaky, monotonous or just plain irritating. Minor annoyances, on the surface, but voice quality, delivery and articulation play an enormous role in communication. According to the exotic-sounding Mehrabian Survey of Factors of First Impressions, only eight percent of our impact comes from what we say. Fifty-five percent is based on appearance – no surprise – but 37 percent of the impression we make is created by the way we speak, and we're judged on that basis in the first six to 12 seconds.

Delivering the Right Voice

Few of us spend much time grooming our voices – and we should. . . . Alright, you say, but this is how I sound. If I spoke differently, it wouldn't be me – and I'm satisfied with me the way I am. But you're multi-faceted, and, just as you act differently in different settings, you can learn to speak differently when the occasion calls for it. Once you've found a new voice, you can put it on and take it off. . . .

The Corporate Voice

While voices help us to create a personal identity, they're crucial to company identities, too. Sometimes a company's image rests with the voice representing it. [Christine] Harvey, [founder of Voice Dynamics, a Toronto voice-training firm], specializes in tailor-made programs for corporations. Her client list reads like *Canadian Business* magazine's top 500 – big brokerage firms, telemarketing companies, computer sales offices, customer service departments. Using tape recorders, she lets clients hear for themselves what they're projecting. Often they're shocked at how quiet . . . monotonous, shy or garbled they sound. Then she "tricks or cajoles them into trying different sounds" on a second tape. One man repeated a story on tape with what he considered exaggerated emphasis – but the class agreed when the tape was played back that the new version sounded more "normal" than the first one. It turned out the man had made a pact with his wife that he would never raise his voice – and he was holding back to the point of being monotonous.

Next, Harvey provides exercises to relax and train the jaw and tongue, change resonance, regulate speed, add variety of pitch and improve enunciation. To eliminate "word whiskers" – verbal tics such as "um" and "ah" – she suggests clients put five cents in a jar for every whisker, the money to go to charity. "They find they don't get up to five dollars," says Harvey.

For Karyn Baker, Harvey's classes paid off – with dividends. Her stint as M.C. at her brother's wedding was an unqualified success. Guests complimented her on her presentation, wanting to know if her job called for a lot of public speaking. Said Baker, "People said that I was the only speaker they could really hear."

[Opera singer Christine] McMahon coaches groups of about 15 for three nights, and holds more intensive classes for students interested in advanced work. Her group exercises, designed to lessen inhibitions, sound like a heavy-breathing prenatal class one minute, and the Indianapolis 500 the next. Students, wearing loose, comfortable clothing so they can lie on the floor, start out slightly embarrassed, but thanks to McMahon's relaxed, down-to-earth demeanor, soon get into the spirit of the class.

Occupational Hazards

Occupational hazards and behaviour can damage or change the quality of your voice. Christina Harvey sees aerobics instructors with unusually husky voices caused by shrieking over loud music. People who whisper a lot, such as pharmacists providing confidential information over the counter and people who sit closely together in open-plan offices, can end up with chronically subdued speaking voices and even damaged vocal chords. Dry or polluted office air, cigarette smoke, heavy-equipment noise, excessive use of the telephone (especially if it causes a stiff neck) can all hurt your voice. If you suspect a chronic ailment underlies your inability to speak clearly or at the correct volume – vocal chord nodules or polyps, blocked nasal passages, spastic dysphonia (a vocal chord malfunction), allergies, hearing loss – see a doctor. Many hospitals have voice clinics.

The Root of the Problem

A growing number of foreign-born Canadians seek voice training of a special kind – they hope to eliminate an accent. In spite of the claims of some trainers, linguists stress that it's nearly impossible to drop an accent completely. But McMahon and Harvey point out that exercises can often relax the jaw and tongue enough to enable the speaker to form many new sounds. Schools with programs in English as a second language often include accent adjustment courses. Toronto-based speech therapist Christine Gandy coaches business people – many of whom feel they've been blocked in some aspect of their careers because of their accents – to replace some of the sounds of their mother tongue with those common to the English language.

Your ethnic background may also have provided you with a home environment where family members were either exceptionally quiet or loud. But nationality may have little to do with it. Only you can determine the role models you imitate that have resulted in an inappropriate speech characteristic – and only you can decide if and when you want to change.

SCARED SPEECHLESS

Afraid Of Speaking In Front Of A Crowd? Relax, And Follow These Expert Tips

By Nancy J. White

Terror strikes. You stand there looking at the audience and all you can think of is your sweaty palms and churning stomach. You open your mouth. Nothing comes out. Your heart races and your knees shake.

Pure panic, that's how many people describe making a speech.

"The last time I made a speech, my blouse stuck to my body I was so nervous," says one 22-year-old sales representative. "I felt myself freeze up, which made me even more nervous. My mouth was really dry and my voice started changing."

While many are horrified at the thought of talking in front of a group, some even have trouble one-on-one, seizing up in impromptu encounters or simply making a pitch to the boss.

They're afraid of making fools of themselves, that others will think they're stupid.

"They may be perfectionists about their interpersonal relationships," says Norman Endler, a psychology professor at York University who specializes in anxiety. "They may have a high need for achievement."

They definitely have a high need for help.

'Aristocratic Syndrome'

"Unless you're a lighthouse-keeper, you have to speak to groups of people," says Hugh Thompson, who teaches public speaking at George Brown College. "It's the [person] who speaks up at the meetings who gets pushed ahead."

But even some got-aheads – corporate presidents and vice-presidents – need help. They have no idea how to engage an audience or speak effectively.

"It's the aristocratic syndrome," says Christina Harvey, president of Voice Dynamics Inc., which helps people improve their speaking. "The further up the corporate ladder, the softer and more confidential the style of speaking. The higher up, the more secrets you have."

While a microphone helps a bit, the message can still sound flat and lack energy.

But mumblers and timid talkers need not despair. It's possible to learn to speak up – or even give a speech – without having a nervous breakdown.

Take University of Toronto chemist Tom Francis, once the coldest of cold-feet communicators. By the time he was 22, he had a bachelor's degree and a PhD, but had never asked a question in class.

He hid out in a research lab in Saskatoon for several years, then changed jobs and joined a Toronto lab.

"I realized I'd have to go to the coffee room and say, 'Thank you' for my going-away gift. That kept me awake at night for months," says Francis. "Talk about a basket case."

He was so nervous, he taped his farewell and played it at the gathering.

Francis eventually joined a Toastmasters Club and slowly became an accomplished public speaker.

"I still get nervous, but I know I won't fall on my face or lose my dinner."

He now teaches effective public speaking at the Junior Board of Trade and at York University, in the ongoing education department.

"Nobody's born with it," he says.

Francis doesn't believe in phony crutches, like imagining everyone in the audience is a head of cabbage. . . .

"That just made me feel hungry . . . " he says with a laugh. "You have to learn to use your adrenalin to your advantage and you have to be totally confident in your material."

But a good speaker shouldn't be too relaxed.

"You should feel on edge," says Thompson. "People who say they're as cool as a cucumber sound like a cucumber. I like controlled fire."

Here are some pointers:

Content

In writing the talk, Francis nixes the silly opening joke or the rambling preamble about what happened on the way over. Get right to the point with a strong opening, he says.

Never apologize about yourself or the listeners will start to look for faults, says Thompson.

And stay away from abstract concepts, he says. "People don't want to hear a discussion of free will versus determinism. Talk about something near and dear to them."

The general advice is to beware of straying from your themes in the body of your speech and to close with a snappy, memorable ending.

Then practise, practise, practise. If you must write the speech out, highlight the main points.

"Concentrate totally on the message," says Thompson. "It should be something you're busting to tell them."

Eye Contact

When speaking, don't focus above people's heads or look just at one person, says Francis. And don't do a rhythmic scan, left to right, left to right – you'd look like a machinegun.

Instead, make eye contact with a person very briefly, then move on, in a smooth random pattern.

"The master of this is Pope John Paul II," says Francis. "He looks at a crowd and everyone says, 'He looked right at me.'"

Voice

You must control your voice.

If you're very nervous, your voice becomes tense and doesn't project a credible sound, says Harvey of Voice Dynamics Inc. She suggests taking a deep breath and holding it for maybe 30 seconds, until you can feel your heart slow down and body relax.

A good speech needs volume, a variety of volume and emphasis, according to Harvey.

Hands and Feet

"Don't grasp the lectern as if it's the last thing on earth or stick your hands in front of you like a fig leaf," says Francis.

He advises gesturing as if you were in normal conversation, avoiding repetitive hand motions.

And whatever you do, don't rock and roll. If you sway at the podium, you'll distract the audience, never mind making them dizzy.

"Plant your feet solidly about 10 inches apart," says Kai Rambow, a Toastmasters Club member who teaches public speaking through the Learning Annex.

Rambow, 27, is another former shell-shocked speaker. "I was your typical wallflower," he says.

Now, after three years with Toastmasters, he says he's more self-confident.

A major hurdle is to stop being so self-critical, he says.

"Only about 10 per cent of what you feel on the inside shows up on the outside," explains Rambow, a training specialist with an insurance company. "When I tell my students that everyone has some strengths – perhaps humor, energy, a good voice – I hear a tremendous sigh of relief. Most think they're weak in everything."

GIVE SPEECH OR DIE: SOME LIKE THE LATTER IDEA

By Cathryn Motherwell

Ask business people what strikes terror in their hearts, and it is unlikely the answer will be an unfriendly takeover or being fired. No, their greatest fear is public speaking.

"People fear dying less than getting up and talking in front of people," said Henry Flattery of Con-Ryan International Consultants Ltd. of Toronto.

While that may slightly overstate the case, the seemingly simple task of making a speech generally does bring on a terrible panic and a host of nervous ticks that could have a bearing on who climbs how far up the corporate ladder.

Consequently, everyone from clerks to chief executives are swallowing their pride as well as the lumps in their throats and seeking professional assistance for their speech and presentation techniques.

"I was nervous," confessed Leslie Luciani, a business analyst with the Toronto Stock Exchange who was apprehensive about making a staff presentation. She suffered from some common problems: sticky hands, dry mouth and a shaky voice. And at a course on presentation skills given by Mr. Flattery at the TSE, she made another discovery.

"The first thing I noticed was that one of my hands has a mind of its own. It just kept slowly circling at my side. I had no idea it was doing that," she said.

Ms Luciani overcame her nervousness and not only used her new ability to make a successful presentation at work, but also applied them to something even more important: a toast at a friend's wedding. "That was tough for me because not only was it in front of 200 people, but in front of my parents as well."

Some people are naturally gifted public speakers, but most mortals seek outside help to overcome their fluttery stomachs and fidgety habits. Business schools have recognized the importance of giving students experience in public speaking, and many companies now offer in-house training to help their employees hone their verbal skills.

There is a wide variety of companies and organizations that offer public speaking assistance, ranging from Dale Carnegie and Toastmasters International to private consulting firms such as T/K Training International Inc. of Vancouver. It offers a seminar pioneered by former language commissioner Keith Spicer called Think on Your Feet.

"What we focus on almost exclusively is

that before putting your mouth or pen in motion, you have to get your mind in gear," said John Priddle, T/K's academic co-ordinator based in Ottawa. People want to be more relaxed when they face a group of people, to quickly collect their thoughts and competently handle any questions or objections raised about their presentations, he said.

When called upon to make impromptu remarks, Mr. Priddle said people often fear their remarks will be incoherent. Think on Your Feet offers advice on organizing your thoughts before a presentation, and anticipating what questions members of the audience might ask.

Most people need public speaking ability for two reasons: they want to sell their ideas and themselves. Whether they are pitching a product to a client or advocating a change in office equipment, many people feel they are not putting their ideas across as well as they could.

"I could recall sitting in meetings and having something to say but having no breath," said chartered accountant Karl Ruban.

He attended a course offered by Voice Dynamics Inc. of Toronto, which helps people improve the sound of their voice. The courses offered by former opera singer Christina Harvey focus on how people speak, and she emphasizes that people can change the sound of their voice. "Your voice might be suited to college years but it doesn't fit anymore for a vice-president."

Most speech classes and organizations are informal and use aids such as tape and video recorders to allow students to hear and see themselves at work. They often involve making impromptu speeches, and can offer an opportunity to try out your big sales pitch in front of the class instead of in front of the board of directors.

In Think on Your Feet, for example, Mr. Priddle encourages students to practice by assuming the role of a popular personality or historical figure who talks on a topic familiar to them. Charles Dickens, for instance, would talk about poverty. But not all the roles students play are quite so commonplace.

"We've had many people make successful speeches as the Marquis de Sade and Mata Hari," he said. . . .

The techniques supplied in the courses are not quite as likely to put the speaker into fits of laughter, however. They include such basic tips as speaking slowly and establishing eye contact with members of the audience.

Here are a few hints from the experts that help make public speaking an easier experience:

- There is no real trick to controlling nervousness, said Mr. Flattery but it helps if you can make presentations as often as possible. This way, the experience becomes more familiar and you grow more comfortable.

- Some nervous habits can be addressed directly. If you are jingling the coins in your pocket, leave them in the office before you make your speech. If you fiddle with a pencil do not place one within reach.

- Arrive early. Establish your bearings, familiarize yourself with any of the equipment you will be using during the presentation, and greet people as they enter the room.

- If you are unexpectedly called upon to speak, Mr. Priddle suggests two useful structures to organize your thoughts: put them into the classic journalistic framework of who, what, when, where, how and why, or put them into the context of past, present and future.

- Memorize your opening lines. You can use notes and memory prompts later, but show the audience off the top that you know your stuff.

FOLLOWING THROUGH

Now that you have examined various opinions and broadened your own opinion on the concept of vocal image and vocal improvement, you should be prepared to apply the ideas and information and to put your best voice forward.

SUGGESTED APPROACH

Select one or more of the following activities.

1. Prepare and deliver group oral presentations that answer Neffie Pike's question, "Who said we all have to talk alike?" These presentations could be done in various ways:

- as a seminar, having each group member deal with one aspect of the question;
- as a dramatization, having some members role-play various characters in the story and/or authorities in the articles and interview Neffie Pike;
- as a talk show, having a "host" interview some of the authorities in the articles and two or three "celebrities."

Also, if they are to be evaluated, you should design a criteria checklist from the "do's and don'ts" you listed earlier.)

2. Prepare and deliver a speech in which you evaluate the whole concept of "vocal image." (This could be done seriously, humorously, or satirically, and two or three people could work together creatively to deliver one speech, demonstrating some of the do's and don'ts of oral presentations. You should adapt the criteria checklist designed earlier.)

3. Set up a formal debate or series of debates on one or more of the issues raised in the reading material and general discussions.

SOME FURTHER FOLLOW-THROUGH SUGGESTIONS

Some of these suggestions may be done as independent study activities, either individually or in small groups, or as whole class activities.

- Invite a speech teacher in to the class to discuss vocal image.

- Design and conduct a survey of students who have learned English as a second language to determine the validity of the concepts put forward in the articles concerning the attitudes and language problems of non-native English speakers.

- Design and conduct a survey of businesses in your area to determine the validity of concepts put forward in the articles concerning the importance of vocal image in the world of business.

- Watch two or three newscasters deliver the news on television and compare their vocal images. Develop some criteria to decide which one is the best. (This would be a good activity to do as a group and then you could compare observations.)

- Conduct a survey of various radio stations to determine the range of accents exhibited by their on-air personnel.

- Select a television personality or a political figure and conduct a vocal image analysis of the person using criteria developed from the articles and your own observations. (You may wish to communicate your analysis to that person, if it would be helpful in any way.)

- Examine your own vocal image, using either a tape recorder or a video recorder. Conduct a vocal image analysis using criteria developed from the articles and your own observations. (This project is only for the brave!)

- Find an interesting speech or a passage of dialogue (it could be from a variety of sources) and re-write it in a variety of accents and/or dialects for various audiences. This could be delivered in a variety of ways to the class and they could identify the intended audience.

- Read the play *Pygmalion* by George Bernard Shaw. It is one of the most famous stories of accent adjustment that has ever been written. (Seeing the play itself or the musical version, *My Fair Lady*, would enable you to see the transformation of body language as well.)

T O P I C
five

The Wild, Wonderful, and Weird World of Advertising

··

FOCUSING IN

Advertising is so much a part of our lives that it generally is something we take for granted. We seemingly give it little of our attention, unless, as consumers, we are in the market for something specific or are interested in a bargain. Many of us tune out the commercial breaks on television by "zapping" to other channels or by using the commercial time for a viewing break. When we read a newspaper or magazine, we often flip past the advertising or give it only a cursory glance if something about it catches our interest. But companies and advertising firms think that advertising works and they spend billions of dollars every year on it.

SUGGESTED APPROACH

This could be done in pairs or small groups.

Step 1

In your opinion, just how powerful is advertising? How much have you been conditioned to associate a general product with a brand name? In your notebook write your responses to the quiz on the following page. Do this quickly and put down the first answer that comes to mind. If nothing comes to mind, go on to the next one.

Product Association Test

Toothpaste   _____

Ketchup   _____

Chocolate bar   _____

Soap   _____

Baby powder   _____

Jeans   _____

Fast-food outlet   _____

Shoes   _____

Car   _____

Ice cream   _____

Pickles   _____

Pancakes   _____

Frozen cake   _____

Shampoo   _____

Mayonnaise   _____

Mouthwash   _____

Razor blade   _____

Grape juice   _____

Coffee   _____

Diaper   _____

Running shoe   _____

Television   _____

Wrist-watch   _____

Headache tablet   _____

Car tire   _____

Pet food   _____

Step 2

Once everyone is finished, tabulate the range of responses for each item. Examine the patterns that emerge and determine to what extent they indicate how conditioned we are generally and in what areas particularly. Consider whether your results reinforce the position of advertisers or undermine it?

Step 3 (Optional)

You may wish to test your conclusions by adding a few products in certain areas to see if they support your thinking or by having another age group take the test.

···

FINDING OUT

Advertising is a serious business. Billions of dollars are spent on it yearly. From the perspective of the business world, advertising is crucial because it often determines the financial success or failure of a product or service. From the perspective of advertising companies hired by businesses to promote their products, their success depends on their ability to figure out the psychology of consumers and make them buy. However, from the perspective of certain social and political bodies, advertising needs constant monitoring because of the impact it is said to have in shaping the consumer's self-image and social and cultural values. It should be noted that from the perspective of some artists and art critics, advertising is a modern art form, perhaps the greatest art form of the twentieth century. For example, Andy Warhol painted a Campbell's Soup can and turned it into an object of art. The material that follows explores advertising from two major perspectives: the business and ad worlds that create the advertisements, and the consumers who are the targets of these advertisements.

As you explore this topic you will develop skill in organizing and consolidating information, weighing evidence, and exploring possibilities and seeing new patterns.

Suggested Approach

These activities may be done individually, in pairs or small groups, or as whole class activities.

Step 1

Examine the following material and develop a strategy for reading and sharing the information given in the first six articles which examine advertising from the perspective of the advertisers.

Step 2

Describe the picture of the advertising world that is presented in these articles. What did you already know, what didn't you know, and what really surprised or even shocked you?

Assess the extent to which advertising may now be seen as a "science."

Step 3

Examine the remainder of the material, beginning with "Ad Modelling Misleads Youth," and decide on a plan for dealing with the information.

Make a list of the various effects of advertising on the consumer and society as a whole.

Step 4

Based on your reading of the material and your own experience, decide whether or not advertising needs to have some controls put on it, and, if so, what controls?

BLUE IS FOR TRUST – AND FOR PEPSI

....

By Kenneth Kidd

"See Red, think Coke."

Wandering through the grocery store, that's what most people apparently do – at least when they cruise past the soda section.

Then again, the sight of red also makes shoppers reckon the product is mild on taste and nutrition.

Some of us might have reached this conclusion in the absence of extensive research but Cheskin & Masten, a California marketing firm, made its discoveries after a survey of American consumers.

Cheskin & Masten tallied a number of color and value associations for soft drinks which, taken together, make an interesting portrait.

Coke 'Owns' Red

The study showed, for instance, that 71 per cent of consumers associate red with Coca-Cola, meaning that Coke has carved out a pretty enviable place on the shelves. Advertising types would say that Coke "owns" the color red.

But Coke has also bought into a color that suggests, at least to the consumers tested, such things as "danger, love, safety, speed, warmth and strength."

With such a lethal mix of emotions, no wonder Coke has been having a few problems of late.

Pepsi also has a strong image on the shelves, since 64 per cent of people associated blue with Pepsi, while only 13 per cent connected red with Pepsi. (Red, white and blue are the Pepsi colors, although blue is arguably the dominant one.)

The emotional baggage for blue: trust and tradition, which sounds more like the CTV National News than Michael Jackson and the Pepsi Generation.

Yet consumers also think of blue as a color for the 1990s, which provides some solace for the Pepsi people. It can also mean "cold" and "filling."

Interesting Question

An interesting question is whether Pepsi's ad agencies, when designing a new campaign and slogan, should take a close look at the sorts of images evoked by Pepsi packaging.

Since the Pepsi cans and bottles seem to be so well established in the public eye, a change here wouldn't be taken lightly.

But, if the new research is to be believed, there seems to be some conflict between what the Pepsi can says and what the Pepsi ads try to convey.

"Whether it's something Pepsi ought to be thinking about, I don't know," says Davis Masten, who heads up Cheskin & Masten.

Masten reckons a big part of his job is to provoke the marketing managers, not provide them a pat answer.

The survey results "should only be taken in the context of food for thought," he says. "A lot of what we do is help clients question their own judgment."

Thinking of pink?

It might help to know that 24 per cent of consumers associate pink with Cherry 7-Up, as well as with "love, trust, calm and friendly." Things like "natural" and "good for children" also come to mind.

Further down the shelf, however, particular brand identification falls off dramatically; nobody "owns" any color.

Among consumers, for instance, green is linked with 7-Up (61 per cent of those surveyed), Slice (48 per cent), Canada Dry (44) and Cherry 7-Up (32).

Emotionally, though, green is pretty solid: "for the family, for kids, progressive." It brings "trust, good taste and strength" to mind.

But a big irony awaits with orange.

Seventy-nine per cent of shoppers connect that color with Sunkist products, and 57 per cent link it with Minute Maid, of orange juice fame. So we're talking the health food set, right? Not quite.

Orange apparently makes us think the product is "artificial."

Moving up-market, however, may not be the best way out of the color syndrome.

A bit of silver foil does suggest a scientific, progressive and cold product, according to Cheskin & Masten.

That's good news for the purveyors of ginger ale. Thirty-seven per cent of people associate silver with Schweppes, while 35 per cent connect it with Canada Dry.

But roughly one third of consumers apparently connect silver with "bland, artificial and expensive."

All of which, in a roundabout way, might explain why the soda pop giants spend megabucks clogging up the airwaves with their messages.

Get the consumer bent on buying a Coke and he'll find the cans, regardless of what the color of the package tells him.

SELLING FEELINGS

Advertisers Are Using Powerful Images and New Marketing to Connect with Consumers

By Patricia Chisholm

Attractive young women flirt with handsome men, rebellious teenagers leap off soft-drink machines, and small children munch happily on cheese. Alternately sensuous, energetic and heart-tugging, more and more television commercials and magazine advertisements are directed at the viewer's heart – fighting to deliver a message before he [or she] changes the channel or turns the page. It is all part of the fierce new warfare for the attention of consumers. To gain that attention, Canadian advertisers will spend $9 billion this year on advertising and sales promotions. Said Ann Boden, national media director for McKim Advertising Ltd. in Toronto: "It is much more difficult for traditional advertising vehicles than it was five years ago. Advertising budgets are not high enough now for campaigns in both print and broadcast, so often one has to be cut."

High stakes and savage competition are creating high-pressure conditions in the advertising industry. Ad revenues are the life-blood of television, magazines and newspapers. And the commissions generated by advertising campaigns also support Canada's advertising agencies. But stagnant corporate advertising budgets and the burgeoning number of television stations and publications across Canada have resulted in cutthroat competition for advertisers, as well as fragmentation of the reading and watching consumer audience. Zapping – changing television channels by remote control when a commercial begins – also has caused concern among advertisers, as has the growing use of video cassette recorders, which can flash through advertisements at high speed. Sales promotions, including direct mail, and colorful store displays are also continuing to cut deep into revenues from other forms of advertising, such as television commercials. Said Linda Saul, vice-president of the Toronto-based Environics Research Group Ltd.: "The competition is ferocious."

Advertisers are now in a position to demand – and receive – far more value for their dollar. Peter Swain, president of Media Buying Services Ltd. of Toronto, said that firms are now paying far more attention to where their money is spent, partly because 80 to 90 per cent of any particular advertising campaign budget goes directly toward the cost of the space or time purchased in a publication or on a radio or television station, with the remainder going toward the cost of producing the advertisement. To convince companies that they are getting their money's worth, special deals are becoming more and more common.

Newspapers, accustomed to historically steady ad revenues, are fighting hard to increase advertising linage as competitors launch aggressive raids on their traditional customer base.... Other media outlets are also offering more inducements. Radio stations increase revenues by offering perks to their major advertisers, including free sponsorships of traffic reports and other promotions.

That strategy is helping combat competition from such sales promotions as direct mail, price discounts and in-store displays, which are on the upswing. Those promotions attract advertisers because they deliver strong sales results in a relatively short period of time. As a result, more and more advertisers are siphoning off dollars from their traditional advertising budgets for promotions. Some industry experts estimate that sales promotions now account for between 50 and 60 per cent of total advertising spending.

But for many advertisers, even good deals may not help them reach a wide range of consumers. Fragmentation of some advertiser's target audience increases every year as magazines, radio and television become more specialized and consumers become more selective about what they watch and read. General-interest magazines are also benefiting from the trend toward increased advertising revenues. Said Linda Saul: "Revenues are up at news-magazines because, in general, the population is better educated and reads more. The percentage of women readers is also up." Television, which could once guarantee almost total market coverage, is particularly susceptible to fragmentation. Swain said that the booming market for video cassette record-

ers as well as zapping are "very disconcerting for advertisers, because ratings then come into question." That is because zapping decreases the number of viewers who may see a particular commercial, without the decrease being monitored by normal television rating techniques. Zappers actually account for the loss of less than five per cent of the viewing audience, Swain said, but the perception by advertisers is that it is a much higher figure.

Still, the attraction of television for advertisers is almost irresistible. It is commonly perceived by advertisers as the leading medium because of its powerful combination of sound and motion, and advertisers who can afford it still line up for prime-time spots on large networks. To help fight the fragmentation effect, more television commercials try to get the viewer's attention quickly and impart a single, strong message. They are becoming shorter, more direct and frequently emphasize image and emotion, rather than long lists of information. Said Terrence O'Malley, president of the Toronto-based Vickers & Benson Advertising Ltd.: "Emotion is one of the most common platforms of understanding." He added, "There is a new discipline with the 15-second commercial – they are much more focused."

The approach seems to be making an impression. Consumers polled by Environics about advertising campaigns last year particularly remembered those which concentrated on image and feeling....

But while advertisers are now also placing more emphasis on tangible results, it is still not clear that they are receiving them. Traditionally, the connection between advertising and sales has been difficult to make. Saul said that "nobody can really measure whether advertising works, in terms of increased sales," adding, "You just hope that they will notice and pay attention to the product." And last week, Gerard Tellis, an associate professor of marketing at the University of Iowa, released a study that concluded that television commercials may indeed have little or no effect on the buyers of detergents – the product he studied. Coupons and in-store displays affected most decisions to switch products, he found.

Still, most experts say that advertising's dominance will remain for a lengthy period. Said Saul: "Everybody believes in advertising – there is no loss of faith. But because it is harder and more expensive to reach consumers, advertisers are looking for other avenues as well." And many advertisers say that they have never doubted the force of their campaigns. Ray Verdon is president and chief executive officer of Nabisco Brands Ltd., a Canadian subsidiary of RJR Nabisco, one of the world's largest advertisers. Said Verdon: "There is a direct link between advertising and sales, no question." He added that some types of advertising, including image commercials, simply take more time to work, and he pointed to Nabisco's long-standing success with its "Mr. Christie" series of cookie commercials. "We look for 'charmth,'" he said, "a combination of warmth and charm." For advertisers, the psychology of cozy feelings could well be the ultimate selling tool. And the ability to deliver that message to the right viewer at the right time will help determine the future outcome of the ever-escalating advertising wars.

A LOOK THROUGH ADVERTISING'S BAG OF TRICKS

The Want Makers:
Lifting The Lid Off The World Advertising Industry: How They Make You Buy

By Eric Clark
General Publishing Co. Ltd.

....

Review by Bertrand Marotte

Over the course of this informative but ultimately wishy-washy trek through the magical-mythical world of advertising, author Eric Clark offers up the following gems:

- Ernest Dichter, aging guru of motivational research, wants to know why some people save shopping coupons and some don't: "What's behind it?" he asks. "Are coupon users more [thrifty] or are non-users afraid of being identified with cheap money grabbing? Coupon Saver – Greed or a sign of love?"

- An ad campaign in India by Roche Vitaminets Forte plays on naked fear: "Your child is intelligent, but is he alert?" The ad lists "symptoms" said to be associated with "vitamin starvation," including an unwillingness to go to school, leaving books or pencils at home or complaining about other children.

- Chicago consultant Leo Shapiro lays claim to discovering the "grazing society" in 1978: "... we have as many as 20 'food contacts' a day – and spend as little as 20 minutes eating together."

- *Seventeen* magazine tells potential advertisers, in no uncertain terms: "Reach a girl in her Seventeen years and she may be yours for life."

- One of the rough guides of children's advertising: Children envy children slightly older than themselves – so if you want to get a seven-year-old to buy a product, show him a 10-year-old enjoying it.
- Research shows that single-color pills look too much like candies. Pastel is seen as weak. Two colors connote strength and achievement. Dark blue is the best. It means safety, calmness, gentleness.

One gathers from these and other nuggets that the high-stress, high-flying, high-paying world of advertising is one of outlandish promises (to both consumer and advertiser); of the tapping of human fear, envy, greed, desire; and of flaky "consultants" indulging in pseudo-scientific research of the most dubious kind.

Mr. Clark is quick to make clear from the outset that he is "pro-advertising" and not a crusader aiming to ban or seriously restrict the freedom of the business.

He takes a middle-of-the-road approach in which no solid conclusions or revelations are made, besides a call for more stringent controls, more awareness through education and alternative financing for advertising-supported media, and a vague admonishment at the end to be "eternally vigilant."

There are enough instances brought to light in this well-researched book that lead one to wish the author had been more daring in attempting to distill from his rich blend of detail more insight into advertising's impact.

Thankfully absent, though, is the paranoid squawk emitted by certain critics who see conspiracy everywhere.

Without resorting to conspiracy theories, Mr. Clark shows us the latest from the adman's bottomless bag of tricks: the time-compression of speakers on radio to make them sound more energetic and enthusiastic; actors who incorporate into drug commercials

a selection of 45 different grimaces of pain that researchers collected from interviews with diseased people; members of focus groups being asked to "model their feelings" in clay. . . .

One is left with the distinct impression that advertising – despite the increasingly feverish use of computer models, grids, focus groups, psychographics, nanosecond response measurement, brain-wave research and the rest – is still very much a hit-and-miss, seat-of-the-pants operation – a brilliant fiction that helps both advertisers and consumers live out lives based on illusions, on little lies.

To the advertiser, the ad agency is selling reassurance, confidence in the product, a scientific aura. To the consumer, on the other hand, it is selling magic, image, fantasy, lifestyle.

"Agencies and individual [advertisers] disagree over whether it is possible to formulate meaningful rules for creating advertisements. Many are skeptical," writes Mr. Clark. . . .

From its very beginning, advertising's practitioners and theoreticians have been unable to agree on just exactly what works and what doesn't. The careful, research-oriented camp continues its pitched battles with the "creative," intuitive group.

⸬

ART OF SELLING BECOMES A SCIENCE

Researchers Say Ad Effectiveness Can Be Proven

. . . .

Determining whether advertising works is becoming more of a science – much to the relief of advertisers.

A University of Michigan marketing researcher says he can now substantiate the effectiveness of an ad.

Christopher Puto, assistant professor of marketing at the School of Business Administration, University of Michigan, says an effective advertisement can change the way a product tastes, smells, feels, looks, or operates.

Puto says effective ads transform lemons into limousines, make a hamburger taste better and breath feel fresher.

"We've always done research to discover if sales improved after a campaign has run," says Dick Berndt, vice-president and media director at Foster Advertising Ltd., Toronto.

"And we also do research to determine the level of public awareness before and after a campaign."

Puto, who has been studying the impact of advertising on the human mental process since 1983, says an advertisement can make or break a product by transforming the consumer's experience of using the advertised brand.

Transformation

He says: "What happens is that after people are exposed to an advertisement, their experience using or consuming the advertised brand becomes transformed, so that it's different from what it would have been if they hadn't seen the ad."

"It's what the ad industry calls 'user imagery,' " says Bill Booth, executive vice-president and general manager of Toronto-based ad agency Baker Lovick Ltd.

"We recognize that most consumer product categories are perceived as being roughly equivalent by the public.

"But if you can sell the product so it better reflects the attitudes of the consumer you are targeting, the better the response will be."

Berndt points out that sophisticated computer models can quantify–if not an ad's

effect–at least the success of a campaign. And that, to most advertisers, is still the bottom line.

According to Berndt, several U.S. computer models have been developed to measure advertising's effectiveness.

"The models use a client's reported performance based on the amount of advertising activity over a period of time," Berndt says.

"The result is that trends emerge."

Berndt says the Canadian Media Directors Council, based in Toronto, is developing a similar program for Canada.

Puto maintains that his theory is also measurable.

For example, researchers asked one group of consumers to drink a bubbly brown liquid from a plain bottle and evaluate its taste.

They asked a second group to watch a commercial of handsome people frolicking on a beach and drinking the same beverage.

The second group then drank the brown liquid and evaluated its taste.

"The liquid is unchanged," Puto says.

"Yet, the scores on the rating sheets will be much higher from the second group of subjects because they saw the ad. The ad has made the beverage taste better."

This change in attitude is accomplished by what Puto calls "dimensions."

Consumers first must see themselves in an ad and believe its message is aimed directly at them.

They must then experience the same feelings projected by actors in an advertisement. This projection is the ad's ability to elicit empathy in a consumer, to make a consumer wish for the same experience the actors are having.

The third dimension of a successful advertisement is the information it provides. Factual, relevant, brand data make consumers feel more confident about their buying decision.

For example, advertisements for Mercedes-

Benz automobiles are information oriented.

The information transforms the experience of driving and owning a Mercedes into that of driving and owning a very special luxury car.

"Objectively, the car may not perform any better than a Chevrolet Eurosport, yet its perceived performance will be far superior as a result of the advertisement," Puto says.

The fourth dimension is how an ad is presented.

This has to do with how likeable and memorable an ad is – how long it sticks with you.

CLASSIC MARKETING

A Revolt Against Things That Have Gone Too Far

By Nina Killham

Above the desks of advertising executives, above the tips of their spit-polished Gucci shoes, hangs a motto. It reads: If a product is new, label it NEW. If it's been fiddled with, label it IMPROVED. If its sales are declining, label it CLASSIC.

Classics don't die. They don't even fade away. They are created every year to be snapped up by nostalgia-hungry consumers. . . .

"It reflects a return to traditional values, a swing to the right," says Al Ries of Trout and Ries Advertising Inc. in New York. . . .

Classic, Ries says, is a "revolt against the music, the drugs and the food that's gone too far. People are asking, 'What's this pineapple doing in my roast beef? What's all the spice on my fish, this blackened-catfish stuff?' People are saying, 'Wait a second.' "

Advertisers, their ears ever to the bleached hardwood floor, are responding to this reactionary trend.

221 Classics

In the 1985-86 *Trade Names Dictionary*, 221 products are called Classic, from Classic roofing shingles to Classic Silver hair coloring, Classic Series theft-proof desk pens to Classic Pet Food. In the 1974 issue only 60 Classics appeared; that's almost a 300 per cent jump.

In *Positioning: The Battle for Your Mind* (Warner Books), co-authored with Jack Trout, Ries argues that the most successful way to launch a product and keep it at the top is to be first – like Xerox in copiers, Kodak in photography, IBM in computers. And if you can't be first, you can always pretend you were.

Classic: It fools people into thinking you were there all along.

Take Classic French Fries. "Using this word identifies with the classics from the past, and it looks like you also have that longevity," says Kelley Atchison of the Simplot Co. in Idaho, manufacturer of the fries. . . .

WCXR-FM (105.9) in Washington has even declared rock 'n' roll a Classic. According to station manager Bill Sherard, the name emerged from audience research, in which a group of 25- to 40-year-olds rated phrases like Rock and Roll Oldies, Rock Hits of the '60s and '70s, Album Rock of the '60s and '70s. At least $40,000 later, the Classic Rock format clicked in January of this year [1986].

"That makes me feel old," Ries moans. "All this time I thought rock was young. Now I find it's so old we have to go back to it."

The name Classic Rock "seemed to be the one that best summarized the music we were playing," Sherard says. "People didn't have any trouble positioning in their mind what we meant. It sure isn't Barry Manilow. At the same time it wasn't the Monkees."

Odds Improve

"What's classic today may not be classic tomorrow," he adds, "although the norm is if a song has endured five to eight years and is still popular in people's minds, the odds are that it will be a classic."

WCXR is so sure about this formula that it's now predicting future classics, calling some newly released songs Neo-Classics.

"These are new songs by artists that are the mainstay of the WCXR library – John Fogerty, the Rolling Stones, Dave Mason, Joe Cocker," Sherard says. "All these artists are still recording, are still popular. Yet these artists have the patina of time."

Classic Coke is only 4 years old. Of all the Classics it's probably the most authentic – so authentic it couldn't be improved.

" 'Classic' conveys to consumers that the product is traditional and is a standard of excellence," explains Randy Donaldson, media director for Coca-Cola USA. "We felt both ideas applied to the original formula."

Burning Bottles

So did the public, which was burning New Coke bottles in effigy. "There was no time to do extensive marketing testing," Donaldson says.

According to WCXR's Sherard, a company runs a risk if its label doesn't match its product. "You can't sell a 1974 Ford Fairlane and call yourself the Classic Dealership of Washington," he says.

If a company makes a mistake, its sale pitch will be perceived as a lie. "If they say it's classic mustard, it better . . . have something classic about it," Sherard says. . . .

"Classic" isn't the first attempt to bring back better days. Remember "Old Fashioned," as in Dad's Old Fashioned Root Beer?

Ries says the idea is the same, meant to evoke a time when life was supposedly sweeter, but isn't sophisticated enough for today's market.

Wendy's, however, still chooses it to describe its hamburgers. And Ries can understand why: "Classic sounds so good you don't want to eat it."

Not a Yearning

Yet Wendy's has succumbed to the trend with its New Big Classic Hamburger.

Ira Bachrach of NameLab, a name-development and testing laboratory in San Francisco, says that buying Classics does not indicate a yearning for the good old days.

Classics are popular because "Americans are less secure about their tastes these days. There is so much information about what's happening that they get nervous about keeping up. With something 'Classic' they are more sure."

The word, he says, comes from the Latin "classis," which in ancient times described the sound made to summon people to a meeting. "It has connotations of safety for the consumer. . . . The consumer is defending herself – it's funny, we usually use 'her' – against these lifestyle instructions by not responding, by becoming less interested."

And so companies are now introducing new products designed to exploit the consumer's resistance to new products.

But today's Classic might be tomorrow's museum piece.

As Ries says, "Life is a clock. It's 5 minutes to midnight, and it's back to basics. Time to go around the clock again."

MARKETING WARFARE BEARS DISTINCT ECHO OF GEORGE ORWELL

....

By Kenneth Kidd

Karl von Clausewitz, the 19th century Prussian who wrote what many believe to be the definitive book on the art of war, is very much in vogue among the marketers of today.

This is an eminently sensible approach, at least as presented by ad executives Al Ries and Jack Trout in their . . . book, appropriately titled "Marketing Warfare."

But what is disturbing about the book is its underlying assumptions about marketing and capitalism in general, either stated blatantly or running obliquely through every page.

It is as if Ries and Trout begin by accepting as fact every scathing rebuke of corporations and advertising ever voiced by critics. Marketing warfare, in short, has everything to do with beating corporate competitors and almost nothing to do with serving consumers.

True Nature

"Why do the hundreds of definitions of the marketing concept almost never mention the word *competition*?" the authors ask. "Or suggest the essential nature of the conflict?

"The true nature of marketing today involves the conflict between corporations, not the satisfying of human needs and wants."

This cynical but brutally honest thought fits in rather nicely with another frequently-voiced notion about today's market-place: There are precious few consumer needs or wants left out there. So why bother looking for them?

Marketing research thus involves, not the discovery of consumer wants, but getting a handle on how consumers perceive company X and its competitors. And "truth" is always on the side of the company consumers perceive as the market leader; If your widget is so good, then why aren't you the market leader? Might is right.

Having thus moved the marketing function to a different level, Ries and Trout then apply Clausewitz's maxims about war to corporate competition, which they divide into four distinct categories.

- Defensive Marketing. This is the tack only the market leader should take, and it involves attacking oneself – i.e., coming out with new products that make your old ones obsolete, thus retaining leadership. Any strong competitive moves by other companies should be blocked with extreme prejudice.

  As a prime example, the authors cite Gillette, which keeps coming out with new razors that fundamentally compete with its own previous line. This is not only smart defensive marketing, but also lessens the chance of arousing the interest of anti-trust investigators.

- Offensive Marketing. Something that strong number two and three-ranked firms can indulge in, offensive marketing means your main consideration is the leader's strength. Find a weakness in that strength, and attack solely on that narrow front. Thus Burger King rightly attacked the pre-fabricated nature of McDonald's hamburgers with its "Have it your way" campaign.

- Flanking. Under this strategy, strong also-rans will attack the competition in an uncontested area, a market that doesn't yet exist. Surprise is the key element here, and the flanking firm must maintain the pressure.

  A classic bit of flanking, we are told, was perpetrated by Haagen-Dazs, which created and dominates a market for super-premium ice cream.

- Guerrilla Warfare. This should be the strategy of the smallest competitors. Find a market small enough to defend, never act like a leader and be prepared to "bug out" on a moment's notice.

  Rolls-Royce, dominating the market for cars priced above $100,000, is the most spectacularly successful guerrilla.

Monstrously Idiotic

These strategic tips are undoubtedly useful to the *real-politik* marketers of today, but that doesn't make the approach less disturbing. At the back of this military framework is the unstated assumption that consumers are monstrously idiotic, susceptible to the most cynical of manipulation.

Ries and Trout may be right, but they are not pleasant as a result.

In the pages of their book, one hears a strange echo of Gordon Comstock, the brilliant but disillusioned advertising copy writer in *Keep the Aspidistra Flying* by George Orwell.

Comstock observes that New Albion, the agency that employs him, is thoroughly modern in spirit. His fellow employees are the "hard-boiled, Americanized, go-getting type.

"They had their cynical code worked out. The public are swine: advertising is the rattling of a stick inside a swillbucket."

AD MODELLING MISLEADS YOUTH

By Morning Star Trickey

Advertising reaches a huge audience – according to marketing statistics research, the average person is bombarded by approximately 7000 broadcast messages daily.

The impact the fashion and cosmetic advertising have on youth concerns many persons: It sets a standard for attractiveness that most teens, whether consciously or subconsciously, attempt to adhere to.

Critics complain the standards in fashion and cosmetic advertising are unrealistically high. For example, the model in an advertisement is always beautiful, with flawless features, and a perfect body. It is unreasonable for anyone to expect to reproduce this contrived appearance.

For instance, Deborah Samuel, one of Canada's top fashion and advertising photographers, says, "A model can spend hours with her hair and makeup alone. It could take several hours to get the right shot. No one should expect to look like that."

In Ms. Samuel's opinion, physical perfection is not something to strive for.

Fashion and cosmetic advertising may also be a contributing factor to a youth's low self-image. Sunshine Martinez, 18, a student at George Harvey C.I., says, "Every girl I know thinks she's fat. Girls have this picture that you have to be a bone rack to be attractive. And I think most fashion advertising reinforces this negative concept."

According to Dr. Elaine Borins, a psychiatrist, and the director of The Women's Clinic at Toronto Western Hospital, many advertisements convey this destructive image.

Furthermore, Dr. Borins believes that a certain product can't give a person a certain lifestyle; nor can it give the person happiness. Advertising only shows people what they want to see, and what they would like to be, she says.

If teens think positively of themselves, they will not take seriously the perfect images created by advertising: "Teens follow trends because they are not comfortable with themselves. If you like yourself, then you don't need to look, or act like anyone else," says Ms. Samuel.

Danielle Gagnier, a young Toronto model, says that she has considered giving it up. "I felt like a product, not a person. I really think people's expectations are too high. The money is great, but I sometimes feel like I'm being used."

She also says fashion and cosmetic advertising do seriously affect many teens. Many girls feel inadequate because they don't look like the model in the advertisement. And Ms. Gagnier feels, "Teens really don't need that kind of pressure on them."

PUSH TO BAN BOOZE ADS HEATS UP

....

By Ingrid Abramovitch

Many Canadians would like to see advertising for alcoholic beverages dry up, much as cigarette ads appear headed for the ashcan. . . .

"Health and Welfare gets more letters complaining about alcohol marketing practices than on every other issue combined," says James Mintz, chief of Marketing and communications for Health and Welfare Canada.

A recent Gallup poll suggests 54 per cent of Canadians favor a total ban on alcohol advertising, says Mintz.

Two years ago, responding to pressure by health groups – and by Health Minister Jake Epp, who pushed through the cigarette legislation – the federal broadcast regulator established a code of restrictions for alcohol advertising on television and radio.

Restrictions Ignored

The code included prohibitions against associating alcohol with "youth symbols" or with any activity requiring special skills or mental alertness.

A study of alcohol advertising on Canadian TV shows that many ads passed by the Canadian Radio-television and Telecommunications Commission do not abide by the new restrictions.

"Our findings were that the CRTC code is ineffective . . . and is founded on erroneous assumptions," says George Spears, president of Erin Research Inc., which conducted the study for Health and Welfare Canada.

"And whatever the flaws or merits of the code, many ads don't abide by it at all."

Spears found that among other violations of the code, at least 20 per cent of Canadian ads for booze include what he categorizes as youth symbols – Frisbees, skateboards, ice-cream carts, stuffed animals, roller skates and others.

'Weak Variable'

And a new study by the Toronto-based Addiction Research Foundation appears to confirm that view.

"Current research suggests that advertising is, at best, a weak variable affecting human drinking," says Dr. Reginald Smart, who conducted the study.

"Those interested in effective alcohol controls would be better to spend time controlling prices and availability than advertising."

But in the United States, some research has shown that alcohol advertising does increase consumption, says Dr. Lawrence Wallack, professor of public health at the University of California at Berkeley.

"Everyone agrees on one point: alcohol advertising appears to shape people's feelings about the product," says Wallack.

The alcoholic beverage industry says people determined to ban alcohol advertising are misguided. Tackling social problems, like the peer pressure that leads to drinking, would be more effective.

"People who believe banning advertising will have an impact (on alcoholism) will be tremendously disappointed," says John Hay, vice-president of public affairs at Carling O'Keefe.

Industry [spokes people] also cite the principle of free speech as an argument against banning ads and note that even in the event of a ban, Canadians would still face a barrage of American alcohol ads.

More important, they argue the public does not see a single advertisement that has not been approved by a CRTC tribunal or by provincial liquor boards.

The complaint by many is that Ottawa has not forced advertisers to comply with existing regulations.

"It's a lack of enforcement not a lack of the law," says John Bates, president of People to Reduce Impaired Driving Everywhere.

"The beverage industry contributes a lot of

money to government coffers. People are dying and legislatures are not doing anything about it.''

"The industry is aiming at young people," says Mintz, "they don't even deny it anymore." He cited one recent ad campaign, Labatt's Blue Zone, as particularly "troublesome.''

Launched last July, the campaign is designed to make Labatt's Blue the "cool" brand among beer drinkers between the ages of 18 and 24, reported an article in the Oct. 3 issue of *Marketing* magazine.

"We wanted Blue Zone to be very hands-on, to let the kids discover it," the campaign's account manager says in the article.

Edward Stewart, executive vice-president of Labatt Breweries of Canada Ltd., says the brewer has no intention of luring underaged drinkers.

"This is a highly competitive industry and there are people of young – but legal – drinking age who do like to drink beer," says Stewart.

Counters Mintz: "If a 19-year-old is watching (these ads), then so is a 15-year-old."

Mintz says the intensive marketing aimed at youth is especially disturbing in light of recent federal statistics suggesting that about 50 per cent of Canadian teenagers now begin drinking at age 16, compared with 25 per cent in 1971.

Studies show a quarter-million teenagers are considered high-risk drinkers, and teen drunk-driving accidents are at a dangerously high level.

Braced for the attack, the Canadian alcohol industry has been arming itself with numerous studies suggesting there is no link between advertising and alcohol consumption levels.

"They (the studies) have shown just the opposite: that there is no impact on over-all demand," R.A. (Sandy) Morrison, president of the Brewers Association of Canada, said in a recent speech.

TV STATION PICKETED OVER BEER COMMERCIALS

A small group of students picketed in front of CITY-TV's headquarters Saturday to protest airing of Labatt's Blue Zone beer commercials.

Seven students, all members of Students Against Drunk Driving, said CITY is being "irresponsible" in showing the ads on MuchMusic programs without accompanying them with drinking-driving messages.

LABATT'S SAYS IT WON'T STOP 'BLUE ZONE' ADS

By Nomi Morris

Labatt's Ltd. has no plans to cancel its "Blue Zone" advertising campaign in response to a request from federal Health Minister Jake Epp.

"We don't accept the thrust of Mr. Epp's comments," said Dr. Edward Stewart, a Labatt's vice-president.

The ads feature many young people in bar and nighclub settings, dancing and enjoying themselves.

In a letter to Marketing magazine, Epp accused Labatt's and other breweries of making "a deliberate and insistent attempt" to promote beer drinking among young university students.

He urged breweries to adopt "a more ethical approach" to beer promotions.

Epp contested the beer industry's claim that advertising seeks to win drinkers over to particular brands, rather than recruit new drinkers.

Epp said the campaign is aimed "at young drinkers aged 18 to 24 years, although 18-

year-olds cannot legally consume alcoholic beverages in Ontario and some other parts of the country."

"We deny vehemently that we are trying to appeal to anybody under the drinking age," said Stewart.

When asked about a Blue Zone promotion in bars and on campus, he confirmed it was a follow-up campaign for the Labatt's "Blue" brand, aimed specifically at young people.

"We are trying to sell our brand of beer to those eligible to buy it . . . we'd certainly prefer they drink Labatt's," said Stewart.

He said Blue Zone television ads were approved by both the Canadian Radio-television and Telecommunications Commission in Ottawa and the Liquor Licence Board of Ontario.

ADS, HEADLINES CRITICIZED FOR MOCKING MENTALLY ILL

Mental health advocates in Manitoba say they're fed up with newspaper ads and headlines that makes jokes about the mentally ill.

"I don't think we're being sensitive," said Jim Fisher, the Canadian Mental Health Association's public education [chairperson] for Manitoba.

Newspaper headlines and ads regularly use derogatory humor about the mentally ill, Fisher said at the recent annual meeting of the association's local branch.

He illustrated his point with slides of clippings from the Globe and Mail and the Winnipeg Free Press.

The slide show kicked off a year-long, $35,000 education campaign against mental illness stereotyping.

Fisher said throw-away phrases such as "mad as a hatter," upset him. He also pointed

to an advertisement for Krazy Kelly, a Winnipeg electronics store, that talks about "going insane" over price cutting.

The jokes are harmful because they reinforce existing discriminatory stereotypes of the mentally ill, said psychologist Harvey Miller, Manitoba president of the association.

As a result, mentally disturbed people feel stigmatized and lose hope in a potential recovery.

'MISLEADING' FOOD ADS WIN ROTTEN APPLE AWARDS

A TV advertisement comparing the virtues of Aero chocolate bars with those of milk has won the top award for misleading information about nutrition from the Quebec Corporation of Professional Dietitians.

The ad, which won the dietitians' Rotten Apple Award, shows Africans dancing in a tropical forest while comparing Aero with milk.

"The ad implies that Aero is such a good source of milk that it could replace milk as a food," Louise Desaulniers, president of the 1,200-member corporation, said.

It was the second time in three years that Rowntree Mackintosh Canada Ltd., the maker of Aero bars, has won a Rotten Apple.

In 1984, Rowntree was cited by the dietitians for another Aero ad showing two Inuit comparing the bar with milk.

Rowntree officials were not available for comment about the latest award.

Runners-up for this year's Rotten Apples were Kellogg Salada for a TV ad suggesting that Pop Tarts are a nourishing food and the Canadian Sugar Institute for magazine ads implying that sugar is good for children, the association said.

FOLLOWING THROUGH

Read the following article "Bugged by advertisements? Here's How to Complain." It talks about a code of ethics for the advertising industry and demonstrates that the consumers can have a powerful voice in directing advertising if they know how to follow through on their reactions.

SUGGESTED APPROACH

Step 1

Read the article and build on your previous discussion about controls by deciding on the merits of having a Code of Advertising Standards.

Step 2

Follow-through by selecting a current television commercial or a magazine ad (either individually or in groups) that offends in some way, and write a letter of complaint to the Advertising Standards Council. (Make sure your complaint is clearly indicated and that you specify what action you would like taken.)

BUGGED BY ADVERTISEMENTS? HERE'S HOW TO COMPLAIN

....

By Joan Irwin

Almost everybody has opinions about television commercials, and not all of them are flattering. Only a few weeks ago grown men at *The Star* were counting the raisins in their breakfast cereal boxes in an effort to find out just how big (or small) that scoop is that supplies "two scoops of raisins." The commercial, of course, didn't say. The scoop could have been the size of a jigger or a measuring cup.

Let the buyer beware, or if you prefer, *caveat emptor*. Whatever the language it's a reasonable approach for any consumer to take. If there aren't enough raisins in the cereal the buyer can switch to another brand and register a mental black mark against the company that put out the under-raisined brand. "Two scoops" is deliberately vague but being vague is a long way from being deceptive.

I suppose an occasional truly deceptive commercial makes it to air, though it's hard to imagine how considering the number of federal and provincial laws that have to be complied with. The Canadian Radio-television and Telecommunications Commission (CRTC) still plays a role in approving broadcast commercials, but not quite as active or far-ranging a role as it once did before the voice of deregulation was heard in the land.

In addition to legislation, the industry itself has supported a self-regulating organization for many years which enforces a code of advertising standards that has been revised and updated regularly since 1963 when it was first published.

The Advertising Standards Council (ASC) of the Canadian Advertising Foundation is funded on a voluntary basis by advertisers, media and advertising agencies and is responsible for developing and administering the industry-endorsed codes of ethics.

Cynics will by now be saying, "Oh sure, I can just imagine how tough *that* code would be. It's just a public relations gimmick to con us into thinking the ad game has a conscience. Those guys will do anything they think they can get away with."

Crass and Tasteless

Maybe some of them will try, and certainly some of them will make TV commercials that are crass, tasteless, abrasive, insulting, manipulative ... you name it. We're not discussing personal taste: You may like what I loathe, and vice versa. The ASC codes are concerned with such things as accuracy and clarity, the use of research and survey data, honesty in testimonials and guarantees, and other specific standards and practices in areas such as advertising for children and advertising of feminine sanitary protection products.

In the case of the latter two categories, the commercials must be cleared by ASC committees before they're accepted by stations, and the Broadcast Code for Advertising to Children has been made part of licence agreements by the CRTC.

The Code of Advertising Standards is surprisingly (to me at least) tough and uncompromising in tone, and it's available to anyone who asks for it. So are the codes that cover particular forms of advertising, which include: advertising directed to children; advertising feminine sanitary products; comparative advertising in food commercials; advertising practices for non-prescription medicines and for cosmetics, toiletries and fragrances; and advertising horticultural products by direct marketing. There are also guidelines for the use of research and survey data in comparative food commercials, and guidelines for avoiding sex-role stereotyping.

If you'd like to send for copies of any or all

of these codes, the address is: Advertising Standards Council, 350 Bloor St. E., Toronto M4W 1H5. For French-language versions, it's Le Conseil des normes de la publicité, 4823 ouest, rue Sherbrooke, Ste. 130, Montreal, Quebec H3Z 1G7.

In the general Canadian Code of Advertising Standards there's a section on how to complain. However, if you're inclined to complain without having read the codes, you must do it in writing to the above address. (There are regional offices but it would take more space than I have to list them.)

Contravenes Code

If it's a print advertisement you should enclose it and say why you think it contravenes the code, or what you consider to be acceptable. If it's a broadcast commercial, give the station, approximate time, name of product and any other relevant information, including why you are complaining about it.

Each complaint is reviewed, and if there appears to have been a violation of the code, the advertiser will be contacted by the ASC. If the violation isn't corrected, the subject may be taken to the full council. If that still doesn't get any action the council will notify the media involved that the message contravenes the code, and in that case the media will usually refuse to accept the message.

Since this is a voluntary association of media, advertisers and agencies, the code has no real teeth and depends for its success on consensus and the desire of all concerned to retain public confidence in the standards of the industry. Last year there were 541 complaints (there had been 998 the year before) and about 20 per cent were sustained.

Whatever happens, the complainant will be informed, and all correspondence is handled in a confidential manner.

So there you are. No more kicking the wall in frustration if you should happen upon a commercial that strikes you as downright misleading. Armed with the codes you can become an active and responsible participant in the consumer society. And what's more, you can do it without having to get out of the hammock.

Some Further Follow-through Suggestions

Some of these suggestions may be done as independent study activities, either individually or in small groups or as whole class activities.

- Invite a commercial artist from an advertising company to class to discuss advertising from his or her perspective.

- Select a magazine and analyze the kinds and frequency of ads it prints. You might also wish to write to the editor asking him or her to explain the magazine's policy and how they go about selecting their advertising material.

- Send away for a copy of the Code of Advertising Standards and copies of the codes that cover particular forms of advertising and the various guidelines (as described in the article above) and analyze their strengths and weaknesses in controlling advertisers.

- Locate works that examine the psychology of advertising. Analyze one or two commercials or ads from that point of view.

- Create a television commercial, script it, and videotape it. (You will need to know something about film techniques to do a good job with this project.)

- Organize a debate on the issue of whether or not there should be any controls on advertising. Is a Code of Standards simply a form of censorship? Should advertising be censored?

- Make a selection of "prize-winning" magazine or newspaper advertisements and write a "Foreword" explaining your rationale for selecting these particular ads.

- Organize a debate on the issue of whether or not advertising should be considered an art form.

- Working with your teacher-librarian, locate research that examines the purported effects of psychological and subliminal elements in advertising.

- Select a product that interests you (a car, a stereo, etc.) and compare its "image" as seen through advertising with its product reality as described in Consumer Reports or some other consumer publication.

SOME FURTHER FOLLOW-THROUGH SUGGESTIONS

The Ethics of Using Animals
to Conduct Research

....

FOCUSING IN

Often an issue can be so controversial, so emotionally charged, that the mere mention of it polarizes opinion into opposing camps. Instead of discussion, compromise, and resolution, the issue becomes deadlocked between warring factions, each determined to impose its perspective, its will, on the other.

Any issue that provokes intense emotional response and creates polarized perspectives usually has a strong moral principle or value at its centre. Dealing with such an issue can often be very threatening because it requires us to examine our values and our ethics, the very bedrock which gives meaning and purpose to our lives. For example, think about the kinds of responses and reactions provoked by such contemporary value-laden issues as abortion, mercy killing, capital punishment, and genetic engineering.

Increasingly, however, such sensitive issues are very much a part of our everyday lives, and, therefore, it is crucial that we learn to deal with them in a way that keeps the lines of communication open rather than closing them down.

One such sensitive issue is the use of live animals to conduct research. It often provokes intense polarized reactions because of the moral and ethical questions involved. On the one hand, there are those who are opposed to the use of any animals for any kind of research; on the other, there are those who point out all the benefits that have accrued and will yet accrue from using animals for such research. But does it have to be such an "either-or" issue? Is there not some middle ground that would permit some compromise, some way to deal with this ethical dilemma?

Examining this issue may help you to deal with other sensitive issues by making you more aware of approaches you can use to work toward consensus and resolution, rather than those that end up in deadlock and silence, or worse, outright warfare.

SUGGESTED APPROACH
Step 1

You may or may not have given the issue of using animals to conduct research much thought. However, if you are like most people, you no doubt will have an opinion when you do think about it.

In your personal response journal state your opinion on the use of live animals in research. Then reflect on your opinion by exploring your level of knowledge and by identifying any moral or ethical foundation upon which your opinion is based.

Step 2

Conduct an opinion poll to determine the range of opinion in the class and the general level of information on the topic. In your notebook, write down the number of responses to the following questions.

Opinion Poll

My position on the issue of using animals to conduct research is as follows:

- ☐ I am in favour of the use of animals for research in all circumstances.

- ☐ I am opposed to the use of animals for research under any circumstances.

- ☐ I am in favour of the use of animals for research under certain circumstances.

- ☐ I have no opinion on the issue.

- ☐ I am uncertain how I feel about the issue at this point.

- ☐ Other opinion (please specify) _____

My level of information on the topic may be described as follows:

- ☐ I feel very informed.

- ☐ I am fairly well informed.

- ☐ I know very little about the issue.

Step 3

Tabulate the results and examine the data. Determine to what extent the class is polarized in its opinion and the general information level of the class. Use the data to determine if there is any relationship between people's opinions and their level of information. Speculate on the possible meanings and implications of the results.

Step 4

This may be done as a whole class or small group activity.

Read the following accounts of the uses of animals for various kinds of research. As you read decide which ones you would approve of and which ones you would not, if you had the power to approve such research. After you have made the decisions, reflect on what criteria you were using to make your decisions. Make a list of these criteria in your notebook.

OVERFED BABIES MAY TURN INTO FAT TEENS

By Fran Smith

An overfed infant is not likely to become a fat baby but probably will grow up to be an obese teenager, animal studies suggest.

The research on baboons shows that early overfeeding leads to enlarged fat cells in adolescence, especially among females. The message to parents: Don't shove bottles at babies after they indicate they have had enough to eat.

"I think the take-home lesson is try to let your child self-regulate its food intake," said Dr. Douglas Lewis, an assistant scientist at Southwest Foundation for Biomedical Research in Texas.

Childhood obesity – once viewed as a sign of rosy health – has only recently been implicated in a variety of medical problems. Studies indicate that the child and teen with layers of "baby" fat run higher-than-average risks of developing high blood pressure, high cholesterol levels and high blood concentrations of fatty acids. These are conditions associated with heart attacks, strokes and blood-vessel damage.

In an effort to prevent heart disease, researchers have tried to determine how people become obese. Although some scientists have speculated that chunky babies have more fat cells and will be heavy throughout their lives, human studies have produced conflicting results.

Lewis and his colleagues sought to crack the mystery by deliberately overfeeding newborn baboons. The animals – which develop fat in patterns similar to humans and suffer heart disease at nearly the same rate – are considered good models for what happens in children.

From birth to 4 months, animals in one group got formula portions that were 30 per cent bigger than normal.

At 4 months – the equivalent of one year in a child's life – the baboons were weaned and placed on diets of monkey chow. They were allowed to eat as much as they wanted.

The investigators found that in the first year, the overfed infants grew bigger and faster, but not fatter, than the others. By the time they were 1½, the differences disappeared.

At 2½, however, female baboons that had once been overfed gained more weight than the others. And by 5 – the age of puberty – the overfed females were 39 per cent heavier than their counterparts.

DOLPHINS USED IN SECRET PROGRAM NOT MISTREATED, SAYS U.S. NAVY

By Molly Moore

Navy officials have confirmed that at least two bottle-nosed dolphins in its secret program to train marine mammals to detect underwater threats have died in the last year. However, they denied published reports that the creatures have been subject to abuse and mistreatment.

Navy officials said one dolphin died last month while participating in a research experiment at an underwater weapons testing facility in the Pacific Northwest. They said the other died of pneumonia after being shipped to the Persian Gulf to help provide underwater surveillance of an anchored barge used as a command base by the U.S. military during the Iran-Iraq war. Five other dolphins remained on duty in the gulf until May, officials said.

A former trainer at the San Diego-base where the program is headquartered recently told a convention of mammal trainers that he had witnessed "specific incidents of abuse, weight loss, corporal punishment and damage to animals after transport," the Seattle *Post-Intelligencer* has reported.

The newspaper also quoted two unnamed former trainers as saying some dolphins and sea lions have been blinded or suffered crippling injuries because of poor training procedures and that four dolphins have died in the past 18 months. The *Post-Intelligencer* said anonymous sources also alleged that dolphins were being trained to attack or kill underwater divers.

"In all of our training we use nothing but positive reinforcement," said Navy spokesman Lieut. Ken Ross. "We do not punish mammals for not performing a task; we will reward [them] for a satisfactory performance."

Navy spokesman Lieut. Cmdr. Craig Quigley said the mortality rate of the 240 mammals that have been trained since the program began in the 1960s has been less than five per cent, less than the mortality rate of those in the wild.

Navy officials denied reports that the dolphins have been trained to kill enemy divers, allegations that have surfaced periodically during controversies surrounding the training program.

"We have never trained dolphins to kill," Ross said. "We have never put dolphins in any kind of training curriculum that would cause them intentional injury in any way."

Navy officials said the marine mammals have been trained for numerous undersea tasks, ranging from identifying enemy [divers] and driving them to the surface, as well as for locating submerged mines and other weapons.

The dolphins are trained to attach sensors or acoustical beacons to intruders or underwater obstacles.

MDs DEMAND COMPANY STOP STAPLING DOGS

More than 13,000 doctors have petitioned U.S. Surgical Corp. to stop sacrificing live dogs to train its sales staff on how to use the company's surgical staplers.

"Using live dogs for stapler practice is not the sort of thing that endears a company to doctors," said Dr. Neal Barnard, president of the Physicians Committee for Responsible Medicine.

But the company said only a few dogs were used to train sales people and most were used to train surgeons after a sale was made.

The physicians committee charged that the company kills about 1,000 dogs a year to train its sales force.

The company's Norwalk, Conn., headquarters was the target of a bombing earlier this year.

TESTS SHOW CAROTENE SHRINKS TUMORS

A form of carotene, the substance found in carrots and leafy green vegetables, has been shown to shrink and prevent cancer tumors in the mouths of hamsters, and that might lead to a non-toxic treatment for human oral cancer, Harvard University researchers say.

"It would be wonderful if we could have something that works in humans that wouldn't be as toxic as the current chemotherapy," says Dr. Gerald Shklar of the Harvard School of Dental Medicine.

In one part of the experiment, Shklar, Dr. Joel Schwartz and their associates painted a cancer-causing chemical solution on the pouches found inside hamsters' mouths.

Then, for several weeks, they applied a carotene solution to the same area. They found that the carotene solution reduced the number and size of tumors that could be expected to develop from the cancer-causing chemical.

In the second part of the trial, the researchers induced cancerous tumors by either painting the cancer-causing chemical on the inside of the hamsters' mouths or by injecting the mouth tissue with cancer cells. After tumors formed, they painted them with the carotene solution or injected them with it.

Two weeks later, most tumors had disappeared, the researchers reported in two journals, Carcinogenesis, and Biochemical and Biophysical Research Communications.

"We're cautiously optimistic that it will work in animals other than the hamster," Shklar said.

Shklar, Schwartz and Dr. Diane Suda wrote in Carcinogenesis that carotene could have a cancer-inhibiting effect similar to the effect his team found with vitamin A since carotene is used by the body to produce vitamin A.

HOPE SEEN FOR SPINAL CORD INJURIES

Nerve Cell Regrowth Possible, Researchers Find

By Marilyn Dunlop

Medical scientists may be drawing closer to the day when they can repair spinal cord injuries that now leave sufferers partially paralyzed.

At Toronto Western Hospital, researchers have found that, in animals, nerve cells can be made to grow across a cut in the cord and restore some movement to previously paralyzed hind legs when an electrical current is applied to spur the cell growth.

Fetal Cells

At the University of Ottawa, scientists have devised a way to create a bridge across the gap in a severed spinal cord and give it a new blood supply to speed nerve cell growth.

And at the University of Toronto, a researcher has found that, in nerve cells growing in the laboratory, growth can be enhanced with vitamin A, which mimics an electrical current.

At the University of Miami, scientists are studying transplants of fetal brain cells in rats into the spinal cord and have found they can partially restore lost function.

The doctors cautioned a Canadian Paraplegic Association symposium on spinal cord injury at Carlton Place Hotel last week – some attendees in wheel chairs – that there is no cure for spinal cord injury on the immediate horizon.

But they have disproved the long-held belief central nervous system tissue, once damaged, could not regenerate.

It can, but the puzzle of how to make it do so is just beginning to be unlocked.

Nerve cells produce long fibres called axons to make connections with other cells. Messages between the brain and spinal cord travel by means of these fibres.

A day after a spinal cord is cut, "axons on both sides of the gap are standing at the junction waiting to go like motorcycles lined up for a race," said Dr. Jack de la Torre, associate professor of neurosurgery at the University of Ottawa.

But, he said, for an axon the gap is gigantic.

He creates a bridge over the gap made of collagen, a protein gel, and provides a blood supply by moving over a piece of omentum to wrap around the gap. Omentum is a thin piece of tissue, rich in blood vessels, in the abdomen.

After 90 days, de la Torre said, the spinal cords of animals whose cords had been severed and then treated with collagen and omentum looked almost normal.

Reflex Activity

Ten times as many axons had grown into the gap as in animals in which omentum had not been used. The rate of growth of the axons was "phenomenal" he said.

But in an interview, de la Torre said more needs to be known before the treatment can be tested in patients.

Dr. Ake Seiger, director of basic science for the Miami Project – a program funded by money raised by the family of a football player who suffered a paralyzing spinal cord injury – said transplants of nerve cells into the spinal cord will only work if the cells come from fetuses in the early stages of development.

In his studies in animals, embryonic brain cells have been transplanted into severed spinal cords. Some reflex activity has been restored below the cut, he said.

"But it does not reconnect the spinal cord (below the cut) to the brain. It is a sort of mini-brain downstream. It does not help the brain talk to the spinal cord."

Dr. Michael Fehling, a researcher at Toronto Western Hospital's Playfair Neurosciences Unit, said implanting electrical stimulators on the cover of the spinal cord of paraplegic rats brought about a significant improvement in function in the animals.

Vitamin A acts on periphery nerve cells in the same way as an electrical current, "tremendously enhancing fibre growth," said Dr. Umberto De Boni, of the U of T department of physiology.

FINDING OUT

The following articles examine the issue of the use of animals in research from two opposing perspectives: those who are in favour of using animals for research and those who are against it.

Some of the articles present descriptions that you may find upsetting. However, you will see that the writers have felt such descriptions were necessary to reinforce the perspective being emphasized.

As you read these articles see if you can decide if the opinion, the perspective, is based mainly on a moral, value-based position, or on an information-based position, or both.

The key thinking skills you will develop while working on this topic include identifying and assessing bias, formulating questions of inquiry, planning strategies, solving problems, and predicting and speculating on potential outcomes.

SUGGESTED APPROACH

The following activities could be done by students working in "pro" and "con" pairs, either in a real-life or a role-playing context.

Step 1

Examine the articles and decide which are for animal research and which are against it, and have each pair of readers read the articles that support his or her pro or con position.

Step 2

Take turns reporting the position of two opposing sides. Each "reporter" should articulate the essential position and describe the various evidence cited to support the position. Each listener should listen intently to get a complete picture of the opposite position, repeating to the reporter what he or she has heard.

Step 3

This may be done as a whole class activity, in small groups, or in the original pairs from Step 1.

Now that you are aware of the issue from the two opposing sides, assess the extent to which they are truly opposing sides. To what extent are they opposed on basic moral grounds or on some other basis? Determine to what extent there is, or could be, any common ground that could lead to compromise, or resolution of the issue.

Step 4

This should be done as a whole class activity.

Reflect on the issue as it has been presented and on your discussion. Decide which of the important elements need to be considered when dealing with a sensitive issue. For example, when someone holds an opinion because of a belief or a value, you have to deal with the issue at that level. More evidence simply won't change the person's opinion.

ANIMAL RIGHTS MOVEMENT PLANS DAY OF PROTEST OVER RESEARCH

....

By Barry Kent MacKay

In Canada, the use of animals in experiments is so protected from public scrutiny, so lacking in accountability and so devoid of legislative constraint that its benefits are difficult to evaluate. Quite simply, the public is kept largely ignorant of what is being done and why.

This secrecy has occasionally been penetrated by members of the Animal Liberation Front after they trespass into research facilities and acquire photographs and animal research subjects we would not otherwise know about.

Occasionally the secrecy is broken when a researcher or laboratory technician rejects his profession and publicizes the plight of laboratory animals. Some of the leaders of the animal rights movement once worked on research projects involving laboratory animals.

A third way to learn more about the normally hidden fate of laboratory animals is to examine scientists' own published research papers. . . .

A large number of experiments are never published. Of those that are, many are endlessly repetitive. They undoubtedly add tiny bits of data to the overall sum of human knowledge, but not necessarily to the benefit of suffering humanity. An accumulation of data becomes an end in itself.

In 1980, Dr. Stanton A. Glantz stated in *Circulation,* an official journal of the American Heart Association, that "approximately half the articles published in medical journals that use statistical methods use them incorrectly."

Animal experimentation is no panacea. Drugs dangerous to humans have been given to human patients because those drugs were safe to other species. Potentially beneficial drugs have been kept from people they could help because those drugs have been harmful to some other species.

Although we know better, many of us live lifestyles that we know are potentially damaging to our health but sanction the destruction of millions of animals annually in hope of alleviating the problems we cause ourselves. We actually have to make and enforce laws in order to force ourselves to take such elementary safety precautions as fastening our seatbelts and being sober when driving.

Excessive fats, sugar, alcohol, caffeine, salt and tobacco can cause health problems, but we consume them anyway, and then sacrifice animals to find cures for the injuries and ills we make too little effort to avoid.

Toxic chemicals, for which there are no safe levels of contamination – only varying degrees of risk – permeate our environment, but too often those who sound warnings against them are dismissed as unrealistic alarmists.

Diseases and disabilities resulting from personal habits and environmental degradation, including cancer, heart problems, severe allergies, respiratory problems, birth defects and car deaths and injuries, are epidemic.

Meanwhile, money which could be directed into the development of preventable measures, education and rehabilitation programs is diverted into endlessly repetitive animal experiments. . . .

Animal experimentation has, within an atmosphere of secrecy, become big business, nourished by our fears of pain and death. A massive support industry sells researchers anything from "small mammal emulsifiers" to endangered primates and stolen pets.

Unlike Belgium, Denmark, France, Germany, Italy, Japan, Netherlands, Norway, Sweden, Switzerland, the United Kingdom and the United States, Canada has no national legislation designed to help protect laboratory animals from needless abuse. There are no laws that allow outside observers to make unannounced inspections of laboratories where animals are used in experiments. In parts of Canada, provincial legislation actually prevents humane society inspectors from examining such facilities.

Ignored by Most

The easiest way to handle the issue is to ignore it. Most people do, presumably in the hope that their tax money and charitable contributions are invested wisely and that if animals are sacrificed in laboratories they suffer for the benefit of us and our children – as we are taught to believe, of a superior species.

However, when the secrecy surrounding research on animals is penetrated we find rats being fattened with soft drinks while a large percentage of this superior species of ours is trying to lose weight and a still larger percentage is simply concerned with not dying of malnutrition.

When humanitarians try to make us think of such things on World Day For Laboratory Animals, they will, I believe, be doing so not only in the interest of animals, but also in the interest of our own species.

ANIMAL RIGHTS ABSURD, PHILOSOPHER SAYS

By Jack Cahill

The animal rights movement illustrates the incoherent nature of a moral passion become immoral by virtue of its extremism, according to American philosopher Charles Griswold Jr.

He is among many philosophers and scientists who have discounted one burgeoning animal rights movement as "absurd."

"The absurdity of the 'animal rights' position stems from its assumption that animals enjoy an ethical status equal to humans," Griswold says. "If [humans] and beasts possess the same fundamental rights, it is because [humans] and beasts are equal in the essential respects. This argument is to be rejected because it ignores the ethical consequences of the manifest and decisive differences between us and animals, particularly our capacity for discourse, reason and free will.

"In the name of the laudable quality of humaneness, the animal rights movement prohibits the use of animals for food, clothing and medical experimentation. Thus, research that could save your child's life, or save you from an excruciating disease, is declared unethical. The result is inhumanity toward [humans]."

Scientists insist that, despite technological advances, animals are still necessary for research that provides enormous benefit to both [humans] and animals and that they are treated humanely and seldom suffer pain in laboratories that are regularly inspected for any signs of unnecessary cruelty.

One of the most outspoken of the Canadian scientists, Dr. Bessie Borwein of the University of Western Ontario, says:

"Researchers using animals have contributed enormously to our ability to understand the normal body and to counter disease.

"Animals are and have been involved in the control of diabetes and in all the developments of new surgical techniques for heart disease, brain disease and cancer, for organ transplants, in understanding multiple sclerosis and muscular dystrophy, in the development of antibiotics and analgesics, antimalarial and cancer chemotherapeutic agents, vaccines, pacemakers and on and on.

"The scourges of childhood that afflicted us until recently – diphtheria, whooping cough, polio, red measles, scarlet fever, pneumonia and other bacterial infections – have almost disappeared from our society because of the advent of vaccines and antibiotics developed through both basic and applied experimentation on animals.

"Mental hospitals are very different places since antidepressant and antipsychotic drugs have become available, again after experiments on animals. Significant advances have been made in the prevention and treatment of strokes and some cancers.

"In the history of animal life on earth many species have become extinct through the forces of nature, even before the advent of [humans]," Borwein continues.

"I sympathize very deeply with those concerned to save some animal species from extinction at present, although we might be glad enough to wipe out some terrible insect pests such as locusts that ruin our crops and mosquitos that give us malaria.

"We regularly kill vast numbers of animals for food. Few of us wish to watch the process in abattoirs. We all want the beneficial results of surgery, but many of us could not stand to watch the operations. As long as human lives are considered to be more important to us than animal lives, animals will be used in research.

"There are over 250 animal diseases that are very similar to, or identical to, those that afflict people," she adds. "Animals are appropriate for research studies, and, in general, men, women and children are not.

"It must not be forgotten that research on animals benefits animals as well as [humans] and has resulted in the improvement of the health of livestock, pets and wildlife. The use of living matter, animal and plant, is an integral and inescapable part of biological research.

"Who among us would refuse, especially in times of illness and distress, the countless benefits that have accrued to us from experiments on animals?"

ANIMAL WORSHIP IS A 'DANGEROUS NEW RELIGION'

By Tom Harpur

The room where I do my writing looks directly out on a lake. One morning, not long before the freeze-up, I was startled by a huge splash.

It was as if somebody had dropped a cannonball about 25 metres from shore.

I thought it might be a very large fish jumping or rolling. But suddenly I could see the upward thrusting of powerful wings. An osprey, or fish-hawk, was struggling to clear the water with a good-sized bass in its talons.

As the magnificent bird of prey gained height, it shook itself like a dog retrieving a stick; the sun danced on the cascading drops, on the soaring pinions, and on the wriggling victim.

It was a glorious sight. I had never seen an osprey dive at such close quarters before. As the bird circled towards a distant pine to consume its lunch, I felt the same kind of thrill I knew as a boy on discovering my first song-sparrow's nest.

I was pleased; the osprey, I assume, was quite satisfied. The bass, however, was another question.

Pierced mercilessly by those razor-sharp claws, suffocating, out of its element and destined to be torn apart while still living – what about the torture of its suffering?

What of the countless eons of time since creation during which billions of other creatures great and small have been killed and devoured by their fellow creatures?

Nature, "red in tooth and claw," is unbelievably cruel. It is a world of eaters and eaten almost ad infinitum.

This is something the extreme animal activists – with their extraordinarily romantic and sentimental attitudes to animal suffering – want to ignore completely.

Unfortunately, the omission distorts their entire argument.

So, too, does their credo in which they affirm that human life has no intrinsic value above that of any other living being and that, as a result, there is no justification for using animals in medical research.

Let's be quite clear. The Judeo-Christian ethic, as well as the ethical systems proposed by most western philosophers in the past, are based upon the self-evident truth that our ability to reflect on our experiences and to make moral choices makes us unique in the created order.

There is a major value judgment stated in the belief that we have been made "in the image of God." There is an essential difference between a pup or a monkey and a child.

This does not mean we can treat other species any way we like.

And it is indeed true that our commitment to human values has often led us to the grossest form of hubris in which we try to deny our animal nature, our bonding with all other life forms, and our need to live in harmony with the rest of the planet.

Yet it is one thing to be aware of all this and to act to remedy excesses.

It is quite another to fly into the extremism currently threatening to close down all our medical research with animals.

For some of these fanatics, animals have totally replaced people as objects of loyalty and love. For others, the so-called "animal rights" movement is a new kind of religion – a cult of animal worship.

As with the extremists in the anti-abortion camp, this mentality holds considerable potential for violence. Some of it has surfaced already in attacks on various research facilities. Some of it takes the form of hate campaigns and attempted character assassination.

With this in mind, it is urgent that not just doctors and scientists, but all reasonable people everywhere, speak out in opposition to this dangerous, world-wide phenomenon.

Put the emotionalism to one side. Virtually every major health advance can be shown to have developed from basic studies involving animals. That means, among other things, that the extension of the average lifespan from 45 years in 1900 to 70-plus today has been largely dependent on animal research.

As Dr. John A. Krasney, professor of physiology at State University of New York, Buffalo, has warned:

"If the current antivivisection movement is allowed to continue unchallenged ... the steady advance of medical science would cease. All hope of cures for cancer would be lost. . . ."

I hate to think of any living organism suffering or dying before its time. But, to be consistent, the activists would have to reorganize all biology so that every creature was a vegetarian.

There is something much worse than cautious, humane animal experimentation. It is the sight of someone you love in agony or dying because a cure for his condition has not yet been found.

A STRONG RESPONSE TO USE OF ANIMALS IN MEDICAL RESEARCH

By Tom Harpur

Ralph Waldo Emerson once wrote: "To be great is to be misunderstood." There is, however, an easier way to come up with the same result. All you have to do is attempt to be a communicator of ideas, especially in the field of morals and religion.

I discovered this first when I was a preacher – twice each Sunday.

Shaking hands with people after the services was a real revelation. There were always those who would say: "Great sermon, only I wish my husband (son, mother-in-law, or whoever else needed improvement) had been here."

Others, however, would stun me with their remarks about what they thought I had said. What they heard and what I thought they would hear were two different realities.

In journalism, you experience this phenomenon on a vastly larger scale. Some people are so keen to have their own prejudices confirmed they read them into nearly everything. They do the same with their hopes, fears, and hates.

A recent column on the use of animals in medical research (Jan. 4) provides an excellent example of what I'm getting at.

I put forward what I thought was a reasonable, compassionate argument for "cautious, humane animal experimentation" where possible cures for chronic diseases such as cancer are at stake.

This has unleashed a vehement response – a lot of which exhibits the very extremism and fanaticism I was criticizing.

Some of it was sadly funny. One woman, in a three-page, single-spaced, typewritten missive, vigorously attacked what she called my defence of "the right to slaughter" the innocent.

"During the past 20 years, I have lost three members of my immediate family, and my mother-in-law. In all but one case I had the most extraordinary difficulty in shedding even a few tears.

"If my older brother dropped dead this very instant, I would feel that the world had become a considerably healthier place. . . .

"Yet last January, when my dear old dog died, I could not stop weeping, nor can I to this day whenever I think of her – which is often.

From her I received nothing but loyalty, affection and companionship. She never criticized, carped, nagged, smoked, complained (though for many years in poor health), drank, ingested illegal drugs . . . or in any other way contributed to the pollution of the planet. . . ."

Much of the mail was abusive. But I was more interested in the extent of misinformation and falsehoods firmly held as though they were knowledge – even by some of the most level-headed protesters.

A young man, who says he has had first-hand experience in an American research facility, was hotly opposed to animal experimentation in the search for cosmetic purposes. I, too, am totally opposed to this frivolous, wanton sacrifice of other beings just to sell mascara and lipstick, just as I am against all use of animals in war or other military research.

But, he went on:

"I have never heard of any impartial, let alone compassionate, policing being practised anywhere at any research institution. It is naive to assume that scientists will police scientists. Can you really vouch for the 'cautious, humane animal research' in your bafflingly absolute defence of current intemperate research?"

This truly astonished me. I know there have been some terrible things done in the name of science in the past, but to believe and tell others that most laboratories are void of policing and to imply that untold cruelties are going on in them is a pernicious untruth.

I have inspected typical medical research facilities. I have seen the care given to the animals and the measures taken to ensure there is no unnecessary pain. For example, the animals operated on to perfect transplants of human hearts and other organs are given all the preliminary sedation and ongoing anaesthetic used on human patients.

I have met with and talked to scores of

medical specialists who rely on animal experiments for their innovative techniques in healing.

Their chief aim in the laboratory is the avoidance of suffering for any animals being used. These are caring, intelligent men and women – and they are watched and checked by several policing bodies.

To the many who wrote saying there is no reason to believe that medical experimentation with animals has "anything whatever to do with our extended lifespan" I can only say: "You haven't the foggiest notion of what you're talking about. The hard facts prove otherwise."

Summing up, to hold that it is morally right to use some animals, under certain conditions, in medical research is not to say or imply that animals have no rights; nor is it to bless cruelty in any form.

In most ethical dilemmas there is no clear choice between good and evil. Instead, it is one between two evils, a lesser and a greater. I agree with those who are convinced it is a lesser evil to experiment with animals than to allow human beings to continue under the curse of chronic pain and disease.

TESTS ON ANIMALS CRUEL, OUTDATED, COMMITTEE TOLD

Animals are being blinded, tortured and killed in outdated and unnecessary tests, a Queen's Park committee has been told.

Dr. Neil Barnard, chairman of the Physicians Committee for Responsible Medicine, told the Standing Committee on Resources Development yesterday the doctors committee strongly supports Bill 190. The private member's bill seeks to amend the Animals for Research Act, and regulate the use of animals in tests for levels at which products become toxic and irritating.

He and others told the committee they oppose the current testing of cosmetics and household products on animals in such tests as the Draize test, which involves administering harmful substances to animals' eyes, and the Lethal Dose 50 test, in which harmful substances are force-fed to animals until half the subjects die.

Sought Hearing

"How much mouthwash has to be fed to a dog before it will die?" he asked. "This is not science!"

Bud Wildman, MPP for Algoma, requested the scheduled hearing on his Private Member's Bill 190. The bill is designed to prohibit such tests. "It specifically sets forward that tests related to biomedical research would not be restricted," he said.

But Ronald Calhoun, executive director of Partners in Research, a pro-science group, said the bill's real issue is not product safety, but has a "hidden agenda to open up the attack on biomedical research through the legislative route."

Bessie Borwein, an associate dean of research at the University of Western Ontario, sided with Calhoun. She said the use of cosmetics and consumer products in some circumstances becomes a medical issue, as such products are often absorbed, inhaled, swallowed, put in one's eyes and so on.

Animal testing is a regrettable but unavoidable necessity, she said.

'Wise Use'

"The big divide is between that small group in society who would ban all use of animals by [humans], and the great majority, who wish to see the wise use of animals," she said. "Product safety at present requires the wise use of animals."

Cali-Allen Dixon, whose salon advocates "beauty without cruelty," said there are a variety of products on the market that do not involve cruelty to animals, products that are "practical and humane."

There are 11 alternatives to the current Draize and LD50 tests being addressed, said Dr. Harry Rowsell, the executive director of the Canadian Council on Animal Care.

"Let's get on with the validating alternatives and eliminate animals from testing," he said.

Hearings on Bill 190 will continue, but no date has been set.

[*NOTE: At time of publication, Bill 190 was in its second reading in the Ontario provincial parliament.*]

USE ROBOTS NOT DOGS IN THE LAB MD URGES

By Robert Brehl

Medical students can experiment and practise more effectively on computers and robots than on animals, a Washington physician says.

Dr. Neal Barnard, 34, a psychiatrist who founded the Physicians' Committee for Responsible Medicine in 1984, told a seminar yesterday at a Toronto hospital that the medical community must weigh the interests of the animals before using them.

He said students can learn more from computer simulations and lifelike instructional robots than laboratory animals because they're closer to humans in makeup and can be used again and again.

For instance, dogs, goats and sheep continue to be used for training students in emergency airway procedures, he said. . . .

But a simulator made of vinyl skin covering plastic "human" cartilage has been developed and is being used in more and more medical schools, he told about 100 people at Hugh MacMillan Medical Centre.

Barnard was invited to speak by the Toronto Humane Society. Most of the audience appeared to be animal activists; others were hospital staff workers.

Rat Suffered

He became a vegetarian 10 years ago when he saw the agony a lab rat named "Ratsky" went through after developing cancer. He'd let Ratsky out of her cage to play like any other pet and he felt pain as she suffered.

"Any use of animals is hard to defend ethically," Barnard said.

Too often animals are killed needlessly for medical research and training, he said, adding that each year more than 5 billion animals – the equivalent of the world's human population – are killed in the United States for research, training and consumption.

FOLLOWING THROUGH

The last group of articles on using animals for research describe some of the effects of polarization of opinion, pose some further dilemmas, and examine the issue from yet other perspectives. Some situations are threatening, some are worrisome, and some appear downright bizarre.

SUGGESTED APPROACH

Step 1

Read the articles. To what extent do they alter your perspective on the issue? To what extent is information important when dealing with a sensitive issue?

Step 2

Now that you have read a variety of perspectives on the topic, do the Opinion Poll again. Compare results with those of the original poll. Are there any significant differences in responses? If there are no differences, how do you account for this? If there are differences, how do you account for them?

Step 3

Make a final journal entry in which you compare your position at the beginning of the topic with the position you hold now, citing reasons for any change or reinforcement of your original position.

ANIMAL RIGHTS ACTIVISTS USE EDUCATION, VIOLENCE

....

By Jack Cahill

"Animal liberationists do not separate out the human animal, so there is no rational basis for saying that a human being has special rights. A rat is a pig is a dog is a boy. They're all mammals." – Ingrid Newkirk, People for the Ethical Treatment of Animals

There is a powerful, world-wide belief by animal lovers that this statement by one of their leaders is at least partially true and they are prepared to prove their point to the rest of the world through action that ranges from education to violence. . . .

These people are influenced mainly by the teachings of Australian philosopher Peter Singer, whose 1977 book, *Animal Liberation,* invented a new "ism" portrayed as even nastier than racism or sexism. Singer became the guru of "speciesism" which is the crime of treating animals unequally and more specifically denying them freedom from suffering and the right to life.

According to Singer, and now his many followers, if we eat meat, hunt, or accept the benefits of drugs or cures resulting from experiments on animals, then we are guilty of "speciesism."

Instead, he says, we must not interfere in any way with any living creature – right down, that is, to molluscs such as oysters, which he concedes probably can't feel much in the way of pain. It also seems to be okay under the philosphy to kill mosquitoes if they bite you, but there are some followers who claim the keeping of pets like dogs and cats is a form of enslavement.

The philosophy has spread, in interpretations that range from fanatic to loose, from Britain to North America and is gaining ground rapidly now in Australia, New Zealand and Europe, especially West Germany. . . .

The radicalization of local humane societies has become a North American phenomenon. Says Ingrid Newkirk, co-director of People for the Ethical Treatment of Animals: "Humane societies all over the country (the U.S.) are adopting the animal rights philosophy, becoming vegetarian, and working harder to get inside labs."

Other high-profile American humane organizations that have shifted from traditional animal-welfare goals to an anti-research stance include the 50-year-old Animal Protection League, the Animal Rescue League, and the American Society for the Prevention of Cruelty to Animals.

The world-wide movement helping bring this sort of thing about comprises a network of many organizations in which the members often intermingle. Some of these organizations are anxious to use violence in support of the cause. Some will go only as far as civil disobedience, which they describe as nonviolent but including break-ins at laboratories using animals for experiments. And some support only peaceful political and educational methods to enforce their ideals. But they are all linked. . . .

The new animal politics are complex and puzzling and break all the rules. Within the maternal British segment of the movement, according to David Henshaw in a recent BBC broadcast, "you find anarchists all right, but alongside are fascists, life-long conservatives, and people with deep socialist convictions. This is a one-issue movement: What unites the activists is the conviction that direct action – the destruction of property, and even life – is morally justified in a war to free the animals."

Certainly, it's beginning to look like a war in Britain, with a strike rate of 2,000 acts of violence a year, causing more than $12 million in damage – to farms, laboratories, the meat trade.

In four years 16 bombs have been thrown or planted at the homes of scientists and politicians and Scotland Yard has established a special squad to hunt down animal rights extremists. Recently the extremists have been prowling the river banks, pushing fishermen into the water.

In the United States, there have been fewer violent activities, but they are intensifying. In three years the Animal Liberation Front has issued more than a dozen threats of death or violence to individual scientists and has raided 15 research institutions, including two separate raids at the University of Pennsylvania.

The violent activities also are increasing in Canada, where animal rights activists have in recent times broken into the University of Western Ontario's laboratories in an attempt to liberate a baboon; attempted to free animals and issued bomb threats at the University of Toronto; staged a sit-in (dressed as cats) at a meeting of the Canadian Association for Laboratory Animal Science; clashed with security guards at Connaught Laboratories in North York, and claimed responsibility for a series of attacks on Toronto slaughter houses, fur stores and even a Kentucky Fried Chicken outlet, causing about $20,000 damage.

Almost miraculously, or because the animal activists operate with great skill and care, nobody has been killed in any of their illegal forays, but there is now great fear among some of the more moderate members of the movement . . . that somebody will soon, creating a harmful backlash against the cause.

U OF G CITED FOR "TORTURE" OF ANIMALS

By John Roe

Cruel and needless scientific research is being conducted daily on animals in laboratories at the University of Guelph, an animal rights activist charged Thursday.

Denouncing all animal research as "torture" and "mutilation," Mike Schwab, president of the Canadian Vegans For Animal Rights, clashed verbally with a number of U of G students and faculty who had travelled to hear him speak at the University of Waterloo.

"We have to keep people aware of the holocaust going on in the labs, in the environment, in butcher shops and slaughter houses," Schwab, a Toronto chartered accountant told the crowd of about 85 people, his voice shaking with emotion. . . .

Schwab, an outspoken vegetarian, told the audience all animal research is "barbaric" and scientifically unnecessary and, zeroed in on Guelph – which has large populations of experimental animals at its agricultural and veterinary colleges.

Relying on what he called "verbal confirmation of abuse" at U of G, Schwab said: "There's a tremendous amount of cruelty to farm animals there. They're trying to produce the perfect cow with growth hormones. . . ."

Schwab also accused the university of trying to cover up its treatment of animals and said the university has refused to let other animal rights groups tour its facilities.

"They won't open the doors, they refuse to let us in," Schwab said.

In a telephone interview later Thursday evening, Dr. Ron Downey, U of G's director of animal care services, defended the university's record of animal treatment and said no animal rights group has ever asked to tour the laboratories.

"I'd be glad to show anyone around if they turned up," Downey said, adding that a special university committee conducts weekly inspections of the laboratories to ensure humane treatment of animals.

He said there is "no cruelty" in using the growth hormone which helps increase milk production. Likewise, while admitting veterinarians place holes in the sides of cows to observe digestion and learn about the value of certain feeds, he said the operation causes "no discomfort" in the animals.

"We're not at a point yet where we can get away from animal research," Downey said. "As a veterinarian, I wish we could."

At the Waterloo meeting, veterinary students and faculty supported their university's record and angrily defended the need for animal research.

The evening started when Schwab showed a grim videotape that showed how the University of Pennsylvania researchers in 1983 deliberately inflicted brain damage on baboons to learn more about automobile and sports-related head injuries. . . .

But few in the audience with scientific backgrounds believed the film accurately portrayed the kind of experiments that go on in Canada.

One U of G faculty member called Schwab's examples of abuse "cheap propaganda." Others disputed Schwab's statement that diabetics don't need insulin – which is produced from animal pancreases.

Schwab countered with the accusation that some research animals are killed without first being anesthetized. He said animal research could easily be replaced by studying tissue cultures and using computers.

"He used a few isolated instances to generalize about all animal research," second-year veterinary student Morris Belanger contended. "It doesn't wash – we learn from animal research.

"You minimize the damage on humans by using animals. If they were going to try a drug on my child I'd like to see them try it on an animal first.

But not everyone in the crowd disagreed with Schwab's views.

"You seem to think animals are objects," Michelle Duff, of Kitchener told the students. "They're living, breathing things with feelings. If it's acceptable to raise animals in cages, why isn't it acceptable to put people in cages? We have to learn to share the world."

VOLUNTEERS, TOYS IMPROVE LIFE FOR RESEARCH ANIMALS

By Daniel Melanson

The University of Guelph is getting high marks for its treatment of research animals.

It's here that the care of animals on the cutting edge of both veterinarian and medical science are monitored by "the best operating animal care committee in Canada."

That's the assessment of Dr. Frank Flowers, director of assessment for the Canadian Council on Animal Care (CCAC) which toured the university this week in a visit it makes only once every three years.

Animals, like the very rare Specific Pathogen Free colony of cats in the Animal Research Centre at Guelph are kept in complete isolation from other animals, their environment completely controlled.

But they're attended to by university students and animal technicians, as are all the animals, and are even visited by volunteers who "socialize" with the cats.

Cows used in respiratory virus experimentation by Dr. Peter Conlon are raised as calves in the building, have toys, and actually enjoy the company of people. "I think (the toys) do make a difference in their attitude towards people," he says.

Cows are fed hay rather than pellets because of the benefits it has on their behavior and dogs are walked as many as three times a day by volunteers.

According to animal care workers, a happier animal not only means a better treatment of research subjects, but leads to good research results as well.

Animal handlers at the university not only ensure the optimum health of their research subjects, but are encouraged to socialize the animals with humans.

The results are not only humane, but research data is better because bad environment complicates the experiment results, says Denna Benn, Director of Animal Care at the university. A happier animal has less stress and will therefore produce consistent test results and less variability in the results also means fewer animals are needed.

Until "all the answers are known" CCAC panel members agree that animals will be needed in research to serve as research models for studying disease in humans.

For example, Dr. Anne Croy, who has developed an immune-system deficient mouse, has a worldwide demand for her animals for use in AIDS research.

Of the 100,000 animals that go through the university every year over 80 per cent of them are fish or chicks.

But all levels of species are protected from neglect or abuse by a network of animal care officials. The university is inspected by animal care groups on the municipal, provincial and federal level.

"What hurts for a horse, hurts for a monkey, hurts for a fish," says Benn.

"Just because they don't make a noise and are not furry doesn't mean they don't feel pain," says Dr. Hugh Ferguson, who is trying to discover the cause of "the commonest disease in today's fish farms," a disease so common it does not have a specific name.

Beginning with 10,000 trout fry, the experiment proceeds until the fish develop the naturally occurring bacterial gill disease, at which point it is ended.

During the 26 years of his private practice, Flowers saw "more abuse and misuse than I've ever seen in all the institutions in Canada combined."

The most critical animal care body is actually often the institution's own animal care committee, says Benn. The U. of G.'s committee is made up of members from the humane society, the philosophy department, a graduate student and a person from every college, says Ed Bailey, committee chairman.

An institution's animal care committee will often create "a mountain of paper work (for researchers) . . . taking three weeks to complete," says Benn. But it helps ensure that any experimentation is absolutely necessary.

The myth of a "diabolical" researcher is not really a myth at all says Bailey. "It can happen and it did happen," at one time but with an active animal care committee the chances of it happening now are very small, he says.

An abused animal is "extremely rare now," says Dr. Ron Greenwood, a panel member of the CCAC. Neglect or ignorance of what the animal needs, is the more likely cause of concern, he says.

Animals are used for research only when necessary. "People will move away from animal research the instant they can use a better technique," says Flowers.

1,000 LAB ANIMALS FREED BY U.S. ACTIVISTS

A group identifying itself as the Animal Liberation Front claimed responsibility for setting two fires yesterday and freeing more than 1,000 animals from three research facilities at the University of Arizona. Thirty of the mice freed carry the disease cryptosporidium, which can cause severe diarrhea.

CHIMPS GET CONDO AFTER AIDS RESEARCH

Chimpanzees at the forefront of the fight against AIDS have their own pension fund and soon they'll be living in luxury condominiums, complete with televisions and exercise equipment.

The chimps are used in experiments by the Southwest Foundation for Biomedical research in San Antonio, where they are injected with acquired immune deficiency syndrome and hepatitis viruses.

While both diseases are deadly to humans, the chimps are apparently immune to them, making them ideal research subjects.

After "working" for three to five years the chimpanzees, which often live to be 50, are retired. Zoos won't accept them because of the viruses so the research foundation looks after them.

In addition to a $1.7 million pension fund to ensure their welfare in the future, $63,000 condominiums are being built for the chimps, equipped with exercise sets and 19-inch color televisions, said Jorg Eichberg, a veterinarian and microbiologist at the foundation. "At this moment, we have no plans to build a golf course," he said.

RESEARCHERS WORRY ABOUT DECLINE OF WORLD'S CHIMP POPULATION

By Wendy Leopold

Just as science is documenting remarkable similarities between the thinking and behavior of humans and chimpanzees, [humankind] may be on the verge of destroying its brother species.

That cruel irony emerged from a four-day conference in which most of the world's leading chimpanzee researchers for the first time compared notes in person on 25 years of chimpanzee observation and study.

The symposium was organized by famed researcher Jane Goodall, who has spent more than a quarter-century living among the chimpanzees of Gombe in Tanzania.

Environmental changes and the desirability of chimpanzees for bio-medical research were both given as factors pushing the animals toward extinction.

"Chimpanzees fascinate us because they are so very like us," said Paul Heltne, director of the Chicago Academy of Sciences, sponsor of the conference, which, he said, brought together for the first time world scientists to compare long-term observations, not data based on relatively short periods of study.

"You cannot drop in to one of these life history situations where animals live for 20 to 50 years and think you're going to find out about (how they live and learn) in a one- or two-year study," Heltne said.

"There is a great deal in chimpanzee relationships to remind us of our own behavior," Goodall said, "more perhaps, than many of us would care to admit."

Indeed, there is a controversy among scientists over the relationship between [humans] and chimpanzee, with some scientists strongly holding the view that [humankind] is unique among Earth creatures.

But at the conference the emphasis was on similarities ranging from childlike game playing to adult-like politics.

This became readily apparent as participants in session after session reported on different aspects of chimp behavior. For example:

- Chimpanzees use tools, such as a stick to fish for biting driver ants or to force carpenter ants out of their nests in tree trunks.

- Chimp children play in much the same way and some of the same games as human children. For example, they make faces just for the fun of making faces, they have their own form of blindman's bluff, hiding their eyes with their forearms and they apparently enjoy spinning their bodies until they get dizzy, just as small children like to turn and turn.

- Chimpanzees gently chew and then swallow the leaves of a shrub known to have medicinal properties, leaves also used by [humans] for ailments like stomach aches.

- They not only can learn sign language but, having learned it, can transmit it to other chimpanzees.

- Their leaders are politicians, earning their right to rule not through mere strength but by enlisting group support, by coalition building.

- Chimpanzees demonstrate love, compassion, regret, frustration, and most other emotions known to [humanity].

"I would be surprised if we have any emotions that they don't have," said researcher Frans de Waal, a primatologist at the University of Wisconsin.

"They are closer to [humans] than a zebra is to a horse, a dog is to a fox or a chimpanzee is to a gorilla," said Geza Teleki, a George Washington University anthropologist.

In one study of communication and cognitive skills, chimps outperformed researchers when both were asked to reconstruct a symbol composed of geometric shapes after it was flashed on a screen.

Controversy has swirled around claims that chimps using sign language were doing little more than aping their human teachers. To answer the challenge, Roger and Debbi Fouts, researchers at Washington State University, gave up signing to their four sign-language-trained apes for two years.

In that time, remote videotapes showed that the chimps not only continued signing to themselves but also transmitted sign language to a new member of their study group with no previous exposure to sign language. After two years, the chimp had acquired 63 separate signs from his adopted family.

But for all this research, the overlying problem was one of survival.

The population of wild chimpanzees has been seriously reduced by the destruction of habitat, as [humans] demands more space for living and agriculture, and because the chimpanzee is hunted for biomedical research.

"For every one chimpanzee that makes its way into Western laboratories, another five are destroyed," said anthropologist Teleki, who led a session on conservation.

While it is impossible to tally precise numbers of chimpanzees in Africa – the only continent on which they are found naturally – Teleki estimated that there are only a few thousand in East Africa (where they are relatively well protected) and between 15,000 and 20,000 in West Africa.

"Each time we have a medical crisis here at home, suddenly the animals in Africa become far more severely threatened," said Teleki, who was selected to head a committee to win endangered species protection for chimps in the United States. Currently they carry the less restrictive threatened species label.

SOME FURTHER FOLLOW-THROUGH SUGGESTIONS

Some of these suggestions may be done as independent study activities, either individually or in small groups, or as whole class activities.

- Expand your Opinion Poll to get a larger and more varied sample. It could include teachers and/or parents, and/or younger or older students. If the poll is to be conducted with a larger group, it might be significant to determine if results are connected to the knowledge level, age, sex, or some other trait of the respondents.
- Based on the results of the wider sample, design an educational campaign to raise people's level of information and awareness about the issue. (It could take the form of an advertising campaign, a television show, etc.)
- Invite an animal rights activist and/or a medical researcher into your school to debate the issue. (Note: This would have to be handled very carefully, with "ground rules" being laid out beforehand.)
- Update your information on the issue by going to the vertical file in the library to see what recent articles have been written. Report to the class on your findings.
- In consultation with your teacher-librarian, locate information on any laws that govern the use of animals in research, either federal or provincial, or both. Report this information to the class.
- Visit your local animal shelter or Society for the Prevention of Cruelty to Animals group and find out whether or not they provide unwanted animals to research institutions and, if so, under what circumstances.
- Make arrangements to tour a local research facility that uses live animals in their work and report back on your findings.
- Find out which cosmetic company or companies use live animals to test their products and write a letter asking for further information.
- Debate the issue as to whether or not unclaimed pets should be made available to research facilities.
- Select another sensitive issue to discuss as a group. This needs to be a timed activity. The object is to keep the discussion going to the point of compromise and consensus rather than end up bickering and deadlocked. Each group should have an outside observer who records behaviours, actions, and statements that lead toward the objective and those that block it. At the end of the timed period, the observer should report to the group. Reporters should then report to the whole class to synthesize observations and information.

Applying the Concepts: Working Through Topics Seven, Eight, and Nine

The last three topics in *Exploring Perspectives* turn your learning over to you to direct and shape. They continue the three-stage learning format used in the previous lessons (that is, FOCUSING IN, FINDING OUT, and FOLLOWING THROUGH), but you are invited to devise the suggested approach and the specific activities in each stage. Now that you have had a number of opportunities to work through the thinking processes that are necessary to deepen and broaden opinion, you should feel confident about using these processes on your own. As well, now that you have applied a number of different thinking strategies, you are ready to use them and adapt them to achieve a reasoned opinion concerning each of these topics. In other words, you are now ready to demonstrate your independence as learners and your depth as thinkers.

The following is a list of some of the key thinking processes that you have applied in various combinations as you worked through the previous topics and that you will be applying as you work through these last two topics:

- identifying main ideas
- summarizing and outlining ideas and information
- finding similarities and differences among a variety of ideas and perspectives, categorizing and prioritizing
- identifying and assessing bias, including language bias
- locating and organizing information

161

- formulating questions of inquiry
- generating hypotheses
- exploring possibilities, seeing new relationships, patterns
- setting goals, objectives
- defining issues, problems
- planning strategies for solving problems, carrying out decisions
- planning a sequence of activities
- identifying and applying criteria in order to assess
- predicting and speculating on potential outcomes
- selecting evidence to support opinion
- weighing evidence to assess its worth
- finding inconsistencies and incongruities
- applying and adapting information to new situations
- justifying opinion

TOPIC

seven

Family Ties–Binding and Otherwise

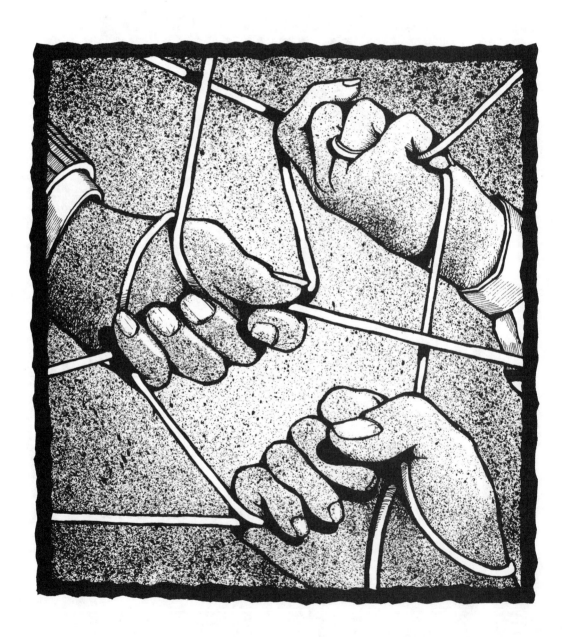

FOCUSING IN

A great deal of research supports the idea that most adults spend their lives trying to live up to or rebelling against the expectations put upon them when they lived within their family unit. It is difficult to imagine anything more intense than the close, daily relationships that surround us as we grow up.

Each of us has had a unique experience within this family structure, and according to research, this experience has been very powerful in molding us into the kind of adults that we become. In fact, a great deal of research indicates that these early relationships set the pattern, both consciously and unconsciously, for all our relationships throughout our lives.

The material collected here focuses on the two most powerful family relationships: that between parents (or adult caregivers) and children, and that between and among children (siblings) within the family unit. The significance of these relationships is verified by the fact that a great deal of the literature and drama written in all cultures focuses on them. In fact some psychologists go so far as to say that all human activity can be explained in terms of these family relationships. "The child is the father of the man" is a paradox which is as true today as it was when the statement was first made, only today we would re-word it to state "The child is the parent of the adult." In other words, if you want to see why you are the way you are, examine your family relationships.

SUGGESTED APPROACH

Any of the following activities, either individually or in combination, would help you individually or as a group to determine your initial thinking, your initial opinion, on the topic of "Family Ties."

- personal journal writing
- thought-webbing (brainstorming)
- conducting a survey
- developing a list of questions you would like answered or areas you would like to investigate
- making a list of all the possible positive elements and a list of all the possible negative elements of family living, from the perspective of various family members of roles
- your choice

•••

FINDING OUT

The following material examines family relationships in terms of the two key relationship patterns within a family: the relationship between parent(s) and child (children), and the relationship between siblings. It looks at these two patterns from a number of perspectives.

SUGGESTED APPROACH

Select a method of dealing with the material that will deepen your knowledge of family relationships and broaden your perspective on the topic.

THE MAN WHO FINDS HIS SON HAS BECOME A THIEF

Raymond Souster

Storming into the store at first angry
at the accusation, believing whole-heartedly
the words of his young one who's told him
I didn't steal anything, honest. . . .

Then somehow becoming calmer, seeing
    that anger
won't help now at all, listening even
    patiently
as the others' evidence unfolds so painfully
    slow.

Then gradually seeing that evidence
almost as if inch by inch tightening around
    the neck
of his son, at first circumstantial, then
    gathering sure damage,
until he's aware of guilt's ugly odour seeping
into his nostrils, choking and horrible to
    bear.

Now suddenly feeling sick and alone and
    afraid,
as if some unseen hand had slapped his face
again and again, for no reason whatsoever;
    desperately wanting
to rush out into the street, the night, the
    darkness, anywhere to hide
the pain that must show to these strangers,
and even more than that, the fear, his
    fear. . . .

It must be like this.
It could hardly be otherwise.

WARREN PRYOR

Alden Nowlan

When every pencil meant a sacrifice
his parents boarded him at school in town
slaving to free him from the stony fields,
the meagre acreage that bore them down.

They blushed with pride when, at
    his graduation,
they watched him picking up the slender
    scroll,
his passport from the years of brutal toil
and lonely patience in a barren hole.

When he went in the Bank their cups ran
    over.
They marvelled how he wore a milk-white
    shirt
work days and jeans on Sundays. He was
    saved
from their thistle-strewn farm and its red
    dirt.

And he said nothing. Hard and serious
like a young bear inside his teller's cage,
his axe-hewn hands upon the paper bills
aching with empty strength and throttled
    rage.

FIRST LESSON

··

Phyllis McGinley

The thing to remember about fathers is,
  they're men.
A girl has to keep it in mind.
They are dragon-seekers, bent on
  improbable rescues.
Scratch any father, you find
Someone chock-full of qualms and romantic
  terrors,
Believing change is a threat –
Like your first shoes with heels on, like your
  first bicycle
It took such months to get.

Walk in strange woods, they warn you about
  the snakes there.
Climb, and they fear you'll fall.
Books, angular boys, or swimming in deep
  water –
Fathers mistrust them all.
Men are the worriers. It is difficult for them
To learn what they must learn:
How you have a journey to take and very
  likely,
For a while, will not return.

WHY DO TEENS AND PARENTS FIGHT?

··

By Nancy J. White

The stand-off lasted for three months. The mother insisted her 16-year-old daughter end her friendship with another girl who had dropped out of school and was doing drugs. The daughter refused. It soured their home life.

"I considered the girl a terrible influence," explains the mother. "But my daughter's answer was that I didn't have faith in her. We went on and on with it. At times I'd forget about it and let it go, but then something would trigger me and I'd be off again."

Finally the mother decided that all her harping wasn't doing any good, and she dropped the subject. The daughter eventually stopped seeing the girl on her own.

"You try to keep 10 steps ahead of a teenager," says the mother resignedly, "but you just have to settle for five."

Parents and teenagers have probably been at each other since time began. No doubt pubescent Cain argued with Adam and Eve.

But today's world seems so riddled with risks. Parents want to protect their kids from drugs, AIDS, and alcohol. And they worry about the heated competition to get into university and land a good job.

Teens, meanwhile, are pushing for more freedom, struggling to find their own identities as young adults.

"Everyone is rubbing each other the wrong way," says Diane Marshall, assistant clinical director at the Institute for Family Living in Metro. "I tell kids they have to learn to handle their feelings in creative not destructive ways. And I tell parents they also have a task – to learn to separate from their kids."

One theory is that teen-parent spats are part of our evolutionary past, that they are necessary conflicts triggered by puberty to push youngsters out of the nest and start their own families.

Necessary or not, they can be hellish. One 15-year-old boy has been stealing from his family. He's taken money, clothes, even the family car for joyrides. He won't go for help and he won't talk about it.

The family now keeps valuables, including pocketbooks and car keys, locked up. "There are days I feel like saying, 'You leave or I'll leave,'" says his mother. "And there are times at work I just don't want to come home. But we'll all live through it."

Trouble doesn't start simply because a youngster hits puberty, says Bernard Stein, head of adolescent psychiatry at Sunnybrook Medical Centre. He explains that although parents say things started to go bad when the child became a teenager, the personality framework was already there.

"We don't see a Jekyll-and-Hyde transformation," says Stein. "The issues are more serious so the fights are greater. The relationship between parent and child is on the same track, but more so."

What does happen at puberty is that the youngster starts to grapple with all the bodily changes as well as issues of sexual and personal identity.

"The teen has an adult's body but still a kid's mind," says Teri Kay, director of family and child services at Jewish Family Services. "They haven't learned that freedom comes with responsibility."

In many families, adolescence is no more intense than other periods, says Peter Crosby, director of program services at Huntley Youth Services. But in those families where it is, fights usually boil down to two issues: limits to what teens can and can't do and achievements.

"Often there's this issue of underachieving," explains Crosby of the cases at the agency. "After years of getting ready for life, there's the clear expectation of doing something."

For Pam Shulman, 17, and her mother, Lynda Freedman, school is the touchy topic. "We fight about my marks, my interest, my initiative–all that stuff I lack," says Pam. "Mom lectures me about once a month."

She says she realizes how frustrated her mother gets with her, but she still gets angry at the lectures. "My teeth are clenched and my brain is pulsing. I'm like, 'Get away from me.'"

Freedman says she regrets that she never went to university when she was young, so she wants her daughter to have the chance. "She reminds me of me. We want to make them what we wish we were," says Freedman. "She's an ideal kid. She's just not cut out to be academic. It's not her problem, it's mine."

Crosby says that teens will sometimes unconsciously create a smokescreen to take the pressure off. For instance, they'll be very rude, so that everyone will be preoccupied with the rudeness instead of the school grades.

Teen-parent fights can sometimes be aggravated by separation or divorce. A teen angry at one parent may think he can simply move in with the other parent, so issues never get resolved, says Rhonda Freeman, director of Families in Transition, part of the Family Service Association.

While adjusting to a new step-parent can be sticky at any age, it's especially tough with adolescents who are more verbal and more used to the way things were, adds Freeman.

Extreme teen-parent fights may be symptoms of other problems, such as physical abuse, alcoholism, drug abuse, or severe economic stress, says Crosby. "If you have two or three factors feeding in, it's more likely the conflict won't get resolved easily."

Different families fight in different ways, depending on their temperaments. While some keep up a cold steely tension, others explode with yelling and screaming.

In some, it's a war of words. "Teenagers are very good at getting you embroiled in an argument when all you meant to say was 'no,'" says one mother. "They're very talented. It seems to come naturally to them as soon as they turn 13."

Rather than resort to heated verbal volleys or constant carping, the experts advise negotiation, sharing some power.

"There is no easy advice, no ABCs," says Anna Crews, a family therapist with Oolagen Community Services. "But you do need to confirm a teenager, to believe in his [or her] trustworthiness and capacity to assume responsibility. When you don't, you have the logical consequences."

For Goody Teachman-Gerner, who has four teenagers, the key is compromise. For example, her son who recently got his driver's licence wanted to take the car up to the family cottage, but she didn't think he was ready for that.

Rather than fight about it, they agreed that he'll drive on out-of-town trips with her in the car to observe him. When she feels confident in his ability, he can take the car to the cottage.

"If you're reasonable, they're reasonable," says Teachman-Gerner.

Privacy is a particularly common teen battle cry. "They have to have their own space," says Marshall of the Institute for Family Living. "Teenagers will stake their human rights on it."

At her house, the compromise was that her teenage son would clean his room once a week and not leave food in it. In return, the door would be kept shut and she wouldn't enter.

Les Fleischer, a social worker at the Adolescent Medicine Unit at the Hospital for Sick Children, says that parents need to "strike a happy medium" in setting up rules for teenagers.

"If they're not firm enough, the teens will be out of control and not feel loved," says Fleischer. "But if they're too firm the teens will rebel."

Another family counsellor tells of a teenager who was stealing from her parents. It turned out that she was angry at the very strict rules appropriate to a much younger child. When the parents eased up on her and negotiated curfews and other rules, the stealing stopped.

One father had terrible fights with a daughter after she turned 14. "My wife and I tiptoed around the house with our stomach in knots," he says. "We got attacked whatever we said."

They joined the Association of Parent Support Groups in Ontario, which has self-help groups that teach parents to change their behavior to better deal with their children.

"A year and a half ago, we couldn't sit together and have a meal, it was so tense," says the father. "Now we can sit and talk."

□

TIPS FOR FAMILY FIGHTING

....

While there is usually no one simple solution to teen-parent fights, experts offer the following advice:

- Teens need to feel respected. Let them make some choices about non life-or-death issues.

- Be clear and consistent about rules, and the consequences of breaking the rules.

- Establish fair-fighting guidelines. Diane Marshall, assistant clinical director of the Institute for Family Living, suggests setting out some parameters ahead of time, such as no name-calling.

- Agree on time-outs. Marshall suggests postponing an argument when everyone is tired or hungry. For instance, before dinner is a terrible time for a fight because everyone is already cranky. A volatile teen or parent may find it useful to take a walk around the block to cool off and then return to a discussion.

- Be creative. Some parents will make an appointment, marked on the family calendar, for a discussion of curfews or whatever issue is in dispute. "It's like a board meeting and makes the teen feel he really counts," says Judith Kennedy, executive director of Parents in Transition, a support group for parents who are having difficulties with their children.

  To avoid harangues, some families will place a timer on the table, limiting each side to a certain number of minutes to talk. This, says Kennedy, helps everyone focus on the main issue.

- Get help. There are self-help groups for parents, such as the Association of Parent Support Groups in Ontario or Parents in Transition.

Peter Crosby, director of program services at Huntley Youth Services, says professional help is needed if: the parent or child feels that the conflict will go on forever; the parent starts thinking of the child as bad and can't see his [or her] good points; physical violence becomes part of the arguments; the teen is seriously underachieving in school and/or seems consistently depressed or anxious.

▭

IMMIGRANTS FACE SPECIAL PROBLEMS RAISING CHILDREN

....

Child-rearing techniques that worked in the old country aren't always effective in Canada. Ask Catherine Ip.

The 40-year-old mother of two immigrated to Vancouver from Hong Kong with her husband, Youn Chan, a property appraiser, 14 years ago. They have two sons, Chung Yan, 13, and Chung Ming, 11.

"When children are born here, they grow up in a different kind of atmosphere from their immigrant parents," says Ip, an academic adviser at Vancouver Community College. "There are dilemmas we face that Canadian-born parents don't because of our cultural differences."

As Canada becomes more multicultural, social service groups are recognizing the special challenges that face immigrant parents raising children in a new environment.

Courses are being offered in Cantonese, Mandarin, Hindi and Punjabi that address the problems of raising children in a bicultural home.

"A second dimension is added when things are done differently than what you are used to," Ip says. "We have to make a great effort to modify how we look at things."

For instance, Ip says Canadian schools train children to think for themselves rather than abide by certain standards, which is the Chinese way. The challenge for Chinese parents is to find a compromise between their children's independence and parental desire for discipline and respect.

"I am more liberal than my parents, but my kids complain that I'm still too strict. My kids say, 'You can't force me to do this because I don't want to.' The way my parents brought me up, I was not allowed to say that."

Shashi Assanand is a family and crisis worker at Oasis, a Vancouver social service group for Indo-Canadians. In her counselling with immigrant families, parenting is a big issue.

She says parents who have lived here for many years with Canadian-born children have as many difficulties as newly arrived immigrants who can't speak English.

Dating among teenage children is a source of conflict for many Indian immigrant families because arranged marriages are the norm in Indian culture, Assanand says.

Also, in India, children are expected to stay in the extended family, while Western culture encourages them to learn self-reliance and leave the family unit during young adulthood.

Family Services of Greater Vancouver also recognizes a need for courses addressing the special needs of ethnic parents. Eight-week courses in Hindi, Punjabi, Cantonese and Mandarin are organized whenever eight to 10 people express an interest, says Susan Silver, director of family life education.

Success, an agency serving the Chinese community in Vancouver, also runs parenting courses.

To help improve parenting courses, Ita Margalit is co-ordinating a project sponsored by several social service groups to compile material available across North America on parenting programs in Punjabi, Farsi, Spanish, Vietnamese and Khmer (the language of Kampuchea).

BY ORDER OF BIRTH

Personality Traits Vary From First to Last Born

By Louise Dickson

"I was the test pilot," says Mike Glunta, an eldest child.

"I was the scrappy middle child," says Becky Rynor, the third of four children.

"I was certainly a mistake," says Max Keeping, the baby of the family.

Eldest.

Middle.

Youngest.

Since the 1950s when Dr. Alfred Adler, a friend and student of Sigmund Freud, pioneered research on the effects of birth order, the subject has fascinated parents and researchers.

According to Lucille Forer, author of *The Birth Order Factor* (PaperJacks Ltd.) 21 of the first 23 American astronauts were first-born or only children.

Her book, like others on birth order and personality, has been devoured by a trivia-loving public. *The Birth Order Book* by Kevin Leman, (Dell, $5.50) has sold more than 107,000 hardcover copies in North America since its publication in 1985.

Ottawa counsellor and mother of three Maxine Gilbert says a child's position in the family affects his [or her] personality.

Gilbert, who led a packed parenting workshop on the subject at the Ottawa Valley Preschool Association spring conference, believes birth order is an important factor which influences a person's behavior and character.

"From the moment of birth, the child acts, thinks and feels in response to his world," says Gilbert. "A child uses his situation to create his style of life and his characteristic traits."

No two children born into the same family grow up in the same situation, she says. The environment changes with each additional child. Parents are older, more experienced and usually more easy-going with each child. Often, too, they are more prosperous.

Another factor in a child's development, says Gilbert, is the number of years between children.

If the age difference between two children is more than five years, it is likely the eldest will develop the characteristics of an only child because he [or she] has spent his [or her] first five years without siblings. If no other children are born, it is also likely the second child will develop the characteristics of an only child.

A child's development in the family will also be influenced by favoritism, a move, step-parents, a sick or handicapped child, being the only boy or only girl or living with grandparents.

As the eldest of six children, Mike Glunta, host of the afternoon radio show on CHEZ 106, shouldered a lot of responsibility from an early age.

He made supper for his younger siblings and helped them with their homework. Because Glunta's father wasn't around a lot in the early years, his mother came to rely on him.

"Mum gave me a little responsibility and I responded positively, so she gave me more. I knew the responsibility of earning my mother's trust. For other people, this would have been an incredible burden."

But looking back, Glunta believes the early responsibility prepared him for the high pressure job he does today.

"I've always been self-confident. I think it's a positive after-effect of handling responsibility and earning trust as a child. I believe in myself and that helps in the kind of job I'm in."

As the big brother, Glunta was careful not to ruin it for the other kids.

"If I did it – go to a movie or a dance or whatever – and it turned out OK, the other kids could do it too."

Glunta laughs when he says his mother used to stay up and wait for him to come home.

"By the third or fourth child, she would ask if they came home at all," he jokes.

One of the disadvantages of being the eldest, says Glunta, was he worried about the others so much, he didn't think about himself very much. It was only after he moved away from home that he started really thinking about his own life.

Today, he still likes to think his siblings will come to him if any of them have a problem.

Local CBC reporter Becky Rynor, a middle child, used to drive her parents crazy at the dinner table.

"I called it debating. They said I was arguing. I pushed the limit as often as I could.

It's an attention-getting tactic. You push the boundaries more to see how far you can go."

While she was growing up, Rynor felt a curious mixture of admiration and jealousy of her older siblings.

"My older sister was very beautiful. I wanted to be like her, but I almost resented her."

Rynor also experienced the typical feelings of being lost in the middle.

"You always feel the oldest is the favorite. My brother was the only boy and my youngest sister was the baby. 'Oh, poor me,' I used to say, 'nobody loves me."

Rynor, 28, believes being in the middle has made her more outgoing and aggressive –characteristics that fit in well with her demanding job.

"Being a middle child makes you less afraid. You're not as easily intimidated."

Rynor is also impatient. She began writing for radio while she was in high school and chose to go to college rather than university because she wanted to get into the working world as soon as possible.

Popular CJOH television host Max Keeping was born in Grand Banks, Nfld., the youngest of three children.

His mother was 41, his sister 14 and his brother 12 when he was born.

Because of the big age difference between Keeping and his siblings, he combines some of the characteristics of a youngest child with the independence and assertiveness of an only child.

Although he doesn't remember a great deal of his early childhood, like many youngest children he recalls being very close to his mother.

"Because I was so unexpected, she made a great deal of me. She was older than most kid's mothers and she spoiled me. I was totally spoiled."

Keeping's father and brother were sailors. In those days in Newfoundland, says Keeping, you could either go to Toronto or do the manly thing and go to sea.

"I looked up to my older brother who went to sea against my mother's wishes. He could do anything. I wanted to be like him and go to sea with my father."

Sadly, Keeping's mother died when he was nine. A year later, his older brother was washed overboard.

During the summer after his mother died, nine-year-old Keeping lived by himself. He says he spent the entire summer cooking french fries for everyone in the neighborhood.

Keeping was rescued from his haven of independence by his older sister who took him under her roof in Halifax and became a second, stricter mother.

"Some of that strictness shaped the rebelliousness in my personality," says Keeping.

To get away from the heavy discipline, Keeping finished high school by the time he was 15, started working full-time and moved out on his own.

"I had a certain streak of independence fostered by my father and brother."

PARENTAL TREATMENT SHOULD MATCH CHILD'S POSITION IN FAMILY

The following lists of major characteristics exhibited by eldest, middle and youngest children, and parenting tips were compiled by Ottawa counsellor Maxine Gilbert and presented at a recent parenting workshop at the Ottawa Valley Preschool Association Conference.

The Eldest

Studies show parents have more interaction with and pay more attention to their first born. A strong bond of attachment between a child and [his or her] parents is established early.

First borns are generally breastfed longer, rewarded more often and over protected.

Because they are the centre of attention they learn to expect praise. They're also more likely to set too high standards and to worry about themselves and others.

They want the best, try to give the best and expect the best.

Because they're usually expected to give help to siblings and parents, eldest children are more likely to have difficulty accepting help. Studies also show eldest children are punished more because parents tend to be more anxious and strict with their first born.

The eldest child is more likely to be self-confident, sensitive, ambitious, persistent, a good listener, independent, studious, autocratic, conscientious, individualistic, a leader, shy in the early years, a perfectionist and outspoken.

Tips for parenting the eldest child: Don't improve on everything [he or she] says and does. Go easy on reminders of what [the child] should be like.

Make sure the child knows exactly what the rules are.

Recognize the child's place in the family. The child should be accorded some privileges to go along with the additional responsibility.

Don't make first borns instant babysitters.

Don't pile on more responsibility as they get older.

Don't be too quick to jump in with corrections when they are reading to you.

Middle Children

Middle children occupy a no-man's land.

They have difficulty knowing who they are because they are denied the privileges of the eldest and the freedom of the youngest. Middle children are starved for attention and love being around people.

They tend to do things just to get attention and often develop a "Hey, remember me?" behavior pattern.

Much of a middle child's motivation stems from resentment. They are more likely to develop an "I give up" attitude and relapse into a self-pitying state in a stressful situation.

Middle children seem to be more vulnerable to peer pressure, become victims quite easily and can be social butterflies.

A middle child is more likely to be unconventional, unpredictable, moody, competitive, dissatisfied, laid-back, easy going, less academic, a class clown, fun-loving, placid and social.

Tips for parenting middle children:

Take special care to make the middle child feel special. Ask for [his or her] opinion once in a while.

Set up special privileges he or she can count on having or doing every day or every week.

Make a special effort to give your child a new item of clothing, rather than hand-me-downs.

Make sure the family photo album has [the middle child's] share of pictures.

The Youngest

The youngest child usually has the easiest time. They get the most attention and the most freedom because parents are usually less demanding or pushy.

The youngest child is more likely to be given the least amount of responsibility. Often they don't learn the meaning of responsibility and have greater difficulty accepting it as adults.

If a youngest child has been waited on in childhood, [he or she] may expect to be waited on as an adult.

The youngest child is also more likely to have difficulty adjusting to a true partnership in marriage because they're not used to the give and take required.

The best thing you can do for a youngest child is to hook [him or her] up with a first born.

A youngest child is more likely to be clever, charming, ambitious, imaginative, egotistical, ingenious, innovative, self-centred, spontaneous, a non-conformist, demanding, creative, lazy and restless.

BEING SECOND BEST SCARS CHILD FOR LIFE, AUTHORS SAY

Decades ago, the Smothers Brothers made a comedy routine out of the notion that their mom always liked Dickie best.

That's what a lot of sibling rivalry is about, of course: Youngsters vying against each other for their parents' attention, and love. Imagining slights where there are none. Keeping score.

But for some children, parental favoritism is more than a "notion," and definitely not a comedy. Their parents really did love one child "best" – and it wasn't them. That is a burden that they carry into adulthood, and beyond.

Sad Stories

Adele Faber and Elaine Mazlish, authors of the best-selling book *Sibling Rivalry*, have heard too many sad stories from the adult children of parents who didn't hide their feelings of favoritism.

Good parents love each child for what's best in them, for who they are as individuals. There's a difference between that and the father who easily announced, "I'm the first to admit that my boys are good kids, but my daughter is the light of my life."

That kind of attitude can cause great pain not only for the man's sons, but also for his life's alleged "light."

One woman wrote Mazlish of her mother's preference for a sister. When she was a child, she said, her family visited a resort hotel. Another mother was there with two children.

"Which one is your favorite?" the woman's mother had asked the other mother, while the children were all in the room.

The woman remembered how terrible she felt, knowing that the other mother would also ask her mother which one was her "favorite."

That young girl knew that her mother would whisper it was her sister she loved best. She had already heard her mother telling her sister, "I love you more than anything in the world."

"I wish my mother loved me half as much as she loves my sister," the woman wrote.

Another woman wrote Mazlish and Faber of a sister who had died at age 14. "The other sister was adored," says Faber. "Even now, as an adult, the woman feels that the wrong sister died, that it should have been her. That's some permanent burden of unworthiness that so many people carry."

Parental favoritism is the raw material of epic tragedy, say Mazlish and Faber. After all, Cain slew Abel after the Lord showed more "respect" for Abel's offering. And Joseph's brothers threw him into a pit in the wilderness because their father loved Joseph more and gave him a coat of many colors.

"Favoritism is not supposed to exist, and parents feel terribly guilty when they feel it," says Faber.

Nasty Truth

"There's always that child who performs in a way that makes you so proud," she says. Not only proud of the child, but proud of yourself for having produced him [or her], and raised him [or her].

The way things work, this child often has a brother or sister who makes the parent feel like a poor parent, who gets on the parent's nerves a lot, who may even turn the parent off – at least at some time during his life.

If parents feel guilty about feeling favoritism, they feel even guiltier about expressing it.

And that's as it should be. Favoritism may be a nasty truth. It may help a parent to acknowledge it to himself [or herself]. But those feelings are dynamite. They need to be kept locked away. Acknowledging them and realizing how dangerous they can be makes it easier to cool our passions, say Mazlish and Faber.

It's also important for parents to be aware of these feelings so that they don't go in the opposite direction and be rotten to the child they adore.

Parents should avoid comparisons like the plague they are, say Mazlish and Faber. Most all parents know they should not compare one child to another, making distinctions between the "good student" and the "bad," or the "pretty one" and the "plain."

But without thinking, they'll declare one child the athlete of the family, or the artistic one. That may give other children the impression that those areas are closed to them.

The best way to praise – or scold for that matter – is with specifics.

Instead of telling a youngster what a great artist [she or] he is, you can say, "This is a very interesting picture of a tree," a parent can say. "I really liked the colors you used."

When it comes to feelings of parental favoritism, honesty is not the best policy.

SIBLING RIVALRY

It's Impossible to Eliminate, But Effects Can Be Minimized

....

By Gary Nyp

Simply defined, sibling rivalry is the term for competition between brothers and sisters, competition for their parents' favor, recognition, attention, time, affirmation, affection and whatever else they have to offer.

Fighting is the most obvious manifestation of that competition. But sibling rivalry takes on other, perhaps more subtle, characteristics.

Kathryn Bosch, family life educator with K-W Counselling Services, says it may take the form of a child convinced she must work exceptionally hard to gain her parents' favor. Another child, considering negative attention preferable to no attention at all, may decide that if "Johnny is good at being good, then I'll be good at being bad." Another may become particularly adept at manipulating his parents. By telling tales – true or false – he may learn to gain the favor of his parents while, at the same time, denigrating his sister in their eyes.

In any case, sibling rivalry is nothing to be taken lightly. . . .

A child who grows up feeling he or she isn't given equal time and attention by his parents, for instance, may develop gradually increasing feelings of rejection, low self-esteem and worthlessness, Bosch explains.

Such children may grow up believing "everything's my fault;" "everybody would be happier if I wasn't around;" "nobody appreciates me. . . ."

Some, convinced of their worthlessness, will grow up afraid of taking risks or setting their sights too high. Others may become the classic over-achievers, those who excel not for themselves, but to prove themselves to others.

The good news is that while sibling rivalry can't be eliminated, it can be minimized. . . .

Coping effectively with sibling rivalry, Bosch says, is much more than intervening in their numerous squabbles – although that is certainly a part of it.

Really, Bosch says, it is based on a parenting approach that treats each child as unique, respects their rights, and recognizes that each has different needs at different times.

It is also a realistic approach that realizes sibling rivalry is inevitable, even in the best of families, and needs to be dealt with the moment [parents] bring that second child into the world.

But many cling to a fantasy that their children will always love each other, be perfect playmates and seldom, if ever, feel such things as anger and jealousy toward each other.

Bosch says such parents tend to negate any evidence of sibling rivalry. The child who approaches them with negative feelings toward a brother or sister is generally refuted with expressions like 'don't be ridiculous,' 'that's not true,' 'you don't really feel that way.'

Take, for instance, the toddler who comes to his mother wishing his baby sister had never been born.

"That's not true," a taken-aback and somewhat defensive mother might respond. "You love your sister. . . ."

The child goes away, feeling put down, not to mention increasingly negative toward the sister who has become the bane of his once-secure existence.

In other words, it's very important to listen to children and acknowledge their feelings," Bosch emphasizes. "We have to remember that everybody has different needs at different times . . . We also have to remember that feelings aren't good or bad, they just are. It's how we deal with them that counts."

Parents, Bosch says, have to realize that the oldest child is bound to feel some degree of jealousy, anger, resentment, fear and uncertainty when a younger sibling enters the picture. Rather than negating those feelings, which only exacerbate them, the most constructive approach is to acknowledge them. . . .

Chances are, children who have their feelings acknowledged, whatever their age, will be left with the feeling 'I count.' More secure in that knowledge, the negative feelings he or she has toward the sibling are more likely to diminish.

Bosch recommends parents make relatives aware as well. Often, she says, relatives will focus their attention on a newborn while all but ignoring older siblings.

To minimize feelings of resentment and jealousy toward the infant, a parent might tell relatives 'I want to avoid a sibling rivalry problem, could you make sure you spend some time at least talking to (the older child)?'

Bosch recognizes that children who feel shortchanged by their parents may only be operating on their perception of the situation. But whether their concerns are perceived or real isn't the issue – if the child feels shortchanged, parents need to acknowledge that feeling and, through listening and open-ended conversation (the kind which doesn't allow for yes and no answers), find solutions.

Bosch says one of the key ways to minimize sibling rivalry is to avoid comparisons between siblings. Unfortunately, many parents, often as an attempt to motivate, do just that.

"In rare cases, comparing siblings may work (as a motivator)," Bosch says. "But in general it either creates an 'I'll never be good enough' attitude (in the child asked to measure up to the standards set by a brother or sister) or one of defiance – 'if she's this, I'll be that'."

Bosch recommends, for instance, that report card time be made up of private sessions between parents and child.

"One child may have a better report card than the other," she explains. "But the only one who needs to know that is you."

Trying, as many parents do, to treat each child equally is another approach that invariably backfires. While parents may have the best of intentions, the children involved will invariably have individual needs and talents overlooked.

"What would be more helpful is to give each child unique treatment," Bosch says. "The approach should be 'what is the special need you have?' How can we give encouragement and recognition to each child for what (he or she) has to offer as an individual?

"If a child comes to you and asks 'Who do you love best?' do you say 'I love you all equally?' Or do you say 'I love you for being you?' . . . It's a good idea to reaffirm the (individuality) of each child by noting qualities, talents or actions (unique to them) you appreciate and admire."

There are many subtle things parents do to unwittingly compound the competition between siblings. Many, for example, expect an older child to share everything he has whenever a younger brother or sister demands it.

But the child, Bosch says, has the right to decide when and if to share what belongs to him.

Parents also need to remember that they chose to bring another child into the world. Which means that older siblings shouldn't be expected to assume too much responsibility for the care of that child.

Siblings can be asked to help out once in awhile, Bosch says, but it's often a good idea to offer them a type of tradeoff – 'If you spend some time helping to look after Johnny now, I'll have more time later to spend with you. . . .'

And what, you ask, about fighting? How do you handle, and hopefully, minimize that?

There is a way. Indeed, Bosch says ... squabbles, if handled constructively, can actually help [siblings] learn some extremely important skills, such as problem solving, the kind of negotiation in which both people come out feeling like winners, and the ability to recognize and express feelings.

Typically, we yell, take sides, lecture, judge – sometimes we even dish out the same treatment one sibling may inflict on another, just to teach them how it feels. But these are nothing more than band-aid solutions which cover up the underlying feelings behind the fighting.

The goal, whenever dealing with a pair of fighting siblings, is to help [siblings] understand why they're fighting and come up with a win-win solution, Bosch says.

☐

FOLLOWING THROUGH

SUGGESTED APPROACH

Step 1

Select one aspect of family relationships that interests you. Go to the library and find more information on the topic, either in the vertical file or through consultation with the teacher-librarian. Don't neglect the potential source of material in autobiographies, biographies, fiction, and poetry.

Step 2

Plan a follow-through activity in consultation with your teacher, either as a group or individually.

TOPIC

eight

Censorship–Yes? No?
or Somewhere in the Middle?

.... FOCUSING IN

The issue of what people should read, hear, and see is one that has a long history. Since ancient times, it has provoked intense interest, concern, and, at times, restrictions and outright censorship.

The issue of censorship provokes strong responses, as you will see from the readings that follow. You may wish to supplement this material with more recent material from other sources. You may wish to focus on one area, such as television, advertising (see Topic Five), textbooks, or films, particularly if any of them is of current local concern.

Once again, this topic turns the learning over to you to direct and shape. You should still be using the approach taken in the previous lessons, but the specific FOCUSING IN, FINDING OUT, and FOLLOWING THROUGH activities are largely up to you. Since you have worked through the process of learning and used a variety of approaches and applied many thinking patterns in Topics One to Seven, you can now apply and adapt activities to suit your own learning needs and learning styles. You are once again ready to become independent learners able to select and organize information and apply various skills in thinking through an issue.

Suggested Approach

Select an approach that will determine what you, both individually and collectively, think about censorship – your level of emotional involvement and your present level of information.

. . . .

FINDING OUT

The following material on censorship examines the issue from a number of perspectives. You may wish to supplement it with material from the vertical files in your resource centre or from current newspaper and/or journal articles.

Suggested Approach

Select a method of dealing with the material in order to develop an overall perspective on the issue.

DID YOU KNOW?

··

1. The following authors have had at least one book banned or challenged somewhere:

   Ernest Buckler
   Geoffrey Chaucer
   Brian Doyle
   Alexandre Dumas
   William Faulkner
   William Golding
   Ernest Hemingway
   Victor Hugo
   Thomas Jefferson
   Margaret Laurence
   Dennis Lee
   Jack London
   Arthur Miller
   W.O. Mitchell
   Alice Munro
   Eugene O'Neill
   J.D. Salinger
   William Shakespeare
   John Steinbeck
   Mark Twain
   Kurt Vonnegut, Jr.

2. Mickey Mouse was banned in Nazi Germany in 1933, in the Soviet Union in 1936, in Yugoslavia in 1937, in fascist Italy in 1938, in East Germany in 1954.

3. The Indiana State Textbook Commission was asked by one of its members to remove *Robin Hood* from a list of approved texts on the grounds that he was a communist – robbing the rich to give to the poor.

4. Rev. Thomas Bowdler revised and edited the plays of William Shakespeare to take out the bloodshed and eliminate the tragic endings. His *Family Shakespeare* published in 1818 resulted in the coining of a new word – "bowdlerize." Look it up in your dictionary.

5. In 1885, the town of Concord, Massachusetts, banned Mark Twain's *Huckleberry Finn* as "trash and suitable only for the slums."

6. The following writers were killed because of their spoken or published words:

   Socrates, the Greek philosopher, in 399 B.C.
   Lucan, the Roman poet, in 65 A.D.
   Maxim Gorky, the Russian author, in 1936

7. The following books have been burned:
   The *Analects* of Confucius – in China, 240 B.C.
   The works of Ovid, Boccaccio and Dante – by Savonarola in Florence in 1497
   The works of Martin Luther – by Pope Leo X in 1521
   The works of John Milton – by the English common hangman in 1660
   The works of Voltaire – in France in 1734
   Ulysses by James Joyce – in several countries, 1932-33
   The Grapes of Wrath by John Steinbeck – by the public library of St. Louis, Missouri, in 1939
   All of Hemingway's novels, along with the works of Erich Maria Remarque – in Nazi Germany, 1933
   (from *The Literary Life and Other Curiosities*, R. Hendrickson. New York: Viking Press, 1981)

   And did you know that Beatrix Potter's *Peter Rabbit* was ordered removed from schools in London, England, on the basis that it was concerned only with "middle-class rabbits?"

BANNING BOOKS ALWAYS A BATTLE OF WORDS

....

By Lindsay Scotton

The organizers of this year's Freedom to Read Week couldn't have wished for a better – or worse – example.

As cries for banning of British author Salman Rushdie's controversial novel *The Satanic Verses* echo around the world, the fifth annual Freedom to Read Week kicks off in Canada.

The event . . . has been put together by the Book and Periodical Development council and the Canadian publishing industry to protest censorship in this country and around the world.

The list of books that are banned, restricted, censored or quietly destroyed every year is long and ranges from the sublime to the ridiculous. . . .

Banning books is an ancient and dishonorable tradition dating back to ancient Athens, where the philosopher Socrates was executed for his writings. In Rome, the Emperor Nero burned the books he didn't like, while Caligula went further and burned the authors.

In modern times, few authors are called on to pay for their words with their lives. But this week, Iran's Ayatollah Ruhollah Khomeini called on devout Muslims to murder Rushdie, whose book has been called deeply offensive to Islam.

The novel ranges in its transgressions from mere bad taste, prostitutes in a brothel take on the names of the prophet Mohammed's wives, to a fundamental questioning of the basic tenet of the faith.

"I'm not aware of any other such edict issued by a (modern-day) head of state" said Libby Scheier of the Writers Union of Canada.

"But there are various ways in which books are banned, or withheld, or censored around the world and in Canada, and most of them are quiet," Scheier said.

Some teachers simply won't teach books that might be controversial, fearing complaints from parents, she said. Librarians may quietly take books off shelves, or keep them on a special, out-of-the-way rack. Bookstores may not carry controversial works and publishers may not publish them.

"There aren't too many people who want to stand on principle and get embroiled in a big mess," Scheier said. "Those who do are heroes and heroines."

And there is also a more subtle form of censorship at work, "Self-censorship," she said.

"The kind of creative pall the threat of death throws over you when you sit at a typewriter . . . it's very effective."

"If I were a writer in the midst of a book about Islam, I'd think twice about what I put in it," she said. . . .

Usually when books are banned in schools or libraries, it's because of pressure from parents or a local religious group.

Pressure is put on school trustees to remove books from the lists of works that are considered acceptable for teaching.

If the library board or school doesn't agree, citizens can ultimately appeal to the courts to have books banned.

Canada's Criminal Code makes it illegal to publish anything that is obscene, promotes hatred or spreads false news.

Last year, Toronto publisher Ernst Zundel was sentenced to nine months in jail on a conviction of spreading false news. Zundel published pamphlets and articles disputing the Holocaust and Nazi extermination of Jews.

Promoting Hatred

Thousands of books, magazines and videos are seized at the border every year by customs officials, who have the power to stop any work that is suspected of being obscene or promoting hatred.

"The really controversial and complex issue has to do with sexism, racism and religious persecution," Scheier admits.

Whatever the Western world may think, it's clear that Rushdie's *The Satanic Verses* is considered hate literature in the world of Islam.

"There are some justified claims that some works may be discriminatory," admits Scheier, who adds that legislators should always err "on the side of civil liberties."

"Once you put the structures to ban books in place, someone will always use them," she said.

COMPUTER PROGRAMMED TO BE SEXIST

....

By Louise Brown

What's in a name?

Some respect, at least.

So you'll be horrified at the lack of respect for women to be found in the new computerized dictionaries swamping the market.

These handy new computer programs magically spit out a definition or synonym with the tap of a keyboard. But they're coughing up some suprisingly archaic words for a business on the cutting edge of technology.

Let's call up on our screen, for example, the popular computerized thesaurus put out by WordPerfect Corp. of Utah.

Let's punch up the word "woman" and see what synonyms pop up:

"Dame, dowager, female, lady, matron, consort, mate, spouse, wife, handmaiden, housekeeper, maid."

Handmaiden? Housekeeper?

Now let's call up the word "man" for synonyms:

"Human being, humanity, humankind, mankind, people, chap, fellow, guy."

How nice for men to be considered human beings. What are women, chopped liver?

Prehistoric thought meets the computer age.

Drop 'Handmaiden'

I called WordPerfect's head office in Utah, where publicist Beth McGill said they had had a complaint several months ago, and had agreed to remove some of the offending words.

But on checking, she learned it had not been done, so she persuaded the company's "development group" to drop the words "handmaiden" and "housekeeper" next time the thesaurus is revised, within the next year.

"It took a while to explain to them why it was offensive," she groaned, "but I finally convinced them it was a little sexist for this day and age. We'll probably also take out 'maid,' although it does have a meaning as an unmarried girl or woman."

I asked her then about the synonym for "masculine": "male, manly, virile, powerful, strong, brawny." The antonym to all this? "Feminine, weak."

McGill shrieked.

"We'd better take out 'weak.' We have a group of professional linguists who come in to update our thesaurus about once a year, and this will definitely be changed."

How nice. But how did it pass last year's revision? What could be more important to update than the very way society thinks of one half of the population? Because what we call women says a lot about what we think of women.

Dictionaries have always been sexist, says Toronto linguist Valerie Alia, who has just finished her doctoral thesis on women, names and power.

"But the scary thing about repeating sexism in computerized dictionaries is that our kids – the computer generation – are the ones who will be pushing the buttons to call up these synonyms. They'll inherit the sexism through computers."

New System

Let's see what else the computer generation will inherit. Let's check the Xywrite thesaurus put out by Xyquest Inc. of Massachusetts, which actually is written by Microlytics Inc. of East Rochester, N.Y.

It's synonyms for "woman"?

"Being, citizen, creature, individual, person, dame, female, gentlewoman, lady, matron, miss, mistress, spinster, cohabitant, widow, bride, consort, mate, squaw, wife, spouse."

Squaw?

I called Microlytics, where spokesperson Carolyn Hodgins asked, "What's wrong with 'squaw'? I have Indian background, and I don't find it derogatory. Mind you, it is a bit obsolete, so it will probably be changed at some point."

Well, they sure find it derogatory over at the Native Women's Resource Centre in Toronto's east end, where women called the word everything from "vulgar" to "discriminatory."

Let's check one more thesaurus, the Multi-Mate program produced by Ashton-Tate software, and based on Webster's dictionary. Its synonyms for "woman"?

"Mistress, miss, inamorata, lover, paramour."

How romantic. Defined solely as a mate. How about synonyms for "man"?

"Human, being, body, creature, individual, life, mortal, party, person."

Enough, enough.

Will computer companies wake up, smarten up and bring their word banks into the 20th century, before it's over?

A LETTER FROM MARGARET LAURENCE

···

Dear Teacher:

I wish that those people who are so keen to ban serious contemporary novels would learn to read properly. I wish that they would not take excerpts and read only these, out of context. I wish that they would learn to hear what my novels are truly saying, which is a celebration of life itself and of the mystery at the core of life; and a portrayal both of human beings' ability to love one another, and of man's tragic inhumanity to man. I wish they would not be so oddly preoccupied with sex, which is only one aspect of life, and only one aspect among many others dealt with in my novels or other serious novels. I wish that they would understand that writers must be true to their fictional characters, and must present them truthfully, as they are, and as compassionately as possible. I wish that they would learn that to tell our young people that they must not read anything about sex, either its joys or its pitfalls, and that they must not know anything about life's tragedies, will not prepare them for life – the reverse, rather, is true. Social injustice, cruelty, exploitation, suffering – these things exist, as do people's love and kindness towards one another. Surely it cannot do other than help in the growing towards a responsible maturity for our young people to read novels in which many aspects of human life are dealt with, by writers whose basic faith is in the unique and irreplaceable value of the human individual. I wish that the people who want to ban certain novels would talk to some of the many Grade 12 and 13 students with whom I have discussed my writing. These students have read the novel they are studying – all of it, not just snippets here and there, and they have no difficulty, under the guidance of sensitive and informed teachers, of seeing that this work is an affirmation (and I think a serious and moral one) of faith in life and humanity.

Margaret Laurence

:::

JOHN MILTON ON CENSORSHIP

....

When someone refers to the Areopagitica, and half a dozen aspiring journalists around the table have never heard of it, where have they been all their lives? Evidently not browsing in the 1644 pamphlet by John Milton that used to be synonymous with the resistance to censorship on which writers in every age rely. A few of his arguments (in the spelling of the day):

I deny not, but that it is of greatest concernment in the Church and Commonwealth, to have a vigilant eye how Bookes demeane themselves as well as men; and thereafter to confine, imprison, and do sharpest justice on them as malefactors: For Books are not absolutely dead things, but doe contain a potencie of life in them to be as active as that soule was whose progeny they are; nay they do preserve as in a violl the purest efficacie and extraction of that living intellect that bred them. I know they are as lively, and as vigorously productive, as those fabulous Dragons teeth; and being sown up and down, may chance to spring up armed men. And yet on the other hand unlesse warinesse be us'd, as good almost kill a Man as kill a good Book. . . . We should be wary therefore what persecution we raise against the living labours of publick men, how we spill that season'd life of man preserv'd and stor'd up in Books; since we see a kinde of homicide may be thus committed, sometimes a martyrdome, and if it extend to the whole impression, a kinde of massacre, whereof the execution ends not in the slaying of an elementall life, but strikes at that ethereall and fift essence, the breath of reason it selfe, slaies an immortality rather then a life. . . .

Bad meats will scarce breed good nourishment in the healthiest concoction; but herein the difference is of bad books, that they to a discreet and judicious Reader serve in many respects to discover, to confute, to forewarn, and to illustrate. . . .

If we think to regulat Printing, thereby to rectifie manners, we must regulat all recreations and pastimes, all that is delightfull to man. No musick must be heard, no song be set or sung, but what is grave and *Dorick*. There must be licencing dancers, that no gesture, motion, or deportment be taught our youth but what by their allowance shall be thought honest; for such *Plato* was provided of; It will ask more then the work of twenty licencers to examin all the lutes, the violins, and the ghittarrs in every house; they must not be suffer'd to prattle as they doe, but must be licenc'd what they may say. And who shall silence all the airs and madrigalls, that whisper softnes in chambers? . . .

And though all the windes of doctrin were let loose to play upon the earth, so Truth be in the field, we do injuriously by licencing and prohibiting to misdoubt her strength. Let her and Falshood grapple; who ever knew Truth put to the wors, in a free and open encounter.

:::

THE CHALLENGE OF HATE LITERATURE

By Mark Bourrie

The Ernst Zundel case has done nothing to stem the tide of hate literature in Ontario, the Canadian Jewish Congress reports.

In fact, the organization says there has been an increase in anti-Semitic mail since Zundel was convicted in two long, sensational trials for spreading false news (denying the Holocaust took place) in order to incite hatred.

First convicted in 1985, Zundel appealed but was sentenced in 1988 to nine months in jail. He again appealed and the conviction was upheld . . . by the Ontario Court of Appeal.

Manuel Prutschie, national director of community relations for the Jewish congress, says he gets anonymous racist mail regularly and has seen an increase in the past two years.

"In a democratic society, there's room for vigorous debate but there isn't room for hateful literature," Prutschie said. . . .

Prutschie has kept track of many of the authors of Canadian underground literature. He said that because of this country's laws against inciting hatred, Canadian writers are more restrained than the authors of the American, South African and European pamphlets circulated in Canada.

"The material from the U.S. is the most vicious. We have laws in this country to stop that kind of hate literature that have certainly played a role in limiting the noxiousness of the home-grown material.

"But the stuff that comes in from the States is really nasty. People here subscribe to it and pass it along. There is a network of these people throughout the world who interchange material, visit with each other and have conferences," Prutschie said.

Canadian authorities "should come down hard on ideas that are outside the pale of constitutional expression," he said. "The authors of material that is false, that is maliciously false, or promotes hatred, must be penalized."

But there is sharp disagreement over whether there should be a crackdown on racist literature.

Alan Borovoy, general counsel for the Canadian Civil Liberties Association, says such material must be tolerated so censorship of legitimate protest doesn't happen.

"The problem you have is, how do you stop them? How do you write a law that's so tight you nail them but you don't risk catching in the same net material that would be unconscionable to suppress?

"How do you draw the line between strong disapproval and hatred? Sometimes minority groups, in their own defence, want to lash out at a majority group.

"Three years ago, a film sympathetic to Nelson Mandela (the jailed South African black nationalist) was held at customs for more than a month. They feared it would promote hatred against white South Africans. That's an irony if I've ever seen one.

"It's just not worth prosecuting these people. Our society can contain the influence of hate mongers without resorting to laws," Borovoy said.

Zundel says there's a market for his work, although it's not as lucrative as his former job as a Toronto freelance commercial artist. All of that work dried up when he went to court for the first time, he says.

No one is sure of the size of the right-wing fringe in Canada, but Jewish community leaders say the country is host to an entire spectrum, from frustrated anti-Semites to white supremacists. Both their numbers and their audience of supporters is growing, say people involved in the debate on whether the law should suppress written material.

Last July, former Canadian Nazi leader John Beattie outraged residents of Minden, Ont., by staging a two-day white supremacist rally.

About 100 skinheads, a group known for its racist views, burned crosses at the gathering amidst chants of "white power" and "Sieg heil."

In an earlier highly publicized case, Jim Keegstra, a former Alberta high school teacher, was convicted in 1985 of wilfully promoting anti-Semitism. He told his students that the Holocaust was a hoax and that the course of history had been manipulated by a group of powerful Jews.

Meanwhile, Jewish community leaders say Ottawa's decision to prosecute alleged Nazi war criminals has also increased hate literature in Metro.

Typical pamphlets target not only Jews but also the city's growing population of visible minorities. Material from the west coast is often anti-Asian.

Many of the hate pamphlets and newsletters are circulated to supporters. But some are also sent to ordinary Canadians who hold contrary views.

A splash of right-wing clippings was sent anonymously to a rural Ontario man after he wrote a short letter to a newspaper supporting the spending of taxpayers' money on war crimes trials. The parcel contained the work of home-grown Nazis, U.S. white supremacists and South African defenders of apartheid.

The inch-thick bundle of news clippings and pamphlets frightened the letter writer. His friends told him to save the $1.52 worth of stamps on the envelope, which strangely were not cancelled, and throw the contents away. But he intends to send the material to Justice Minister Doug Lewis.

The package included:

- A comic book printed in the United States called "Tales of the Holohoax," which mocks the stories of concentration camp survivors. It was printed by Michael Hoffman in New York state and dedicated to Zundel.

- Several Zundel pamphlets urging supporters to write letters on his behalf to Canadian and German authorities and attacking Israeli actions against Palestinians. (Zundel said in an interview he now is careful about what he writes, as he is under a court order not to continue spreading his views on the Holocaust.)

- A copy of an anonymously published magazine with an article on "the Martyrs of Nuremberg" (Nazi war criminals tried and hanged after World War II) and an interview with David Irving, a self-described "alternative historian" who testified at Zundel's 1988 trial and claims the Holocaust never happened.

- A photocopy of a newspaper article about University of Western Ontario professor Philippe Rushton, with his controversial theories relating race and intelligence, sexual promiscuity and criminal tendencies underlined.

- An article from a supermarket tabloid claiming the Nazis sent astronauts into space in 1943.

- A racist U.S. pamphlet that warns against whites marrying blacks and urges supporters to fight against tougher gun laws.

Prutschie said the right-wing fringe in Canada is small but growing.

Zundel disagrees. He says it's already grown to a size that it is close to overthrowing the system. He boasts he has enough supporters to keep him going financially.

He claims he himself does not send out hate mail. He "relies on the market," but says he gets hate mail from his opponents.

CBC NEWS OPENS GATES TO OBSCENITY

....

By Dalton Camp

On several occasions, man and boy, I have been there as a witness to the incremental lowering of the barriers that the general society maintains against the public display or dissemination of indecency and obscenity. The lowering of barriers and the rise of permissiveness – cause and effect – have been triggered by precedent. What we know about this, to our satisfaction or otherwise, is that the results are irreversible; in the good taste wars between prevailing "community standards" and encroaching libertarianism, the momentum is all with the latter.

There was, by way of example, the Oscar-winning movie, *It Happened One Night*, in which Clark Gable removed his shirt, exposing a bare chest. Not really much to that, you might say, but Gable did so in the presence of Claudette Colbert in an overnight tourist camp (yesterday's model of today's motel).

I did not, myself, think much of the event at the time; more mature members in the audience, however, spotted it immediately as a daring breakthrough. Even so, I doubt many realized the true significance, that the baring of Gable's chest signaled the gloves were off, so to speak, and that Ms Colbert would be among the last women to be seen on the silver screen fully clothed.

Scarcely five years passed before Gable lowered the barrier another notch. This time, he cussed. In the movie classic, *Gone With The Wind*, Gable uttered filmdom's first four-letter word: "Frankly, Scarlett," he said, addressing Vivien Leigh, "I don't give a damn." Again, the precedent did not strike me as a turning point, but it appears to have opened the floodgates. Since that event, in 1939, we have inched our way to a time when obscene language is routine (if not artistically

essential) and the performers remove much more than their shirts. One way or another, we owe a lot to Clark Gable.

Obscene language – I know, I know – begs for definition, a plea most often made by those who profit from its use. My own definition – freely offered – is any word or expression I would not deliberately teach my children to use. This should not confuse anyone. I would say to a child: "This is a steam iron. It is very hot. It burns. Do not touch the iron." I would not say: "This is a (expletive) iron. It's (expletive) hot. Keep your (expletive) hands off the (expletive repeated) iron." Few children learn obscenity or profanity from their parents. They pick it up in the schoolyard and – of course – at the movies, among the elsewheres.

Last week – Thursday, at 1800 hours, to be precise – I was witness to another breakthrough, not so incremental, more like an explosion of obscenity, and a landslide precedent.

This took place on television, heretofore something of a sanctuary from hard-core obscenity – at least during the daylight hours – and occurred during two successive newscasts on *Newsworld*, the CBC's new all-news channel. On the world news (beginning with Lithuania), the scene shifted to Canso, N.S., and the troubled site of a fish plant closing. The item carried comments from four of the plant's employees, now unemployed, three of whom expressed their concern in clear and eloquent language, with words in common usage at your average family dinner table.

The fourth and final victim, however, used language I have never before heard on a television newscast. Neither has anyone else. The language could not, certainly, be repeated in this newspaper, other than perhaps in a literary essay on the works of Henry Miller. In one 20-second clip, we heard the f-word twice, the s-word once, and a familiar anatomic vulgarism twice. Minutes later, the item was repeated on *Newsworld*, this time from the originating newsroom in Halifax. (Let the record show that Halifax aired the clip with a warning to listeners offensive language might follow.)

Clark Gable, move over. The CBC, of course, has a policy on obscenity, found on page 97 of its *Journalistic Policy Handbook*. Obscene language, it informs, is an offence (against CBC policy) unless the obscenity is germane to the story (such as explicit testimony given in a trial involving rape, incest, child abuse, and like matters).

Otherwise, the policy handbook goes on to say, "Obscene language is an offence . . . unless its purpose is to serve the public good." This only puts a spin on the more common defence of obscenity wherein juries and judges exhaust themselves in a search for "redeeming social value." But although I count myself as a resolute opponent to censorship, I have – I am now reluctant to admit – always been comforted in the belief the CBC would not seek to serve "the public good" by airing the obscenities of someone who had been sacked by National Sea. Not anyway – and here I am reduced to special pleading – during television's long-established children's hour.

Perhaps it can be explained: *Newsworld* may have liberated itself from the policy handbook, and the Canso clip may be – as when Gable spake to Ms Leigh – a signal to warn that the all-news channel, from here on out, intends to give us all the news unfit to print.

In search of clarification, I have called Joan Donaldson, inventor, designer and chief executive officer of *Newsworld*. The person who answered the phone told me Ms Donaldson "is in a meeting all day." Further, the person answering the phone said she did not expect to see or hear from Ms Donaldson at any time during the day. I was invited to leave a message, which I failed to do. "Tell Ms Donaldson, obscenity sucks," I might have said. But I didn't.

'TONED DOWN' MOZART

The COC Says Its Changes to Sexist Language in *The Magic Flute* Are Not Censorship. But Would the Composer Have Approved?

....

By Ray Conlogue

Mozart's celebrated opera *The Magic Flute* is riddled with sexism, in the form of slighting and denigrating remarks about women. But viewers reading the surtitle translation at the O'Keefe Centre this week won't notice, for the simple reason that all the offending passages have been altered or removed.

"Beware of women's tricks," the guards inform the young hero Tamino as he prepares to be initiated into Sarastro's priesthood. "This is the first principle of our Order!" Of course, they are singing in German. What appears in the surtitles is: "Beware of trickery."

Similar alterations appear throughout the evening. "She is an arrogant woman" becomes "she is arrogant." "Women talk a bit and accomplish little" is altered into a comment on one character specifically. Sarastro's remark to the young heroine Pamina – "A man must guide your heart; without him, all women step outside their proper sphere" – has been emended to an inoffensive wish that everybody should live in harmony.

The COC's [Canadian Opera Company's] Gunta Dreifelds, who wrote the surtitles, acknowledges that the decision to alter the sexist passages was a deliberate one. But she does not feel it is censorship. Rather is is an effort to prevent the audience being antagonized in a way that neither Mozart nor his librettist Schikaneder would have intended.

"The audience would put too much emphasis on the sexism which is not the predominant thought of the opera. If you say 'women's tricks' you emphasize the wrong points. *The Magic Flute* is about love."

Dreifelds says that she and the director, Lotfi Mansouri (who is now out of town), discussed the matter briefly, and that it was understood the language would be toned down. Mansouri, for example, suggested that when the priest Sarastro says "ein Weib tut wenig, plaudert viel" ("a woman does little and chatters much") it should be interpreted as a specific reference to the Queen of the Night rather than to women in general – in spite of the fact that "ein Weib" is obviously intended as a collective noun.

The opera also contains a racial issue, in the form of Sarastro's jailer Monostatos – a black. Monostatos tries to rape Pamina, and in a famous aria (Alles fuhit der Liebe Freuden) justifies himself by saying he is entitled to passion too. "I must shun love because a black man is ugly! Was I not given a heart? Am I not made of flesh and blood?"

This aria ironically echoes Shylock's famous "Hath a Jew not eyes?" speech. Whether Schikaneder intended this or not is beside the point: the rhetoric in either case seems characteristic of Europe's ability at the time to come to grips with racism, and to express some sympathy for its victims. But here too, the words have been altered. Monostatos' heartfelt cry that he was "taken in by a white woman" has been deleted, and the language of the aria softened to the point that the racial issue is all but dissolved.

There is no doubt that the presence of starkly sexist or racial language makes a modern audience uncomfortable. There might be some tittering or hissing. But by removing such material, the COC has deprived the audience of the chance to decide for itself whether these issues are central to *The Magic Flute* or not.

Ironically, the program for the production contains an excellent essay on the issue of

sexism in *The Magic Flute* by Peter Sandor of the Mozart Society. It explains the problem in terms of the Viennese Free-masonry of the time. "A less-than-progressive aspect of Masonic philosophy was the distrust and hatred of women," he writes, adding that while both Schikaneder and Mozart were Masons, Schikaneder also suffered from an unhappy marriage, which might explain some of the jaundiced language of the text. To Mozart, usually a creator of strong female characters, Sandor attributes the otherwise baffling turnabout late in the opera when the hitherto submissive Pamina suddenly defies Sarastro and declares that she is going to accompany Tamino on his terrifying initiation into the all-male order.

Is all this, as Dreifelds argues (and Mansouri would presumably agree), peripheral to *The Magic Flute*? It is hard to agree. This is an unusual opera, which has provoked and inspired many artists. It is set in ancient Egypt, filled with dragons, warriors, and special effects intended to appeal to its intended audience, which was children and young people.

But on another level it is a very adult business. The plot is really about the war between the sexes, and its immediate pivot is a child-custody dispute. Sarastro, the estranged husband of the Queen of the Night, has kidnapped their daughter Pamina – to prevent her, as he says, being infected by her mother's "lies" and hatred of men. The Queen in turn will marry her daughter to anybody who will kill Sarastro, and even charges Pamina herself with the task, under pain of being forever cut off from her mother if she refuses.

There is no doubt that the story is tainted with misogyny. Sarastro is portrayed as the seat of light and goodness, and the Queen and her female warriors as the seat of darkness and hypocrisy. But there are many signs that both Mozart and Schikaneder were disturbed by this black-and-white dichotomy. Among others, we hear the Queen and her warriors as they prepare to attack Sarastro's palace sing of "blotting out the bigots from the earth" – meaning, presumably, their male oppressors.

To an artist like Ingmar Bergman, several of whose films are strongly influenced by *The Magic Flute*, the misogyny of the text is merely a pointer to the opera's real issue, which he identifies as the profound alienation between the sexes. In his 1975 film of *The Magic Flute*, he shows Sarastro and the Queen of the Night as the fruit of a soured marriage, and gives Sarastro a malevolent air which helps create a moral equality – an equality in infamy, as it were – of man and woman. For Bergman, the opera was a powerful venue for thrashing out the malaise of male versus female, and the film foreshadows his later rewriting of Ibsen's *A Doll's House*, and his bitter staging of Strindberg's *Miss Julie*.

But there is a difference between rising above the sexism of *The Magic Flute*, as Bergman did, and simply eliminating it as the COC does. The result in the latter case is an insipid, denatured piece of work that focusses on the only conventional aspect of the opera, the romance of Pamina and Tamino.

Dreifelds justifies this by saying that today's audience would not know how to deal with the sexist language in the libretto: they "would not put it into context."

This kind of assumption is the beginning of what might be called The New Priggishness. Just as Victorians couldn't stand the mention of sex, we are to believe that our contemporaries can't bear the mention of sexism.

If this attitude spreads unchecked, it will soon be necessary to sanitize every masterpiece that has come to us from the past. Surely the better approach is that of the Stratford Festival, which offers the audience of *The Merchant of Venice* pre-show discussions of Elizabethan attitudes toward Jews.

Why not do likewise with *The Magic Flute*, and the many other classics that will offer similar difficulties?

The past, after all, is a foreign country. If we homogenize it to look like the present, there isn't much point in visiting there.

THE DAMAGE DONE BY ILL-CHOSEN WORDS

By Carol Goar

Every day, in small ways, people practise self-censorship.

They keep their thoughts to themselves out of politeness, or to spare others' feelings, or to hide their emotions, or to avoid a confrontation.

No sensitive person would walk into a hospital room and tell a friend: "You look awful." No sensible person would joke to an airport security guard that he was carrying a hand grenade.

Like it or not, one of the unwritten rules of conduct in a civilized society is that some things are best left unsaid.

For politicians, knowing where to draw the line between candor and callousness is especially important – and never more so than right now, with racial and linguistic tensions running dangerously high.

Every public statement is a delicate balancing act. Sometimes it is right for a politician to shock the electorate, sometimes it can do irreparable damage. Sometimes leadership means saying things people don't want to hear, sometimes it means remaining diplomatically silent.

FOLLOWING THROUGH

Step 1

Devise a number of topics or tasks that could be used to extend or apply the issue of censorship in one or more areas.

Step 2

Select one of the topics or tasks, complete it, and evaluate the results.

T O P I C
nine

Perspectives on the Future

• •

The last topic in this text asks you to think about the future. As young people growing up in the last decade of the twentieth century, you will be spending most of your lives in the twenty-first century. What do you think it will look like? Are you essentially optimistic or pessimistic? From your perspective, are we entering a new age, a brave new world full of technological wonders, or are we entering a dark age, full of pollution and turmoil? Or do you have another perspective? Or a new perspective?

The articles collected here are meant to provide only a "starter kit" to get you thinking about the future. The first article "Challenges for the Twenty-First Century: Seeking a New Perspective" gives an overview of five key themes that will need to be addressed in the future. The writer describes the need for developing "a new perspective." The other articles focus on areas that are going to require not only new perspectives but incredible problem-solving skills: genetic engineering, technology, and the environment.

In exploring the future and developing your perspective on some aspect of it, you may wish to focus on the topic in one of the articles and locate further material which gives a variety of perspectives. Or, depending on your interests and the availability of material, you may wish to explore some other area, such as the future of transportation, fashions, art, families, marriage, or religion. Remember, whatever subtopic you choose, your goal is to achieve a well-informed perspective on it.

CHALLENGES FOR THE TWENTY-FIRST CENTURY

Seeking a New Perspective

....

By William Van Dusen Wishard

The twenty-first century is roughly 3,800 days away. How well we cope with its opportunities and problems may depend on five themes that must come to the forefront of our awareness.

- To learn to live in a global community where isolated actions have global consequences.

    Technology now has linked the people of the earth together in such an interlocking system that actions in one country can have immediate consequences around the globe. Argentina's economic growth is affected by America's interest rates, which influence French exports, which affect U.S. farm employment, which can alter Japanese political stability, and so on.

- To assimilate the scientific knowledge gained during the twentieth century.

    Ninety percent of all scientific knowledge that exists has been acquired in the past 35 years. With such a flood of new knowledge, a point is eventually reached where the primary issue is not what new technology we can develop, but whether we are wisely using the technology we already have. Are people happier and is the social fabric stronger as a result of it? Are we controlling technology or is it reshaping us and our institutions?

    The twenty-first century may see the development of new technologies that could alter human existence more fundamentally than any invention thus far. Yet technology, in and of itself, is not an expression of basic human purpose in life. It is an extension of technical means. As such, development of technology in the twenty-first century must be subservient to deeper human goals.

- To restructure our institutions in light of new knowledge and possibilities.

    As new knowledge develops, it changes the context in which institutions operate, and, unless they adapt, they lose their effectiveness. Thus, almost every institution is in crisis today. No government anywhere in the world – whether democratic or totalitarian – is working well. No educational system, on the whole, is producing people equipped to cope with the inter-relatedness and diversity of the twenty-first century. Organized religion of every stripe is in crisis, and people are seeking solace in all sorts of unconventional beliefs. The family is collapsing as the fundamental training ground for social conduct and as the basic unit of government.

    This institutional breakdown is happening not because everyone is incompetent. They're not. It's happening because new technologies have created new possibilities that are altering the context of life in which all our institutions were conceived and developed.

- To reintegrate ourselves as part of the natural order of life, to again feel ourselves as part of Life's Great Process.

    Alienation from this Process is at the heart of our environmental problem today, from the teenager who throws a beer can out a car window to the business executive whose plant dumps toxic wastes into the nearby river. Disregard for nature has, up until now, had only marginal consequences. But further disregard now brings consequences of global proportions, which would fundamentally alter the conditions needed to sustain life on our planet.

- Finally, to see clearly that the key to the

twenty-first century is for all people to become integrated with every part of their inner selves and to be at home with people from every part of the world.

As we look around the globe, we see alienation in many people–especially young people. You see it in America as well as Russia, in China as well as France, in Brazil as well as Egypt.

Alienation has been growing for centuries. It is a byproduct of the trends toward mechanization, standardization, quantification, and uniformity that constitute the core of industrialization. As these qualities were emphasized, the life-giving attributes of sensitivity, autonomy, diversity, meaning, love, and the impulse to higher levels of being were all deemphasized as "irrelevant" to a modern technological society.

The result is that, over the centuries, we have distorted the human personality and alienated ourselves from the deepest roots of our own being. We have created people who can absorb massive amounts of data, who can manage complex mechanical or bureaucratic systems, but who are unable to provide a depth of meaning that links the individual to some larger significance beyond material gain or personal advancement.

Given the pace of change and the interconnectedness of the globe, the task ahead is to seek a new perspective, a new way of seeing ourselves in the context of new possibilities. In sum, we must redefine for the twenty-first century the enduring purpose of the human journey.

Pessimists say that the twenty-first century will be the final chapter of the human story. More likely, it will be the start of a new age of wonder and achievement – an age we can now only dimly perceive. The outcome depends on each one of us as individuals, for the condition of the world is a reflection of the condition of the inner life of its inhabitants.

WHAT KIND OF BRAVE NEW WORLD?

Genetic Technology Is Itself Being Dissected to Answer Its Moral Questions

....

By Debra Black

How many angels can dance on the head of a pin? That's the kind of question ethicists and philosophers have tried to answer since the beginning of time – without much success.

The questions currently involving genetic engineering and reproductive technology seem as impossible to answer:

- Geneticists are mapping the mysteries of the human gene. Will they one day have the power to change human genetic structure, and redesign humanity?

- Reproductive specialists now routinely bring forth life in a test tube. What should be done with the embryos used in this process?

Even Wise Solomon would scratch his head if he had to deal with some of these issues. The answers are not clear-cut, prompting many to cry out: What kind of brave new world might we face?

The federal government's announcement earlier this month of plans to set up a royal commission examining reproductive technology comes in the wake of lobbying by women's groups and academics.

One ethics specialist says we are confronting "a new social structuring of reproduction."

"It's something Canada should be thinking about," says Christine Overall, a philosophy professor at Queen's University and author of the book *Ethics And Human Reproduction: A Feminist Analysis.*

"When we're talking about reproduction . . . we're talking about issues that very powerfully affect women. Women should be very, very heavily involved in policy formation on this.''

Overall warns that, without the royal commission, ''decisions will be made anyway on an ad hoc basis.''

The commission, which will look at issues such as artificial insemination, *in vitro* (test tube) fertilization and surrogate motherhood, will have to deal with a wide-ranging series of ethical and moral issues, including:

- Should offspring from artificial insemination be told of their genetic or family history?
- How many embryos do you plant in a woman's uterus to increase her chances of pregnancy, knowing if some take you'll abort the others?
- How much money should we commit to *in vitro* fertilization programs as opposed to doing research on the prevention of infertility?
- To whom do embryos belong in case of a divorce or death?
- Should we set up commercial sperm, egg or embryo banks?
- Should we legalize surrogate motherhood?

The federal government isn't the first to examine this quagmire. In 1985 the Ontario Law Reform Commission released a two-volume report with 67 recommendations on the legal implications of the new reproductive technology.

Similarly, in Europe, Britain, Australia and the United States, researchers have looked at the issue and tried to establish guidelines.

Rather than set up another commission, some bioethicists believe the public would be better served by first examining the existing studies. And there are many.

''At least they should be reviewed before we start generating an entirely new series of guidelines from the ground up as though no

one had ever done anything on this,'' says David Roy, director of the Centre for Bioethics at the Clinical Research Institute of Montreal. ''This is to me a very unwise way to conduct a study leading to public policy guidelines.''

One of the most touted reports is Britain's Warnock Report, which according to a report in *The Sunday Times*, tried to strike ''a balance between pride in technological achievement'' and ''unease at the apparently uncontrolled advance of science'' with its 64 recommendations.

For the most part these guidelines and other international recommendations have sat on the shelf. And there may be a very good reason for this.

''It's a very complex issue,'' says Dr. Margaret Somerville, director of the McGill Centre for Medicine, Ethics and the Law.

''My current view is there may not be any right answers at the moment. We simply are in a mid-position of not knowing the way we should go on a lot of these issues.''

''We've got to have a group of wise persons . . . plus we've got to have some fairly well-defined and worked out decision-making structures. We can't just let people use ad hoc situations.''

Some say there are, realistically, no absolute answers.

''You've got to recognize you cannot have a right answer technologically,'' adds Bernard Dickens, a professor at both the University of Toronto's Faculty of Law and the Faculty of Medicine.

''You can have a right answer ideologically. One is: Don't interfere. The other is: Control and stop.'' But neither route will satisfy people on opposing sides of the question.

Ever since the birth of the world's first test tube baby, Louise Brown, almost 11 years ago, the field of reproductive technology has advanced rapidly and helped many infertile couples.

But critics have compared the advances in

reproductive technology to "playing God," worrying about the "Frankenstein factor" and "the possibility of influencing not only the present generation but generations to come," explains Abbyann Lynch, director of the Westminster Institute for Ethics and Human Values in London, Ont.

Now an even larger issue hangs over the heads of the international scientific community: the mapping and sequencing of DNA (deoxyribonucleic acid), which contains the genetic prescription for life. It is unlikely that the royal commission will study this complicated area, however.

Yet its impact on humanity will be astounding, researchers say.

Scientists from Britain, the United States, Japan, France and West Germany are all intensely working on this project, hoping to determine the location and identity of each of the estimated 50,000 to 100,000 genes that are in a single strand of DNA. Each of these genes is responsible for the various jobs of cells and organs.

"In doing this they would learn knowledge equivalent to what they learned in undertaking to put a man on the moon," says McGill's Somerville. "We've gone into outer space, Now, we're going into the most inner of inner space."

Indeed, the quest has become a kind of holy grail.

Repair Defective Gene

"Genes are eternal," says University of Toronto's Dickens. "It is us that are mortal. In a sense we're simply containers of genes and through reproduction we pass on our genes. So our genes survive. We don't. If we see some of our own immortality in genes then that perhaps explains why we find them so interesting and powerful."

"We will know what we're made of structurally," explains Louis Siminovitch, director of research at the Toronto-based Mount Sinai

Hospital Research Institute and internationally well-known geneticist. "For diseases we'd be able to put a map on people and know who they are and what they are at the DNA level."

This will mean that through genetic engineering scientists could one day repair, remove or replace the defective gene that's at the root of a disease.

But many worry about the potential problems that could come with this knowledge. Bioethicists are asking themselves a number of questions about what DNA mapping might mean for the future of humanity, including:

Genetically Programmed

- How would parents cope if they were able to know what their children would die of before they were even born, through DNA mapping?
- What if the mapping was used to breed only a certain kind of offspring, perhaps one who is genetically programmed to be the best basketball player or blue-eyed?
- Will genetic engineering or the medical intervention in our DNA change forever the genetic make-up of mankind?

"We don't know the prescription for human survival," says Dickens. "Once we start tinkering with conditions that will affect future generations we are altering the human blueprint. And we ought to do that only by stealth."

For this reason some academics would like to see the question of genetic engineering and gene mapping included in the royal commission.

But the Centre for Bioethics' Roy believes reproductive technology, genetic engineering and the gene mapping program are distinct and different areas of scientific research and should be treated accordingly.

What's more Roy believes it may be jumping the gun to conclude that the quest to map

DNA and genetic engineering will lead to apocalyptic results.

"Some of the concerns are unrealistic . . . We are just about getting ready perhaps to do some of the first attempts at genetic therapy for single gene diseases and certainly not all single gene diseases.

'Power for Evil'

"To jump from there to imagine within a short while we're going to be trying to do genetic modification of behavioral traits that depend on many genes, is totally unrealistic."

That's not to say that scientists and ethicists shouldn't give serious consideration to these issues, Roy says.

He warns, that despite the potential power for good, "it is theoretically possible to turn it around and make it a great power for evil.

"I think even the most committed scientists recognize the need to reflect on the broad social, philosophical questions that will arise with increasing frequency as the mapping of the human genome advances and as the sequencing of those genes advances."

What's needed, Roy and others believe, is a "sober, sombre, totally well-informed, critical, ethical analysis and review," involving people who are not directly involved in the scientific projects but who can understand genetics and speak in an informed way about it.

Ultimately there may be no single or clear cut answer to any of the ethical and moral questions in these areas.

Francis Rolleston, a biochemist and director of scientific evaluation at the Medical Research Council, sums up the complex challenge.

"It comes down to a framework of proper behavior that is set by society, which is called the law, and then within that an enormous amount of individual discretion."

WIRED FOR THE '90s

Digital Technology Promises Electronic Network Capable of Enormous Changes in Daily Living

By Mary Gooderham

It will be a digitized decade.

Digital technology – a computer technique whereby information is coded into numeric patterns – will explode in the 1990s, becoming an increasing part of the consumer marketplace and telecommunications while expanding the amount of information that floods into daily life.

Through it the world will become wired with an integration of communications technologies – voice, data and image – into a common electronic network never before thought possible.

"Digital is coming more and more into our lives," says David Havelock, a scientist in the division of physics and digital signal processing at the National Research Council.

The past 10 years have brought the technology to such consumer products as compact discs, computers and telephones, leading to developments that will have a wide application in the future.

Experts say one of the most important of those is the Integrated Services Digital Network. Called a "global switchboard," ISDN is a set of standards for plugs, switching systems and signals that will enable voice, data, video and text to be sent simultaneously and interactively among the world's 600 million telephone subscribers.

Facsimiles, electronic mail, data bases, high-definition television images, services such as home banking and cellular and conventional telephones – until now fragmented on separate channels – will share one path.

The 1990s will finally bring powerful computers to every office desk and make them an increasing part of everyday life.

Kenneth Grant, a technology consultant for the Toronto firm of Peat, Marwick Stevenson and Kellogg, says the telephone and the computer will merge to become an instrument through which information can be simultaneously sent and shared by several parties.

A mobile telecommunications system is evolving in which everyone will have a personal phone number and will be able to be reached everywhere. By the end of the next decade, international governing bodies for cellular telephone technology hope to establish worldwide standards to make possible such a "personal telecommunications age."

The number of cellular telephones in Canada, which now has one of the highest per-capita rates of usage in the world at about 1.2 per cent of the population, is expected to increase to one million, or 4 per cent of the population, by 1993. Marketers predict that 15 in 100 Canadians will have a mobile phone by the turn of the century. By the end of 1991, cellular telephones will use a digital network for transmission, at least quadrupling the capacity of channels that are now overcrowded.

Telecommunications experts see telephones in offices that are cordless so they can be carried everywhere and telephones in the sky beside almost every airplane seat.

The pressure will be turned up, even more in work and personal lives in the age of instant information and global communications.

"Life gets faster, the time slots for doing things get less and less and the amount of information coming at an individual gets greater," Mr. Grant says.

The explosion of information will reach into automobiles. Intelligent Vehicle Highways Systems – dubbed smart cars and highways – mean improvements in traffic management but could create problems of state control over drivers. They may also lead to pricing schemes for the use of roads through sophisticated computer systems.

An increasing number of electronic items will be brought into the price range of average consumers in a continued surge of mass marketing. They will help to save time and increase the trend to spending leisure time at home.

Houses will become wired through technology once depicted only in science fiction films, where devices and appliances "talk" to each other and can be controlled through telephones.

Miniaturization of technology to make tiny silicon moving parts will lead to flea-sized robots that could be used in space exploration or in performing surgery from inside the human body.

Scientists say there will be more applications for artificial intelligence and robotics, most importantly for dealing with hazardous environments such as nuclear power plants, the sea floor and space.

While hopes for 1990s technology are bright, there are warnings. Sociologists and humanists fear that the world could continue to develop into a split between those who are "technologically advantaged" and those who are not, because of factors such as access to sophisticated computer systems.

There are also concerns that in the 1990s, movements such as environmentalism could bring about a retrenchment against technological advances because of pollution fears. Breakthroughs in areas such as biotechnology and genetic engineering will raise ethical questions.

Scientists counter that technology such as the development of toxic-waste-eating microorganisms will prove to be solutions to some of the world's problems.

"Technology is going to be aimed at mitigating some of its severe effects we've now learned about," says David Bates, author of a 1982 Science Council of Canada study on the regulation of technology. "It will be an interesting decade."

CATERING TO NEW CONCERNS

The Debate About Green Products

....

By David Todd

For Edmonton homemaker Sandi Pryde, environmentalism begins in the nursery. Concerned about the pollution caused by disposable diapers, Pryde has been a regular customer of a local cloth-diaper delivery service since Storm, the first of her four children, was born in 1981. And although Storm Pryde is now nine years old, the same service delivers diapers for Pryde's five-month-old daughter, Spirit Rose. Pryde, 30, whose husband is a business executive, says she wants to do more as a consumer to protect the environment and gives increasing thought to shopping for so-called environmentally friendly products. She says that she is prepared to bear some extra costs. Said Pryde: "I'm willing to go as far as I can with this comfortably. I don't mind sacrificing."

Health: Pryde is not alone. According to public opinion polls, a growing number of consumers are declaring their willingness to at least consider the health of the environment when they make purchasing decisions. And business has wasted little time in catering to their concerns. In the past year, supermarket and hardware chains have begun trying to convert shoppers to new lines of so-called green products, and manufacturers of everything from detergent to batteries have modified and repackaged goods to present a more environmentally friendly face. The potential for profit is considerable. Since a new line of products was first introduced last June, the Toronto-based Loblaw supermarket chain has already generated more than $60 million in sales from its Green-product line. But environmentalists warn that, in many cases, the companies trumpeting their newfound environmental sensitivity are in fact offering products with little or no environmental benefit.

Still, recent polls have shown that mounting concern over the harm to the planet has reshaped consumer attitudes. In fact, 18 per cent of respondents to the 1989 Maclean's/Decima poll rated the environment as the leading issue facing Canada today, the first time that the issue was the top concern in the six years of the poll. And market researchers predict that ever larger numbers of consumers will soon do more than simply pay lip service to environmentalism – they will actually change their buying habits. Indeed, a 1989 survey by the Ottawa-based Grocery Product Manufacturers of Canada, which represents about 150 food and beverage makers, found that 80 per cent of shoppers were willing to consider paying higher prices for environmentally safe products. Said Len Kubas, a Toronto-based retail industry consultant: "People will vote with their dollars at some point."

Few companies have played to public environmental concerns more aggressively than Loblaw. The company markets more than 100 products under its Green label, ranging from toilet paper bleached without chlorine to phosphate-free detergent to recycled motor oil. Said David Nichol, Loblaw International Merchants president: "To be pro-environment is sound business strategy." Finding that competitive edge has lured other major retailers into the green market. Last fall, the Home Hardware Stores Ltd. chain of St. Jacobs, Ont., with nearly 1,000 outlets across Canada, began marketing 40 of its low-toxicity paints and household cleaners under a new Earth Care logo. And in March, the Calgary-based grocery chain Canada Safeway Ltd. launched its Environmental Options program. Shoppers at each of Safeway's 235 stores across Western Canada are now greeted by shelf signs that point out more than 60 different products, ranging from coffee filters to cloth diapers, that the company has deemed "environmentally sensitive." Sherrie Dutton, Safeway communications manager, says the company opted against creating its own line of green products, choosing instead to educate consumers about the choices already available on Safeway's shelves. Dutton added, "People recognize that putting baking soda in a green box does not change the product."

Dumps: In the race to win over environmentally conscious consumers, some major manufacturers have shifted their marketing engines into high gear. Last September, Procter & Gamble Inc. of Toronto began offering six of its popular cleaning products, including Liquid Tide and Mr. Clean, in one-litre plastic pouches, called Enviro-Paks, so that consumers could refill their plastic detergent bottles at home. Since the pouches contain much less plastic than the bottles, company officials predicted that the new system would reduce the amount of plastic being thrown into garbage dumps across Canada by 300 tons annually. Three months later, Procter's leading Canadian competitor, Toronto-based Lever Brothers Inc., trumpeted a new $20-million environmental action plan that included the elimination of phosphates – chemicals linked to excessive algae growth in lakes and rivers – from the company's leading brand, Sunlight laundry detergent.

Hyperbole: While many consumers have embraced the new consumer products, environmental groups have responded to them with skepticism. Michael Manolson, executive director of Toronto-based Greenpeace Canada, said that while a few green goods represent encouraging steps forward, many represent little more than industry hyperbole. Among the companies that have aroused the

ire of activists is Eveready Canada Inc., which has started promoting its Energizer batteries as "environmentally safer." Company officials say that, over the past five years, they have reduced the mercury content of their batteries from one per cent to .025 per cent of total weight and predict that the move will improve their competitive position. But Greenpeace campaigner Gordon Perks said that simply cutting down on mercury – which has been linked to nervous disorders in humans, and is one of several toxic metals used in batteries – does not make Eveready's product substantially safer.

And even Loblaw's successful Green line campaign has been dogged by controversy almost from its start. Colin Isaacs, executive director of the Toronto-based environmental group Pollution Probe resigned last summer after many associates complained of the organization's endorsement of several Loblaw's products, including a disposable diaper. Most environmental advocates contend that only cloth diapers are truly less harmful to the environment. And many activists have complained that Loblaw's Green line includes products devoid of any environmental benefit whatsoever, such as toxic cleaners carrying the Green label simply because they contain bitter-tasting additives meant to discourage children from swallowing them. "To call a product like that 'green' is the ultimate in marketing gall," said Jenny Hillard, who chairs the Ottawa-based Consumers' Association of Canada environmental committee.

Trash: Some companies, meanwhile, already appear to be backing away from their products' environmental claims. Mobil Corp. of New York City recently announced it would drop the word "degradable" from packages in its line of Hefty plastic trash bags because, while the bags are intended to break down under sunlight, they end up in landfill sites covered from the sun. Environment Canada also is trying to offer consumers guidance on green purchasing. Under the department's Environmental Choice program, manufacturers can apply to carry the federal EcoLogo – three doves entwined in the shape of a maple leaf – on products that meet established criteria for environmental soundness. So far, the government has moved cautiously. In the past two years, board members have set criteria for only 10 product categories, including cloth diapers and recycled paper products. And only 10 individual products, including three brands of water-based paint and two brands of recycled motor oil, have received certification to carry the EcoLogo. Clearly, as companies rush to color profits green, they and their consumers may find the business of saving the planet at the supermarket checkout more complicated than it first appeared.

Endnote

In the last topic the following statement was made:

The task ahead is to seek a new perspective, a new way of seeing ourselves in the context of new possibilities.

It is hoped that *Exploring Perspectives* will have shown you some of those possibilities.

Notes on Key Learning Activities

RESPONSE JOURNALS AND LEARNING LOGS

Journals and logs are a useful means of clarifying and keeping track of your thinking and learning experiences.

A **response journal** is an informal, private record of your personal thinking on any topic or issue–your ideas, opinions, questions, and reflections about it. Responses are generally in writing, but at times they may take other forms such as drawings, pictures, even cartoons. Responses may be shared or not shared; that decision is up to you. Your response journal may be a separate book, or a separate section of your notebook or writing folder. Response journals provide a useful record of the progress of your thinking. Sample excerpt:

I guess like most people I've never really thought much about the use of animals in research. I remember learning somewhere that insulin was discovered by experimenting with dogs, and look at the millions of people who have benefited from that research. But then it still really upsets me to think of them suffering. Maybe there's some other way - maybe through technology. Maybe though it's because they were dogs. I'm not sure I feel the same about rats. Maybe I'll know by the time we finish this topic. I hope it's not too upsetting. My nerves can't stand it. Courage!

A **learning log** is similar in many ways to a response journal, but it is a more deliberate, more structured, tracking device. In a learning log you record your reactions or track your response to certain activities as you are engaged in them. A log is also a method of formally keeping track of your progress as you work through a lengthy pre-determined task such as an independent study project. In the independent study log, you record such things as the time you spent, the research you did, the steps you took, any problems you encountered, and how you dealt with them. Such a log becomes an integral part of the project. Sample excerpt:

Jan. 24 – Went to the library today to start my outline. Now that my thesis has been approved I can start thinking about the framework for my outline. Finished reading the material I have but it's too one-sided. Looked in the periodical index and a couple of articles that might give another perspective. Have to check back with the librarian tomorrow to see if they can be located. On track so far.

Jan. 26 – Off track. Temporarily, I hope. The two articles are not available – at least not right away. Can't wait too long, so I may have to either do without them or find something else. Completed the outline and am ready now for Friday's interview. Check with Crighton for other possible sources for articles.

COLLABORATIVE THINKING

Brainstorming is the practice of having a group generate as many ideas on a topic as it can within a short space of time. When brainstorming, you focus on quantity of ideas rather than on quality. You accept all ideas without any evaluative comments. Really good brainstorming occurs when people in the group build on each other's ideas.

Brainstorming may be done by listing ideas one after the other as they are generated. This procedure is useful for selecting and prioritizing your ideas. Sample:

Dealing with Drunk Drivers
- long jail sentences
- large fines
- confiscate vehicle
- therapy
- visit victims
- community work
- drunk-proof cars
- life-time ban on driving

Thought-webbing or **thought-mapping** is a particular kind of brainstorming using a visual technique. The topic on which the group is going to focus is written in the centre of a page (or on a chalkboard if it is whole-class brainstorming), a circle is drawn around it. Then as the ideas are presented, lines are drawn radiating out from it. This procedure provides a visual perspective on your thinking. It is a good procedure for building on each other's ideas, seeing relationships and connections among them, and ultimately labelling, organizing, and categorizing your ideas. Sample:

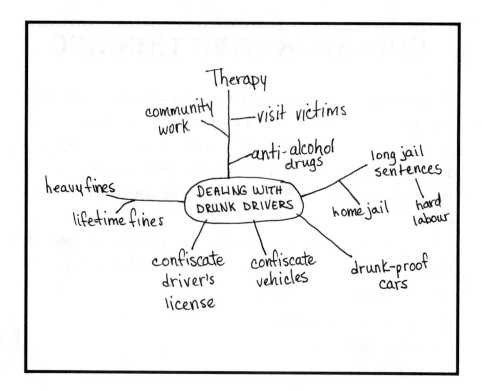

ROLE-PLAYING

One of the best ways to explore perspectives other than your own is to **role-play.** When you role-play, you adopt only the persona, the general qualities of someone else. You are said to be "in-role," when you are improvising written and/or oral responses from the point of view of that character. Good role-playing requires you to use your knowledge of the person you are playing to develop an imaginative response to a situation. In other words you put yourself in that person's shoes. Role-playing may involve all participants working in-role with each other with no intended audience, or role-playing may be an improvised performance done by specific individuals before an audience.

CO-OPERATIVE LEARNING

Thinking things through is often accomplished by talking them through. When people work together to share their thinking on any given topic, they share a wide variety of information, experience, and perspectives. By building on each other's contributions, the group can often respond at a level that would not have been possible for any one member of the group. This is particularly evident when engaging in problem-solving.

As with all successful learning, successful co-operative learning doesn't just happen automatically. In order to function well, group size must be carefully considered, group organization must be carefully structured, groups must interact, and group members must be prepared to perform certain roles and follow certain processes and rules of group etiquette.

GROUP SIZE

The minimum size is, of course, two; four or five is an optimum size. Groups larger than six start breaking down into subgroups. If you are just beginning group work it might be a good idea to start with pairs and then expand to fours by having two pairs work together.

GROUP STRUCTURES

Informal Groups: You turn to those closest to you and form small "spur-of-the-moment" groups to focus on something for a few minutes or more. It's a quick way of getting group reaction.

Formal Groups: This kind of grouping is planned. Members of the group share a common need or interest. One type of formal group is the **home** or **base group** that works together over a long period of time, for example, a group working on a co-operative independent study project.

GROUP INTERACTION

Mixed Groups: The simplest procedure is simply to combine one or two informal or formal groups to share information and consult with each other, for example, combining two informal pairs to make a group of four.

   Reconstituted Groups: This kind of grouping provides a method for organizing large tasks into shared learning experiences. One of the easiest ways to organize reconstituted groups is called the **jigsaw strategy.** First you organize into equal numbered groups in which the members examine a given task. Each group member takes on the responsibility for working on some aspect of the task, such as reading a particular article or set of articles, examining the topic from a certain perspective. Once the tasks are agreed upon, members then move into groups with people who have agreed to explore or examine the same areas. (This could be done as simply as having members number themselves within the original group and then having all same-number people meet in a new group configuration, or the new groups could be made up according to common areas of interest.) Once the task is completed, the "experts" then return to their original or "home" groups to bring back information on what they have learned.

Original Groups   **"Expert" Groups**   **Original Groups Reconstituted**

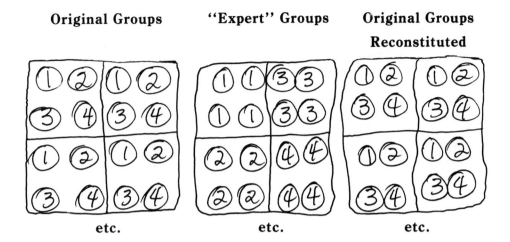

etc.   etc.   etc.

Representative Group: Such a group is made up of a member from every group (home group or base group) in the class. This group may meet apart from the class, or they may meet in front of the class with class members listening to their discussion. The representative group can provide a forum for co-ordinating and reporting on the progress of groups within the class and on the progress of the class as a whole.

GROUP ETIQUETTE

Successful groups practise the following skills:

sharing feelings	seeking clarification
encouraging others	mediating
expressing support	following directions
acknowledging contributions	recording ideas
responding to ideas	staying on task
asking questions	

Sometimes individuals within groups can share specific roles or practise a specific skill as the discussion develops. For example, one person might take the role of keeping things calm or staying on task, another might act as the recorder.

Credits

TOPIC THREE

TOPIC FOUR

TOPIC FIVE

TOPIC SIX

TOPIC SEVEN

TOPIC EIGHT

TOPIC NINE